DELIBERATIVE
AGENCY

WORLD PHILOSOPHIES

Bret W. Davis, D. A. Masolo, and Alejandro Vallega, editors

DELIBERATIVE AGENCY

A Study in Modern African Political Philosophy

—⚏—

UCHENNA OKEJA

INDIANA UNIVERSITY PRESS

This book is a publication of

Indiana University Press
Office of Scholarly Publishing
Herman B Wells Library 350
1320 East 10th Street
Bloomington, Indiana 47405 USA

iupress.org

Manufactured in the United States of America

First printing 2022

Library of Congress Cataloging-in-Publication Data

Names: Okeja, Uchenna B., 1983- author.
Title: Deliberative agency : a study in modern African political philosophy / Uchenna Okeja.
Other titles: World philosophies.
Description: Bloomington, Indiana : Indiana University Press, 2022. | Series: World philosophies | Includes bibliographical references and index.
Identifiers: LCCN 2021047492 (print) | LCCN 2021047493 (ebook) | ISBN 9780253059925 (hardback) | ISBN 9780253059918 (paperback) | ISBN 9780253059901 (ebook)
Subjects: LCSH: Political science—Philosophy. | Philosophy, African. | Deliberative democracy—Africa—Philosophy.
Classification: LCC JA71 .O36 2022 (print) | LCC JA71 (ebook) | DDC 320.101—dc23
LC record available at https://lccn.loc.gov/2021047492
LC ebook record available at https://lccn.loc.gov/2021047493

For my parents, Christopher and Felicia, and Oge.
Ogadinma!

CONTENTS

ACKNOWLEDGMENTS

SOMETIMES, WHEN I TAKE UP a book to read, I start with the acknowledgments page. I often wonder how I will express my gratitude when I write my next book. With this book came an opportunity to write beautiful acknowledgments. The challenge, alas, is that I could not think of a good way to begin the acknowledgment. So I thought I should begin with a note on my lack of words to appreciate all the help I received throughout the long journey of writing this book. My interest in the practice of deliberation goes back many years, so I have incurred many debts of gratitude in the process of thinking through the issues I have tried to work out in this book.

Over the years, Philipp Schink has remained an interlocutor who helps me to think through my ideas on many topics. Thanks a lot, Philipp, for being a wonderful friend over the years. We shall definitely realize our excellent projects pertaining to whales. I am fortunate to have studied with professors who became my friends. Matthias Lutz-Bachmann especially has been gracious with his time and support. From the very beginning of my career, he never failed to offer advice, support, and generous critiques of my work. Through their friendship and generosity, Julian Culp, Dorothea Gädeke, Andreas Niederberger, Katrin Flikschuh, Jörg Disse, Faisal Garba, Chielozona Eze, Cajetan Iheka, Abimbola Adesoji, Maik Nwosu, Onyebuchi Eze, Kenneth Amaeshi, and Paul Nnodim encouraged my research in more ways than they are aware. I am grateful to the members of my department at Rhodes, especially Marius Vermaak, for their kindness.

The real chance to realize the project of writing this book came with the award of an Iso Lomso Fellowship by the Stellenbosch Institute for Advanced

Study (STIAS). I am grateful to the former director of the institute Henrik Geyer and the current director, Edward Kirumira, for their support. I thank Christoff Pauw for his professionalism and friendship. Many things I explored in the process of writing this book would not have been possible without Christoff Pauw's guidance and encouragement. I am grateful to Nel-Mari Loock and the staff at STIAS for ensuring that my residencies were productive and memorable. I am also grateful to the founding director of STIAS, Bernard Lategan, for his interest in my work and support. The fellows at STIAS during my residencies were wonderful people whose wealth of experience enriched my perspective in more ways than I can recount here.

The Forschungskolleg Humanwissenschaft in Bad Homburg offered me the opportunity to continue the work on this book through a fellowship. I thank the director of the institute, Matthias Lutz-Bachmann, for the invitation and also for making my stay memorable. During this time, our son, Beluchi, was born. One could not have asked for better support than what we received from Matthias and his wife, Gitta. While I profited from the discussions and excellent research environment at the institute, I was particularly animated by engagements with old friends and colleagues. I am grateful to Regina Kreide, Rinku Lamba, Maria Kaiafa-Gbandi, Raymond Gbandi, Andreas Niederberger, Mamadou Diawara, and Helmuth Wagner for their kindness. I am grateful to Onyemaechi Ogbunwezeh, Chiagozie Madukife, Innocent Nwafor, Martin Haruna, and their families for their friendship while we were in Bad Homburg. I thank the executive director of the Forschungskolleg, Iris Koban, and the staff for their professionalism and kindness.

It is difficult to express sufficiently my gratitude to Rainer Forst and Stefan Gosepath for their offer of a senior fellowship at the Justitia Ampificata Center for Advanced Studies. Thanks for the support and encouragement. In a special way, I thank Katrin Flikschuh for her support, especially her feedback on drafts of the book proposal. I am grateful to Ajume Wingo for feedback on drafts of the proposal and chapters of the book. Thanks a lot, Ajume, for constantly reminding me of the need to carry on with the project and pointing me in the right direction. I cannot sufficiently express my appreciation to Paul Nnodim for his brotherly encouragement and support. Paul did not only read and provide feedback on the full manuscript of the book; he took on the extra task of language editing. *Dalu*, Paul! I am grateful to Asonzeh Ukah, Enyinna Nwauche, Nomalanga Mkhize, Omedi Ochieng, Adeyinka Alabi, Malebogo Ngoepe, Babalwa Magoqwana, Mutinda Nzioki, Okey Ndibe, John Ganle, and Pamela Maseko for emotional and intellectual support.

Emmanuel Akyeampong deserves special thanks for inviting me to spend time as a fellow at the Harvard Center for African Studies. I am grateful to him for his friendship and support, both on this project and beyond. I thank the executive director, Alex Taylor, Rosalin Salifu, Li-Ming Tseng, Candace Lowe, and the team at the Center for their support during my residency. I am grateful to John Mugane, Jacob Olupona, and George Meiu for the conversations and kind words. Two great friends, Ifeanyi Menkiti and Ife Ogbonna, passed away while I was completing this book. Menkiti not only encouraged me to complete the book; he read with dedication the first drafts of chapters 1 through 4. I appreciate Menkiti's fatherly support. Ife was like an elder brother. His care and concern were incomparable. I pray for the repose of his soul. I appreciate the dedication of Carole, Bo, Nneka, Enuma, and Ndidi to the vision of the Emengini Institute.

A substantial part of section 2 of this book was written while I was in residence at the Neubauer Collegium as a fellow. I am grateful to Jonathan Lear for his invitation and support. I appreciate the hospitality of Carolyn Ownbey, Brigid Balcom, Mark Sorkin, Jennifer Helmin, Adom Getachew, Natacha Nsabimana, Charles Mills, Kevin Irakoze, and Salikoko Mufwene. Caryl Gout and her family deserve special thanks for making my time in Chicago comfortable, productive, and memorable.

I made major revisions to the chapters in sections 1 and 2 while I was a fellow at the Peter Wall Institute for Advanced Studies. I thank the director at the time, Philippe Tortell, for the offer of a fellowship. Philippe and I became friends during my stay in Vancouver, and he made sure I felt at home. Thanks, Philippe, for making your time available. Thanks to Bernadette Mah, Emma MacEntee, and the staff at the Peter Wall Institute for Advanced Studies. I am grateful to my hosts, Handel Wright, Bonny Norton, and Margot Young, for their support. The fellowship at Peter Wall was memorable due also to the kindness of Barbara Arneil, James Stewart, Leila Harris, Bruce Baum, Anna Casas Aguilar, Sara Milstein, Evan Thompson, and Malabika Pramanik. I thank them for being such wonderful people.

Ian Williams has remained a great friend well beyond the time we spent together as fellows at Peter Wall. His ability to carefully think through very complicated issues has encouraged me to develop greater appreciation for the value of patience. Thanks, Ian, for your kindness and encouragement. At Indiana University Press, I started out working with Dee Mortensen. Dee was very helpful right from the beginning of this project and ensured a smooth transition to a new editor, Ashante Thomas, prior to her retirement. I am grateful to Ashante for her professional guidance and encouragement. It was an honor to work with you. I am grateful for the support of the editors of the World Philosophies series and the team at Indiana University Press.

My sisters and brothers are great sources of hope. Joe, Juli, Ike, Mary, Chika, Cee, thanks for being there, regardless of the challenge. I appreciate all of you for your steadfast love and grace. To my wife, Oge, and our children, Aka and Beluchi, your love and understanding provide me the inspiration to cherish every minute. Thanks for answering in practical terms questions regarding the meaning of life. I apologize to the numerous individuals and groups I did not mention. Your support is most appreciated.

DELIBERATIVE AGENCY

INTRODUCTION

IN MARCH 2018, A COURT in Mahikeng, South Africa, considered an interesting case. It was a disagreement between the king and people of Bafokeng. The king had sued the minister of land affairs, asking for the release of properties belonging to the Royal Bafokeng Nation. The argument for the demand was simple. The minister claimed to hold the properties in trust for the Bafokeng nation. However, because such a trust did not exist, the minister had to release the properties. Although it was the highest decision-making council of the Bafokeng nation that decided to sue the minister, serious objections were raised. The objectors argued that the king ought to have engaged in a deliberation with the people prior to suing the minister on their behalf. This step, it was argued, was required by custom. If the king does not engage in a deliberative process with the people, he cannot litigate on their behalf.

The first ruling of the court held that the king should consult his people when making decisions about cases that concerned them. However, the judgment stated further that it was the king's prerogative to decide which case mattered to the public. This implied technically that the king could litigate on behalf of the people without consulting them. This judgment, which was delivered by a single bench of the court, was overturned by a second ruling that was delivered by the full bench of the court. The second judgment ruled that it was mandatory for the king to engage in deliberation prior to litigating on behalf of his people. Bafokeng culture, it was argued, stipulates that the public should deliberate on issues that matter to the public. Thus, it is through public deliberation that a course of action in the name of the group is legitimated.

This story illustrates the importance of deliberation for Africans. Hardly anyone would fail to notice the inclination to approach social and political

1

issues in African societies through public deliberation. The interesting question the story just recounted raises is why it is essential for the Bafokeng people to engage in public deliberation about issues that are relevant to the public. What is the reason for the insistence on a customary practice, even in the so-called modern era? This is a demand for an account of the value of a public political culture in an African society. One of the aims of this book is to inquire into the reasons public deliberation reflects Africa's political culture and how it can help in resolving current political challenges.

In many African societies, the *alternative dispute resolution* process is widely accepted as a means of resolving legal issues. It is common for lawyers to apply to courts to have cases instituted in their jurisdiction resolved privately by means of alternative dispute resolution. Using this means of dispute resolution is considered an important way to prevent future conflicts. It is also seen as a better way to reconcile feuding groups and reestablish harmony. The idea behind all this is that reestablishing a harmonious relationship is essential for coexistence. In cities, ethnic group associations and sundry volunteer organizations carry on the task of fostering deliberation among Africans for different reasons. In some instances, the deliberation can aim to settle disputes. In others, the aim could be to decide the best action to take to address unfortunate incidents, such as death. Even outside Africa, people from the continent rely on deliberation to resolve problems and maintain social harmony.

There are many reasons why public deliberation continues to be important for modern Africans living in the continent and overseas. As an approach to political and social questions, public deliberation is highly valued because of the provision it makes for the exercise of agency by everyone affected by a problem. Taking this observation as a starting point, I aim in this book to show how to harness public deliberation to construct a contemporary African political philosophy.

People familiar with political events in Africa south of the Sahara will agree that the search for a center constitutes a major problem of politics in the continent (Masolo 2000, 17). Recognizing this fact, African philosophers propose political theories that can help resolve political challenges in the continent. Their aims consist of attempts to reconstruct a center for political practice. Whereas some are invested in exploring the reasons the center fell apart in the first place, others direct their focus to conceiving new ways to imagine a novel aim of political action.

The reason for this bifurcation of focus is not hard to decipher. It has to do with the pernicious confusion one encounters in the politics of every country in Africa. Added to this is the anxiety arising from rampant manifestation of the purposelessness of the state in Africa. People are not only uncertain the ends the state ought to serve; they are also not sure what constitutes an overarching ideal of politics in contemporary Africa. Uncertainties are, thus, the essential feature of the current political condition in Africa. The situation is one in which fundamental questions of coexistence are still open, unanswered questions.

Political theorists face tremendous challenges in grappling with the political condition in Africa. In the current situation, where ambiguities and confusions exist regarding the ends of politics and the purpose of the state, how is it possible to think about politics? What is the starting point of a reflection we can call contemporary African political philosophy? It is true that culture plays an important role for how we orient ourselves to politics. The public culture of a people is therefore an important aspect of their orientation to politics as a sphere of human creativity. Thus, to tackle modern political challenges in Africa, I argue that a viable starting point is the analysis of public political culture. I propose that public political culture manifests in the African context as the phenomenon of public deliberation. Thus, by creatively transforming the concept of public deliberation, I attempt to develop a contemporary African political philosophy that is capable of addressing current political challenges in the continent.

Even if we accept that the analysis of public deliberation is where to begin the inquiry about how to resolve current challenges in Africa, that does not reveal the nature of the problem at stake. Therefore, it is pertinent to ask questions about the nature of the problem raised by African political experience. The proposal I defend is that political failure defines the current experience of politics in Africa. This is not just a factual observation but also a phenomenological perspective on the experience. My claim is that people experience politics as a sphere of life where a specific form of powerlessness shapes reality. The powerlessness in question manifests in the feeling by individuals that they can do nothing to change the social and political circumstances shaping their lives. The result is that politics is experienced as a meaningless performance outside the realm of "normal" life.

I argue that addressing the problem of political failure is possible through the development of a contemporary African political philosophy that is based on a reimagination of public political culture. Reimagination is the necessary first step to take because we must begin by making African conceptual resources fit again for theory formation. This view amounts to saying that merely retrieving concepts from a so-called African past will not suffice. The reason for this is simply the fact that the denigration of Africans, at its core, implied a devaluation of the normative potentials of African conceptual resources. The central concepts through which Africans oriented themselves to reality lost reliability as veritable ways to perceive reality due to the experience of denigration and humiliation. The implication then is that addressing the current political challenges in Africa can only succeed if we systematically recast the African conceptual apparatus. I offer a five-step analysis that guarantees a conceptual transformation of deliberation in African thought. I argue for a need to transform the meaning of deliberation from being understood as a process that aims at generating consensus to being understood as a process that aims to guarantee the enactment of agency as the core of political life. Seen as a way to make agency the core of political life, public deliberation becomes a conceptual tool that enables us to construct a new vision of politics.

Constructing a viable contemporary political philosophy, in the sense of developing a new vision of politics, is imperative for many reasons. Chief among them is the limitation of extant responses to the human condition in Africa. Although political theorists have offered answers to questions about inequality, injustice, aims of the state, democracy, human rights, and development, these efforts amount to impracticable outcomes. The reason is that political theorists discuss African political reality from predominantly two angles.

On one side are theorists of human rights and related ideals who focus on poverty, inequality, and related problems. This approach boils down to descriptions of how Africans ought to resolve their problems by respecting human rights and other, mainly liberal, ideals. On the other side are theorists of the state and economy who analyze how internal and external factors shape experiences of poverty, inequality, and other problems in Africa. This approach often amounts to advancing views regarding what external actors ought to do or avoid in the interest of capacitating Africans to resolve their challenges.

The conviction behind this book is that these two perspectives do not adequately address politics as it is experienced in contemporary Africa. The challenge is not to map out the way Africans should aspire to democratic ideals or how to identify relevant external and internal factors driving social and political problems in the continent. The issue is to understand the experience of politics as political failure. The relevant issue is how to understand the reality that there are generations of Africans who have not experienced and will never in their lifetimes experience what it means for a society to be governed properly. The challenge is to inquire into what it means that Africans in the present century must live out their entire adult existence without a prospect of understanding the ends of politics and the goals of the state.

These questions cannot be answered if we merely draw on theories from elsewhere to determine what Africans are doing wrongly or should be doing differently. The starting point ought to be internal. We must begin with an internal exploration, a sort of immanent critique aiming to conceive political theories that are grounded on concrete experience. I show in this book that the best account of the current experience of politics as political failure in Africa would mean to see the problem as a form of cognitive disorientation traceable to the destabilization of African conceptual resources.

The background of this thought is Jonathan Lear's discussion of conceptual loss (2006). Unlike Lear, however, I argue that the African case differs because colonization did not lead to full-blown conceptual loss. Regardless of how it manifested, colonization did not kill imagination. Without the occlusion of imagination, one cannot look at the African situation as arising from conceptual loss. The perspective I defend is that the destabilization of African concepts due to colonization led to a form of cognitive disorientation. Relying on this claim, I develop an account of African political philosophy that reimagines public deliberation as a compelling theoretical response to political failure.

To accomplish this task, I engage in a three-step exploration, corresponding to the three sections of the book. In the first step, which is reconstructive and comprises chapters 1–3, I analyze the current experience of politics in Africa as a phenomenon of political failure and demonstrate why this understanding constitutes a demand for a new approach to African political philosophy. I discuss attempts made so far by social and political theorists to address this problem and show the shortcomings that make the present inquiry necessary.

In the second step of the book, which is constructive and comprises chapters 4–6, I demonstrate how public deliberation constitutes a manifestation of African public culture. By tracing the provenance of conceptions of the meaning of public deliberation in Africa, I map the understanding of the concept by means of five typologies—namely, the understanding of deliberation as (1) ideology of legitimation, (2) ideal of economic interaction, (3) reference point of social interaction, (4) principle structuring social change and cultural modification, and (5) an orientation that enables comprehension of the meaning of being human. In addition, I discuss the problems that arise with attempts to use African concepts to theorize and conceive solutions to current political challenges. I show how the destabilization of African conceptual resources breeds cognitive disorientation, which in turn impedes normative theorizing. To be able to tackle this problem and develop an account of a viable contemporary African philosophy, I propose a turn to conceptual creativity as a method of doing political philosophy.

The third step comprises chapters 7–8. In chapter 7, I use the method of conceptual creativity to distill the meaning of deliberation that has a normative potential. I argue that the best way to reimagine the idea of public deliberation, given current experiences in Africa, is to see it as a performance of agency, a practice whose manifestation places agency at the very core of political life. In chapter 8, I discuss what it means for agency to be the core of political life and propose an account of contemporary African political philosophy as deliberative agency.

I conclude by arguing for an orientation to politics as contradiction. I consider this view an appropriate way to orient oneself to the sphere of life regarded as politics because of the far-reaching damage resulting from the destabilization of the African conceptual world. For Africans, politics will continue to unfold as a contradiction due to the normative instability generated by cognitive disorientation. Adopting an orientation to politics as contradiction is therefore a way to open the mind to a range of possibilities that give meaning to politics, even in the circumstance of political failure.

ONE

—҃ϫϫ—

DEFINING THE AFRICAN POLITICAL CONDITION

The Paradigm of Political Failure

IN 1962, KOFI ABREFA BUSIA (1962, 4) observed that the challenge of Africa to herself and the world consists in "the demands for justice, emancipation from colonial rule, and freedom and dignity for the individual, the aspirations for the high standards of living that contemporary science and technology have made possible, and the search for self-confidence and self-respect based on a past rediscovered and reappraised." This was barely five years after his country, Ghana, had attained political independence. If instead of "emancipation from colonial rule" we were to now say "emancipation from the domination of African political elites," Busia's account of Africa's challenge would retain all the urgency it reflected when he first expressed it six decades ago. How do we explain this situation? How do we explain the fact that Africa's challenges in the 1950s and 1960s have persisted into the present decade? The answer I argue for in this book is that the explanation lies in the political failure that defines experiences in postcolonial Africa. My aim is to demonstrate this point and propose an African political philosophy that responds adequately to the problem.

In this chapter, I develop an account of the phenomenon of political failure and demonstrate how its persistence constitutes a demand for a new African political philosophy—that is, a call to develop a political philosophy that takes a different route in attempting to make sense of postcolonial African experience. To get to this, we must consider the nature of political failure and why this challenge requires us to articulate a new African political philosophy. Instead of defining the phenomenon of political failure in abstract language, a better approach is to explain it through reflection on its manifestation in the history and struggles of people in the African continent. To that end, we must reconstruct some of the attempts that have been made in the scholarship on Africa to explain what is generally regarded as the African condition.

In November 2017 in Zimbabwe, Robert Mugabe was compelled to resign from his position as president after ruling and, many would say, mismanaging his country for almost four decades. Not long after the standoff in Zimbabwe, Jacob Zuma was displaced as president of the Republic of South Africa. Around the same time, people across the world watched with amusement as the drama of succession between Yahaya Jammeh and Adama Barrow unfolded in the Gambia. Meanwhile, in such countries as Cameroon, Nigeria, Niger, Mozambique, and Kenya, a decade of bitter, fierce, and catastrophic battles with such terrorist groups as Boko Haram, Ansar al-Sunna, and Al-Shabaab has shaped the lives of the people there.

Similarly, in Egypt, Tunisia, and Algeria, people's reality since the early 2010s has been defined by the seemingly insurmountable challenge of making the different versions of the Arab Spring translate into a desirable form of politics, economic prosperity, and cultural self-understanding. Libya, since the beginning of the political turmoil of 2011, has devolved into a collection of fiefdoms unevenly divided among strongmen and militias. The menace of the deadly Tuareg terrorists has been at the center of people's lives in Mali for more than a decade. In addition to these political problems, Ebola fever, which claimed many lives in the continent between 2013 and 2016, remains a major threat in the Democratic Republic of Congo. The COVID-19 pandemic brought to light a perennial handicap in Africa—namely, the human costs of poor public health infrastructure in the continent.

DEFINING POLITICAL FAILURE

Every country has its fair share of troubles. In every continent, there are intractable difficulties, regardless of the level of technological advancement and geographical integration. To see that this is the case, we need only take notice of the disaffections currently shaping the politics of the European Union and the bitter disagreements among North American countries about trade and immigration. The question is, why do the challenges in African countries represent a phenomenon of political failure? To answer this question, it is necessary to examine in some detail various experiences that constitute the phenomenon of political failure.

Earlier, I mentioned some events in the African political landscape that have shaped people's experiences in the postcolonial era. It may seem that these events are isolated cases that do not reflect the general mode of politics in the continent. Endorsing this view runs contrary to historical evidence and the signals given by contemporary events. The everyday experiences of individuals in African countries are not the same, of course. However, recurrent miseries unite Africans in their struggles.

These hardships have to do with the powerlessness of individuals in relation to social and political circumstances that shape their lives and determine the future they can imagine. At a fundamental level, this circumstance translates to a form of paralysis, an inertia that suggests that hope is an unaffordable luxury for Africans in the present century. As a result, the struggle of the individual in Africa perennially entails finding a way to cope with the odds of life, leaving issues about politics and social reforms to elites, thugs, foreign powers, and all the various shades of experts offering commentaries on Africa.

Busia observed almost six decades ago that the challenges facing Africa have to do with a quest for justice, emancipation, freedom, dignity, improved standard of living, self-confidence, and self-respect; all of these are still acute concerns. The urgency of this point is acknowledged by ordinary people and presidents in Africa. In a great many African countries, injustices of egregious kinds are too rampant to recount here. Criminal justice, social justice, intergenerational justice, restitutive justice, and transitional justice all jostle at the same time for attention from whoever may care.

Should the individual turn to the courts in the quest for justice, the result most often bitter agony and disappointment. Where personal circumstances, like poverty and illiteracy, do not defeat the appeal to courts for justice, bureaucratic inefficiency and corruption often prevent the realization of the ends of justice. The result of all these is a widespread feeling that the state is inefficient and, hence, that political independence means nothing to anyone but the elites. African states, although politically independent, are seldom accountable to citizens. In fact, they repeatedly demonstrate that they are incapable of holding citizens to account by enforcing their own laws.

Governments borrow from global moneylenders without judiciousness, putting future generations in unjustified and exorbitant debt. It can hardly be disputed that there is a huge challenge regarding justice, both in specific African countries and between African countries and their counterpart countries in the world. Calls for reparatory justice for the descendants of formerly colonized or enslaved people and the quest for global justice bring to the fore the challenge of justice between Africa and the world. In contemporary political philosophy, global justice whose appeal revolves around consideration of what is owed to the global poor regarding the just and equitable distribution of the world's wealth is a direct response to the problem of justice to Africa and other impoverished parts of the world. Sadly, or, should we say, expectedly, the discourse loses steam almost as soon as it begins, failing to lead to any of the anticipated consequences.

If we turn to the challenge of emancipation, freedom, and dignity, the story of Africa does not get any better. The pauperization of African economies, especially the thin middle class, has led to a situation where a vast majority of Africans live and die as prisoners of the freedom wrought by independence. The circumstances that rob the individual of African ancestry of their freedom and dignity are indeed many. If the current spike in outmigration from Africa to Europe and other affluent parts of the world is indicative of anything, it must be that the struggle for the realization of freedom for African people is still a precarious work in progress.

Lampedusa and other spots that have become mass graveyards for the dreams of a better life for Africans fleeing the miserable state of affairs in their homelands bear eloquent witness to the ongoing precarious struggle for freedom in Africa. The dehumanizing effects of poverty, which have provoked bitter conflicts and protests in many African countries in recent history, show the resilience of Africans in attempting to affirm their dignity in the face of trying circumstances. Ensuring the dignity of African individuals—first battered by the humiliating evils of transatlantic slavery, then crushed by the spiteful cultural arrogance of colonization, and eventually neglected by postcolonial African states—remains a central part of the challenge of Africa to itself and the world.

A visit to megacities in Africa south of the Sahara should suffice to convince one of the cogency of Busia's assertion that the quest for a high standard of living made possible by technology and science is one of the major challenges confronting Africa. In many African countries, big cities are megaslums with little care for basic sanitation. Service delivery in many cities has either collapsed or is severely inefficient due to ballooning urbanization and lack of adequate planning to accompany the development. The consequence of this is that anyone aspiring to a decent life must become a minigovernment on their own strength because they must be able to provide roads, sanitation, electricity, and other amenities for themselves.

The problem of service delivery continues to pose a significant threat even in countries like South Africa, where basic infrastructure is more advanced than other sub-Saharan African countries. Evidence for this is the constant service delivery protests in municipalities in numerous parts of the country. It must be considered the most eloquent commentary on the poor standards of living in African countries that a trend among the elites, especially the presidents, is to seek medical treatment in Europe, Asia, or North America for minor such infections as the flu or common cold. Not too long after he assumed office in 2015, for instance, the president of Nigeria, Muhammadu Buhari, a former high-ranking military officer, spent more than three months in the United Kingdom to have access to that country's medical infrastructure because of an ear infection. Not only was he absent from his duty but the nature and costs to the nation of his medical tourism have not been revealed to the citizens to date.

All these make the quest by Africans for self-confidence and self-respect difficult. And this is especially the case when the means to these ends is a reappraisal of the African past as a guide to the present. It is simply not clear how useful Africa's past applies in the present circumstances. For intellectuals engaged in the study of the African condition, a return to the past approach to the study and conception of solutions to social and political problems, often called the *project of retrieval*, is no longer a straightforward or even desirable endeavor because of the realization that the past cannot be recaptured. However, devoid of a starting point, any quest for self-confidence and respect by Africans will remain an intractable assignment. The effect of the seeming permanence of the challenges of Africa to itself and the world, aptly articulated by Busia, is therefore the festering of a pernicious inertia in relation to social and political agency.

The experience of inertia that results from paralyzing social and political circumstances is not new to Africans. Over the years, especially during colonization and after many parts of Africa became independent countries, the image of the continent as a dark continent has persisted for many reasons. In examining what I regard as political failure on the continent, my goal is not to rehash prejudices that the image of Africa as a dark continent evinces. I am instead interested in working through the phenomenology of the everyday experience of Africans to reflect on the nature of the challenge it represents. By examining some of the ideas that have been offered to explain African experience in the present century, it should be possible to grasp the phenomenology of the everyday in Africa.

Certainly, accounts of the continent's political experience are diverse, in the same way the solutions suggested differ. Although the reasons for the divergence of accounts of the problems and answers suggested are many, ultimately, they reduce to disciplinary differences among scholars interested in exploring the African condition. It is reasonable to suppose that where there are disciplinary differences, differences in frameworks and analytical conventions adopted by scholars are normal. However, by pushing to reasonable limits the boundaries of disciplinary distinctions, I attempt in this chapter and in the next two to reconstruct some prominent attempts to explain contemporary African experience in order to demonstrate how the experience constitutes a form of political failure that requires the articulation of a new African political philosophy.

In tackling the matter at hand, I focus my attention in the next three chapters on those materials or studies that may be said to constitute normative African political thought. This is to say that I concern myself mostly with ideas expressed in the literature that have attempted to evaluate African experience through the lens of theoretical, and not empirical or quantitative, analysis. In the present chapter, I begin with an analysis of attempts by Africanists and African social theorists to explain the African experience in the postcolonial era.

AFRICANISTS AND AFRICAN POLITICAL THEORISTS
ON POSTCOLONIAL POLITICAL EXPERIENCE

In the literature that constitutes what I referred to above as normative African political thought, certain dominant perspectives recommend themselves for closer scrutiny. These perspectives include the proposition that African political experience can be accounted for by means of explanatory models of the failed state, the perspective of economic underdevelopment, and values-related deficiencies. Attempts to understand African political experience through the lens of the discourse on failed states generally take a counterfactual route. This is the case because, when we ask what exactly is meant by the notion of a failed state, the answer readily available is that we know failed states because we know successful states. Put differently, the meaning of the idea of failed states can be determined when the states so regarded are assessed in accordance with the standards of successful states.

Following this way of thinking about the topic, Ali Mazrui proposed that there are six crucial functions of a state—namely, that a state should be able to (1) control its territory, (2) supervise the resources of the nation, (3) effectively extract revenue from people, goods, and services, (4) provide infrastructure, (5) provide basic services, and (6) govern and ensure law and order (Mazrui 1995, 28). A failed state, on this account, is one that is unable to perform these crucial functions. With the publication of numerous studies on failed states in the 1990s, this explanatory model gained prominence and became ubiquitously harnessed to explain the African political experience.

According to the story of failed states, African political experience consists of an inability of states on the continent to fulfill all or most of the functions enumerated by Mazrui. In other words, African political challenges can be explained by the fact that they have states that are unable to assert territorial integrity, govern extraction and use of resources, ensure efficient collection of revenue, and provide services and infrastructure, while ensuring the maintenance of law and order.

Images are not scarce to demonstrate this point. When we consider everyday life in countries given as standard examples of failed states in Africa, we cannot but be fascinated by the appeal of this model of explanation. This is mostly the case if we recall that, when features of a failed state obtain, unsavory consequences follow—warlords emerge, epidemics spiral out of control, and refugee and other crises ensue. Thus, failed states are a problem to themselves and the international community. Epidemics that may arise due to the inability of such states to provide what is required for basic sanitation, fragmented authority of competing warlords, and the refugees that will escape to safer havens constitute serious concerns for the international community.

As a result, the African political experience, as conceived by the failed states explanatory model, is not simply a concern for Africans but a global concern, especially today, when nativism is reemerging as a central influence in political decision-making. With the turn to this form of politics, everyone, nativist or liberal, feels challenged to conceive what to do with the most essential exports from failed states—namely, immigrants, refugees, and terrorists. Nativists are bothered because they have an interest in ensuring that their slogan that kindred nativists should come first in political, social, and economic matters is not dismissed as empty sloganeering. Liberals are also concerned because they wish to demonstrate to one and all that the liberal manifesto offers more than a pretentious embrace of people of every land and clime as equals, without a viable plan regarding how to make politics and economics work.

Although the state's failure at carrying out the six crucial tasks noted above is critical, it is the failure at governance that is, according to Mazrui (1995, 29), most telling. Many of the scholars that employ the failed state model of analysis agree with this thought, given that their efforts have chiefly consisted of studies aimed at finding solutions to the governance challenges of failed states. The proposals advanced have ranged from suggestions that the balance of the influence of ethnic groups on the state is the panacea to recommendations about the modifications that must be made to ensure modernity takes root in Africa.

These proposals emerge, however, from varying analytical tracks. On one hand, some of the proposals arise from concerns about corruption or the phenomenon now regarded as *prebendalism*. On the other hand, concerns about the decolonization of political institutions provide another analytical track. While the former analytical track locates the source of problems of governance in Africa in deficiencies caused by corruption, the latter analytical track suggests that the failure to decolonize politics and political institutions on the continent is the reason there are widespread crises of governance in the continent.

The narrative of state failure has not been without dispute. Some scholars have argued, for instance, that the explanatory model of failed states is unhelpful because it does not offer meaningful insight into the African political experience. The point of this claim is that it is misleading to adopt this model of explanation because there is a fundamental sense in which the states in Africa are indeed not states at all. States, according to this objection, have features that are missing in the constitution of postcolonial African states. As Jeffery Herbst (1996/1997, 122) has argued, it is not true that "Africa was ever composed of sovereign states classically defined as having a monopoly on force in the territory within their boundaries."

In other words, African states did not earn their sovereignty; they were simply handed sovereignty by the United Nations' recognition of their membership after independence. Furthermore, African states lacked the requisite capacity to perform the functions they are called on to fulfill. Even in their colonial incarnations, bureaucracies of these states were not sufficiently developed to meet the needs of effective sovereign nations. This is the reason Herbst proposes that the failed state model should be abandoned as a way to explain political experience in the African context.

Instead of focusing on what is needed to remedy the crises that emerge from so-called failed states, attention should be directed to addressing the task of conceiving alternatives to the state model. Regarding this view, Herbst stands out because of his efforts to account for impacts of the imposition of the nation-state model on Africa and ideas he expounded about the rational options open to Africans. To know what should be done in response to the challenge of state failure in Africa, Herbst suggests we need to begin by understanding "what was lost" because of the imposition of the nation-state on Africans. For him, asking this question is the most reliable route to conceive "indigenous alternatives" to the state in Africa (Herbst 1996/1997, 127).

Noting how the unilateral imposition of the nation-state model disrupted African political practice, Herbst (1996/1997, 131) argues that the contemporary, perilous African political experience has come about because "the current state system in Africa has institutionalized weakness and decline, irrespective of the source of failure," the reason being the "complete dissociation between

a country's economic and political performance and its sovereign status."
Guarantee of sovereignty by the international community, regardless of what
obtains domestically, the argument suggests, is an incentive for states in Africa
to not care whether they fail or succeed.

Herbst is not alone in rejecting the cogency of the failed state model of
explanation. The rejection of this model revolves around at least three lines
of argument. As already noted, one strategy is to argue that the failed state
approach is inadequate because the notion of the state does not apply within
the African context. Another line of argument is offered by critics who suggest that, instead of making recourse to the failed state framework of analysis,
what we ought to do is historicize the idea of the state. According to this view,
it is only when we put the state within its proper historical context that we will
discover the underlying reasons that account for the successful or deficient
performance of states in various places. The third line of argument is the proposal that perils of politics in Africa are traceable to shortcomings of either the
composition of the states or the personal weaknesses of those charged with the
duty of running them.

Concerning the second point, it is important to note that historicizing the
idea of the state means more than just recounting the history of the state. It
means, among other things, analyzing the social processes that combined to
give birth to the state. In other words, it requires probing the reasons the state in
a specific context took the shape and composition it currently has. The point is
to ensure that analysis of the current political misfortune of African states does
not proceed squarely from an ahistorical perspective but is, rather, informed by
the complex interactions that shape states in this context.

For the third line of argument, the essential point to underscore is that the
composition of a state and the task of running its bureaucracy must be such
that state neutrality, as an instrument for social and political organization, is
guaranteed. The point then of the third argument is that we can understand the
problems of African politics by considering whether the state, as composed or
run in this context, ensures the realization of its function as a neutral instrument for organizing social and political interaction.

Moving beyond the focus on the state, we find perspectives that focus on the
historical analysis of internal factors, how they came to be, and the implications
of the narratives that justify them. From this perspective, Mahmood Mamdani
(1996) provides a magisterial examination of efforts to explain African political experience in the Africanist literature of the last two decades. According
to Mamdani, modernist and communitarian approaches to analyzing African
political challenges produce a "paralysis of perspective" that must be resolved

so that a viable explanatory model that is built on adequate theoretical frame-work can emerge. To make a case for his theory of "decentralized despotism," Mamdani dissected—and showed the shortcomings of—works that aimed to explain the African political experience.

For Mamdani, the partiality of modernist approaches for civil society as the center of politics and the desire to make African communalism the center of politics by communitarians necessitates a synthesizing critique. Such a critique will produce a new model of explanation or theory. Mamdani thought this was important because of the trend among Africanists to see African political experience through the lens of what he calls "history by analogy" (Mamdani 1996, 12). The concept refers to attempts to explain African experience by sub-suming it under European historical processes. The goal of doing this is to determine how African experiences mirror the European paradigm. This move is problematic because it substitutes "theory formation" with "analogy seeking" (Mamdani 1996, 12). This is important to note because it is impossible to explain a phenomenon if all that is done is to determine the sense in which it differs from another object or experience. I will say more about this point in chapter 6, where I will discuss the idea of *conceptual creativity*.

Among Africanists, explanation of the African political experience revolves around the following theoretical paradigms: patrimonialism, peasantry, civil society, the bifurcated state, ethnicity, and despotism. These explanatory models have served as the main paradigms for analysis of questions about what ails contemporary Africa. The social forces operating within the state or the state itself and those who run it have been at the center of these explana-tory paradigms because of the goal pursued—namely, to specify the source of the ills and failures that constitute African political experience and show the way forward. What is implied by showing the way forward is the modi-fications or changes that need to occur to enable African states to respond adequately to the challenge of political failure. Put differently, what is implied is to analyze African political experience in order to chart a path that will enables Africans to experience true liberation, freedom, development, and democracy.

But these paradigms are insufficient for some Africanists. For instance, con-vinced that the standard methods by which political theorists studied African political experience have exhausted their appeal and efficacy, Patrick Chabal sought to do something different. Rather than focus his study of African poli-tics on the state or objective categories, Chabal (2009) conceived to understand African political experience from below, which is to say, through analysis of the experiences of individuals in African societies. He went further, in his work with Daloz (Chabal and Daloz 1999), to explain African politics in the light of neopatrimoialism, which is considered to be deeply rooted in African culture. The crisis of development in Africa, in Chabal's view, can be reasonably explained without recourse to the failed state model of analysis.

The reputation of Africa as a stronghold of corruption and ineffective public institutions is a consequence of an Africa-specific attitude to development. Although this attitude differs and dismays foreign donors because it does not align with attitudes that lead to modernization, it is nonetheless explainable if considered in the paradigm of analysis Chabal proposes—namely, instrumentalization of disorder. According to this paradigm, chaos, corruption, and disorder are harbingers of Africans' chosen path to development. These behaviors that appear to non-Africans as disorderliness are functional because they order the path to development in this context. Disorder, corruption, and patrimonialism that make institutions ineffective provide a means for politicians and the ruling elite to ensure the sustenance of their people's dependence and, hence, loyalty. By maintaining the linkage of dependence and loyalty, the political elite in Africa ensure they maintain a hold on power.

Amplifying these ideas initially developed with Daloz in a later publication, Chabal (2009) argued that we can better comprehend the challenges of African politics if we direct attention to the way Africans understand themselves as people. The task in this regard is to analyze the way Africans comprehend concrete reality. Weaving together core paradigms of analysis used to study African politics—that is, "development, Marxist, dependency, socialist, indigenous, neo-patrimonial and democratic" paradigms—Chabal (2009, 11) argued that Africanist political theories have become caught up in an "everlasting vicious circle of impotence." The reason for this claim is that Africanist political theories do not offer an account of "Africa that stands before our eyes" (17).

The goal to pursue, Chabal proposes, is to understand African political experience by analyzing the experience of politics by real people. He suggests that an implication of this thought is "to honour the day-to-day lives of those who strive to maintain human dignity in the face of overwhelming odds" (2009, 16). Approaching the study of African politics in the postindependence era from this perspective entails telling the story of African political experience as ultimately a process that reflects a dialectic between lived reality and politics. The question to ask is "how the realities of the lives of those who live affect the workings of politics"(Chabal 2009, 17). To answer this question, Chabal analyzes African notion of being (2009, 25), political morality (2009, 67), and rationality (2009, 71) to show the deficiencies of Africanist political theories as well as "to provide a more ground-level account of how politics is played out locally" (2009, 185).

The literature on patrimonialism, which forms a central part of the inward-looking view of African political experience, is diverse. The truth of this should be evident, regardless of the dominance of this approach as a model of analysis of African politics in the 1970s and 1980s. The appeal of this approach relates to the promise it holds for the explanation of the dismal record of African countries in their different attempts to develop and modernize, especially when the reason for this lack is often sought in the workings of institutions, cultures, and practices, instead of in the composition of the state.

But then, deployment of this paradigm to explain African political experience varies, depending on the aim of the scholar. Gero Erdmann and Ulf Engel (2007) have shown that scholars sometimes appeal to patrimonialism without bothering to question to what extent it is useful and coherent. Notwithstanding the validity of the reformulation of the concept of patrimonialism by Erdmann and Engel, interest in the application of this paradigm in the study of African politics has waned significantly over the last couple of years. And the reason might not be unconnected with unexpected developments in the continent.

Other models of explanation to consider are those dealing with the economic aspects of postcolonial experience. The structural adjustment programs implemented by the World Bank and International Monetary Fund across Africa in part account for the turn to neocolonialism and neoliberal imperialism as paradigms for understanding African politics. Central to these perspectives is the idea that the maintenance of hegemonic domination informed both the formation of African states and the architecture of their postcolonial successors. The point of neocolonial discourse finds succinct expression in Kwame Nkrumah's (1965, 1) observation that "Africa is a paradox which highlights neo-colonialism. Her earth is rich, yet the produce that comes from above and beneath her soil continue to enrich, not Africans predominantly, but groups and individuals who operate to Africa's impoverishment."

Neocolonial theorists argue that while states in Africa are nominally sovereign, they are controlled by external powers and interests mainly through policy prescriptions. Crawford Young echoes Nkrumah in his study of states against the background of colonial history. Young (1994, 244) argues that "one consequential factor in the crisis faced by most African states by the late 1970s—and intensifying since—was the singularly difficult legacy bequeathed by the institutions of rule devised to establish and maintain alien hegemony."

Viewed in this light, structural adjustment program were just another manifestation of the changing patterns of neocolonial and hegemonic control.

Introduced by two institutions produced by the Bretton Woods Conference—namely, the International Monetary Fund and the World Bank—structural adjustment programs were meant to address Africa's worsening challenge of poverty and underdevelopment in the postcolonial era. The programs were designed to enable African countries to redirect their failing economies. Although it is true that experts do not agree on the effects of the programs, an evaluation of the experiences of people in countries where they were implemented shows that consequences of restructuring were not pleasant.

Two of Africa's foremost economists, Thandika Mkandawire and Charles Soludo, recount that evaluating the outcomes of structural adjustment programs in Africa is difficult. They have noted, "The word adjustment embraces too wide a range of policies and experiences to have one single meaning as an independent variable." This means "judging whether the SAPs [structural adjustment programs] are successes or failures and choosing which evaluation techniques to use hinge on one's philosophical view of how real markets operate and on one's perceptions of objectives, policy targets, and instruments" (Mkandawire and Soludo 1998, 51).

Evaluating structural adjustment programs in terms of their successes or failures is possible because "economists agree on several indicators of success" (Mkandawire and Soludo 1998, 51). It is largely acknowledged that structural adjustment failed, as it did not deliver the recovery and growth it promised (Mkandawire and Soludo 1998, 53). The consequences of the underperformance of structural adjustment programs in many African countries were indeed dire. For instance, the outcome of privatization and the retrenchment of workers it created negatively affected many families. Many middle-class families were pauperized across the continent, and austerity measures translated very quickly into stagnation and disaffection, leading to incessant strikes and unrest in urban centers.

As discussions of the structural adjustment programs have demonstrated, the social consequences of the programs were damaging—wages fell rapidly, and what was left of people's savings was wiped out due to spiraling inflation. Moreover, the already pitiable plight of the poor turned into a longer litany of misery due to the collapse of health, education, transport, and other critical infrastructure. In many poor households, food became so scarce that it was rationed. Nigerians, for example, will recall readily some of the formulas for food rationing in families, such as 0-1-1 or 0-0-1 and similar expressions. The numbers stand for the three meals in a day: 1 represents a meal that can be eaten; o, for a meal that must be skipped because of food shortages. The situation was so bad that sometimes, even when one had the money, one could not buy what one lacked.

Against the background of the critique of structural adjustment programs, a renewed attempt to explain African political experience through appeals to neocolonialism and neoliberal domination emerged. However, to many a scholar, these attempts proved insufficient for many reasons, especially because they do not consider the importance of generating home-grown theories for economic development. Dissatisfaction with the accusatory slant of theories based on neocolonialism and neoliberal domination led to the emergence of other paradigms of explanation, mostly theories that sought to explain how Africa could transition from merely "adjusting" structurally to truly developing. The goal was to understand what peculiarly African aspect stunts economic growth and the rapid modernization of society. The paradigm that emerged from attempts to answer this question is a culturecentric approach to understanding the *conditio humana* in Africa.

Although there have been considerations of how such context-specific practices as kinship and patronage intersect with the failure of development, the paradigm that sought to explain African experience through a focus on culture is different. The approach that focuses on culture does not merely look at conventions that are widespread in Africa. It proposes instead that vital aspects of African culture do not conduce to the project of development. In other words, immutable primordial attitudes of mind inculcated by African culture are the cause of the development deficits in the continent. As such, Daniel Etounga-Manguelle (2000) suggests that Africa needs a "cultural adjustment program." The culturecentric paradigm maintains that the main source of Africa's woes is the way Africans are culturally wired. The point of this perspective is to argue that African cultures instill in Africans dispositions that prevent them from being able to initiate and manage the transitions required to attain development.

Etounga-Manguelle (2000, 68–74) enumerates features of African culture that explain the development deficit, including the following: "weak controls over uncertainty," perception of "space and time as a single entity," lack of social mobility, domination of community over individuals, avoidance of conflict, preference for immediate pleasure and irrationalism. These features of African cultures inhibit development because they negatively shape the imaginative horizons of individuals and society.

Etounga-Manguelle observes that African cultures, instead of confronting uncertainty head-on, encourage people to accept superstition and sorcery.

What is achieved in the end is entrenchment of a social imaginery that is unable to deal with uncertainties—that is, a form of thinking that is poorly equipped to harness nature to improve human life. The effects of this inability to deal with uncertainties is further exacerbated by a lack of separation of space and time in African cultures. In Etounga-Manguelle's view, one cannot plan for the future if one is unable to differentiate space from time. Lack of social mobility, domination of individuals by community, and other forms of irrationalism, he suggests, inhibit development in Africa because these factors discourage the personal initiative needed to develop business skills and entrepreneurship.

African and Africanist scholars have long articulated the shortcomings of this approach to understanding the African condition (Odhiambo 2002). Etounga-Manguelle does not make a compelling case for the cultural norms paradigm he adopts to explain the challenges of development in Africa because most of what he identifies as features of African culture can be found everywhere. So, the question is, why do they hinder development in Africa but not in other places where they also obtain? Besides, one cannot fail to notice the sweeping generalization that forms the foundation of his claims and the anchoring of his overall argument in discredited colonial anthropology. Etounga-Manguelle is, however, not a lone voice crying in wilderness of despair. There has emerged in recent years an interest in how culture matters for progress in societies. Two notable scholars, Lawrence E. Harrison and Samuel P. Huntington (2000), produced an edited collection (titled *Culture Matters*) that brought together diverse views on the role of culture for progress in societies. It was in this book that Etounga-Manguelle's views on the impact of African culture on development appeared.

In his preface to the book, Huntington pointed out similarities and differences between South Korea and Ghana in terms of development. In the early 1960s, he says, economic data on both countries were similar. Both "countries had roughly comparable levels of per capita GNP; similar divisions of their economy among primary products, manufacturing, and services; and overwhelmingly primary product exports, with South Korea producing a few manufactured goods. Also, they were receiving comparable levels of economic aid" (Harrison and Huntington 2000, xiii). Looking back thirty years later, "South Korea had become an industrial giant with the fourteenth largest economy in the world. . . . It was on its way to the consolidation of democratic institutions. No such changes had occurred in Ghana, whose per capita GNP was now about one-fifteenth that of South Korea's" (xiii). Although he was aware that a number of factors could account for this disparity, he argued nonetheless that culture supplies a significant explanation for the situation.

The chapters of the book, written by leading scholars in diverse disciplines, discussed the way culture matters for economic and political development in the different regions of the world. Although the different chapters do not make the same argument, the texts focus on offering an analysis of the role culture plays in political, social, and economic development. This is remarkable for many reasons. But central among these reasons is that the return to the cultural paradigm, which for many years had social theory in its firm grip, gave a glimmer of hope vis-à-vis the quest for a viable explanation of the slow progress in economic, social, and political spheres in Africa. The turn to culture was therefore interesting for many scholars because models of explanation—such as dependency theory, colonialism, neocolonialism, imperialism, theories of the failed or weak state, and neoliberalism—had become untenable.

A few years after the publication of *Culture Matters*, Lawrence Harrison and Peter Berger published a book on culture and development. Titled *Developing Cultures*, the book attempted yet again to explain the role of culture in the economic and political progress of different societies. One chapter of the book focused on assessing the case of Botswana as an African success story. The stellar performance of Botswana, as opposed to other African countries, has in essence to do with the appropriation of aspects of the country's traditional culture that were conducive to the flourishing of democratic development. The claim is that, by building on the traditional practice of *kgotla*, Botswana was able to build a secure foundation for its national development plan. Botswana's development was enacted through careful planning, which ensured that "traditional patterns of consultation were extended to national legislative and administrative institutions" (Lewis 2006, 11). The country, thus, developed the means to avoid many pitfalls, especially those that would have led to disastrous consequences for the new nation.

African political theorists do not generally accept the culturecentric paradigm. As one prominent critic of this approach, Claude Ake (1996), observed, the problem is not African culture but the reaction of development theorists. In Ake's view, it is implausible to argue that African culture or norms are inhibitions to development because endorsing such a view will only lead to alienation and not development. It is mistaken to think African culture is inimical to progress due to the mere observation that it is resistant to development projects. The thought that the absence of certain features in a culture accounts for failure of progress in that society is tautological. Arguing in this manner amounts to saying, "The country that is developing or developed has the qualities needed for development, and the country that is not developing lacks them" (Ake 1996, 15).

The implication is that "everything is true by definition. One never really knows why and how a country is developing or why a country is not developing" (Ake 1996, 15). Instead of determining that the solution to a culture's resistance to development programs is to bypass the culture, the goal should be to ensure that development programs are aligned with culture—hence Ake's core argument of "building on the indigenous." According to Ake (1990, 1), this idea means to "take African societies seriously as they are, not as they ought to be or even as they might be." The indigenous is "whatever the people consider important in their lives, whatever they regard as an authentic expression of themselves" (1990, 1). By this Ake aims to underscore that we ought to allow people's self-understanding, values, hopes, and aspirations to determine the process of development.

The problem of Africa is its political condition. Ake (1996, 16) argues that "in postcolonial Africa the premium on power is exceptionally high, and the institutional mechanisms for moderating political competition are lacking. As a result, political competition tends to assume the character of warfare." The focus of elites on power defines every other pursuit as marginal and uninteresting. The consequence is that development becomes an ideology that is co-opted at whim by the elites in competition for power. Ake proposes to resolve this crisis by suggesting that we should shift attention to a paradigm he calls the "residual option"—a paradigm that asserts that "African countries can develop only in the context of democratic politics" (1996, 126).

This raises a question about the relationship between democracy and development. Whereas some think democracy makes development possible and meaningful, others believe that attaining an acceptable level of development is a prerequisite for democracy. The disagreements about the nexus between democracy and development will disappear, Ake argues, if we adopt his residual option paradigm. The assumptions of this paradigm include the conviction that (1) "development is not a project but a process," (2) "people create and recreate themselves and their circumstance through this process to realize better civilization which is in accordance with their own choices and values," (3) "people are the drivers of this process in the sense that they must realize it themselves," and (4) "it is a process that takes people as they are, not as they ought to be, as its starting point" (Ake 1996, 125). Ake's residual option puts people at the center of development. It sees them as not merely active participants in policy or decision-making processes but as the *end* of development. People's well-being constitutes the "supreme law of development" (1996, 124f).

Although Ake (1996, 126) argues that disagreements about the linkages between democracy and development will disappear if we adopt the residual option paradigm, his perspective is not without problems. Democracy may be necessary for development to take root in Africa, but this does not establish whether a democratic approach to development is feasible in this context. In response to this criticism, Ake underscores that the important thing is to discover the sort of democracy Africa needs. In his view, liberal accounts of the nature of democracy in Western social science do not suffice due to the peculiarities of Africa. As such, Ake has argued that a suitable system of democracy for Africa must guarantee that people have real decision-making power. In addition, the goal should be to establish a form of social democracy that guarantees concrete rights and emphasizes both collective rights and individual rights.

Ake suggests further that the viable form of democracy for Africa must be an inclusive form of governance, given the plurality of countries in Africa. The merits of Ake's solution notwithstanding, a question left unanswered pertains to why people would choose democracy as the means to resolve development challenges. Given the terrible history of the struggle for democracy in postcolonial Africa, it is reasonable to be skeptical about its merits. Atrocities of the most egregious kind were committed in the name of promoting democratic values. As such, more needs to be done to show the viability of this perspective. Besides, because of the fragmentary ethnic-group politics one can observe in this context, the *demos* Ake envisages is not clear. By *demos* I mean a common citizenship that makes democracy possible. This is a serious concern because citizenship is often tied to proto-nations, like ethnic belongingness.

Problems about the constitution of the demos in this context are evident in Mazrui's analysis of ethnicity. Mazrui (2001, 97) argues that ethnicity is the "sociocultural" ideology that shaped politics in colonial and postcolonial epochs. Africans, he says, "have responded more to sociocultural ideologies than to socioeconomic ideologies." This means factors of identity, race, and other social variables have been at the core of politics in Africa. Observing that there has been excessive imposition of European categories of political thought on African experience, Mazrui has made a case for reexamining these categories. His convinction is that, although colonialism destroyed the political institutions of traditional Africa, it did not succeed in destroying the values and ideas behind these institutions (2001, 98). He suggests that the following are the major traditions that influence politics in postcolonial Africa: elder tradition, warrior tradition, sage tradition, and monarchical tradition (99).

Elder tradition refers to widespread deference accorded to old age in African politics (Mazrui 2001, 102). Because of the value it attributes to old age, elder tradition prefers consensus as the hub of orientation in politics. The warrior tradition is different in that its cherished political orientation is discipline and not consensus. It pushes for "enforced agreement rather than a quest for compromise" (103). In the sage tradition, political leadership manifests "in terms of teacher-student" relationship (104). The leader embodies attributes of a sage and mentors the citizens, just like teachers would their students. The monarchical tradition is a unique style of politics. It mostly manifests in the elaborate performances of glamour displayed by African politicians, especially those in high office. Mazrui sees the monarchical tradition as an indication of a "quest for aristocratic effect" (105) contemporary politicians consider in most cases necessary for the legitimation of their authority.

The factors influencing postcolonial politics, in Mazrui's (2001) view, embody a normative viewpoint premised on notions of ethnicity. This means that there is "cultural continuity," at least at the normative level, between political experience in traditional Africa and that of the postcolonial era. To this end, Mazrui proposes six traditions that could help illuminate African political experience. He offers the following list: "the tribal tradition," "the dignitarian tradition," "the nationalist tradition," "the socialist tradition," and the tradition of democracy (99). Whereas the tribal tradition emphasizes continuity of ancestry and relies on experience to explain social transformation and political reality, the dignitarian tradition attempts to respond to the humiliation of the African person in history through restoration of dignity. The nationalist tradition is the quest for a basis of solidarity among people of African descent as a way to confront their collective challenges. Finally, the democracy tradition consists of attempts to conceive and entrench democracy in Africa as a way of resolving the continent's problems.

Peter Ekeh (1975), through his theory of two publics, provides a unique conception of politics in Africa. He explains the nature of the public sphere in a context where ethnicization of the political is a default mode. Scholars are paying closer attention to the idea of two publics in Africa due, in part, to the sound argument Ekeh makes regarding the impact of colonialism on the constitution of the demos in the continent. Ekeh argues that, in attempting to understand African political experience, we must consider that "colonialism is to Africa what feudalism is to Europe" (93). Thus, just as one would fail to have a good view of the European political condition without paying close attention to the experiences of feudalism in Europe, so too would one fail to comprehend the African political condition without an adequate grasp of the colonial experience.

Ekeh argues that there are two publics in postcolonial African societies, the *primordial public* and the *civic public*. Although the two publics coexist, the private sphere is not integrated in the way normally taken for granted by political theorists. The primordial public is the public of ethnic groups and reflects sentiments associated with such group identity. The civic public is associated with colonial structures of governance. Thus, whereas the primordial public "is moral and operates on the same moral imperatives as the private realm," the civic public "is amoral and lacks the generalized moral imperatives operative in the private realm and in the primordial public" (Ekeh 1975, 92). Of interest here is that Ekeh proposed this view before Habermas's idea of the public sphere was published in English. Thus, the perceptive insights of his notion of the two publics lie not only in its originality but also in its independent provenance as a way of explaining the African political experience.

Essential in this approach to African politics is the proposition that the cause of the ills in this context is the bifurcation of the public sphere. Without finding an adequate response to the challenge posed by the bifurcated public sphere, hoping for solutions to the problems afflicting African politics will remain futile. There is, in other words, an urgent need to restore to African politics a symmetrical notion of the public sphere where there is no value variance between the primordial and civic publics. Ekeh's conviction is that we find the uniqueness of African politics in the experience of colonization (1975, 111). Thus, attempts to explain contemporary African politics cannot discount the colonial experience because it is the background of the values, practices, and morality that shape politics in this epoch.

LIMITATIONS OF THE LOGIC OF DISCOURSE

When we put the discussion so far in perspective, we find that explanations of the African condition have tended to revolve around a central logic. Scholars attempt to reconstruct the nature of the crisis in Africa and then argue for specific remedies based on their view of this crisis. This can be called a *problem-solution approach* to African political experiences. The paradigms of explanation considered to this point are beholden to this logic. The models of exaplantion that look to the nature of the state in Africa, such as the failed state paradigm and its various modifications or critiques, express this logic by appealing to features of the state to explain politics in Africa.

The problem-solution logic gives us the impression that understanding a problem automatically translates to finding an adequate solution. We see this linearity in the economic development and modernization paradigms. In attempting to explain the African condition through consideration of the failures in the economic sphere, scholars who deploy this model of analysis express a belief in the idea that the solution to Africa's challenges will emerge if the conditions for development and modernization are made to flourish. For instance, if it is determined that the bane of development is the resistance of African culture to development, it is immediately assumed that establishing the condition that will make African culture more amenable to development is sufficient to solve the current crisis of the continent.

Noting that there is a linear logic at the center of the paradigms African and Africanist social theorists rely on to explain African political experience is not enough to invalidate these paradigms. More must be done to show why the central assumption of these paradigms is flawed. We can see why the problem-solution assumption of these paradigms that attempt to explain African political experience is inadequate if we take current African political experience as essentially a phenomenon of political failure.

What I am arguing is not that the problem-solution logic eschews reflection on the complexity of African political experience. Far from that, the paradigms of explanation we have considered undeniably recognize the complex nature of postcolonial African experience. In attempts to understand the political crisis in Africa and propose theories that will ensure a better future in the continent, the paradigms of explanation we have considered indeed acknowledge the complexities involved. In other words, theories of the state in Africa and related models of analysis are complex in themselves and in their dissection of the contemporary African political experience.

The problem of these paradigms lies in the general assumption that the linear logic of the problem-solution approach is fitting for the comprehension of African political experience. The problem-solution logic, which is assumed by these paradigms is linear in the sense that it proceeds by isolating layers of causes to link with effects. In this logic, features of, say, African culture, are isolated and then used to explain such effects as institutional inefficiency, deficient development, and corruption. This leads to the inference that there is a foundational assumption regarding the nature of causality in the sphere of politics; that is, to have an effect B, you must do A. To put it differently, the assumption of this logic gives the impression that an effect, B, is prevalent because a cause, A, obtains. Therefore, to solve B, we only must eliminate A, which is its cause. This is the mode of reasoning that conveys the assumption of problem-solution logic.

The issue, however, is that causality of this sort cannot be validly applied to politics in the African context, the reason being the cognitive disarray in the imagination of politics after experiences of colonial oppression. The linear problem-solution logic is deficient due to the complexity of the political sphere in most of postcolonial Africa. African political experience in the present century is tied to the complex task of finding new idioms, metaphors, or concepts to express the ends of politics. Because of the implosion of indigenous concepts and normative outlook, the African political world confronts the task of reconceptualizing the nature of meaning making in politics. Thus, in this context, political processes are too dynamic, complex, and fluctuational to be amenable to the tenets of a methodology that assumes a linearity of events in politics. Such an approach is incapable of dealing with such situations as we find in African societies, where there exist numerous cognitive confusions engendered by uncertainties about how to make sense of the purpose of political praxis. I will return to this issue in chapter 4, where I will demonstrate the link between African political experience and conceptual loss.

For the moment, it should suffice to note that the linear logic at the core of the problem-solution approach cannot account for the significant aspects of African experience that would persist even should the current challenges be resolved. By this I mean to suggest that the problem-solution approach is severely constrained because it is incapable of accounting for salient questions implicated in the evolution of African politics. To make this point clearer, we need to consider that each of the paradigms adopting the problem-solution approach offer different diagnoses and solutions based on the assumption that solving the crisis confronting Africa demands establishing the link between causes and effects. But then, given the disparity of solutions offered, how should we choose? If we assume that all the paradigms are correct and that they will lead to the resolution of the political crisis in the continent, why should we settle for one option and not the other?

Why, for instance, should we take the advice of the proposal that salvation for Africa lies in advancing economic development, as opposed to the perspective that claims that the essential thing to do is to reverse the tide of failed states afflicting Africa? Merely linking cause and effect and establishing on the basis of this linkage a direction for the future cannot provide an adequate answer to the challenge of political failure. Should one proceed by relying on the linear logic of the problem-solution approach, one will remain unable to provide answers to such questions as why it is good to pursue one option and not another regarding the quest for development in the continent. Without probing further what political failure demands in the context of African political experience, it may well turn out that Africa will modernize and build strong states and economies but remain a perplexing dystopia immersed in debilitating crises of meaning.

The core of my proposition therefore is that an analysis of the political failure that constitutes the core of the contemporary African crisis must do more than propose solutions to particular problems. The reason this is the case can be best explained through reflection on the nature of political failure. What does it mean to view the contemporary African crisis as a phenomenon of political failure? What is political failure, anyway, and how does it apply to Africa's political experience? There are at least three possible ways to understand the notion of political failure. To point out the specific sense I give the concept, let us consider three understandings of political failure: failure of politics, failure of government, and failure of public culture or political culture.

Understood as failure of politics, political failure would refer to a situation where either the ideology of political praxis has failed or is in deep crisis. This may, for instance, occur when liberalism as an ideology of politics fails in its role as the organizing principle of political praxis in countries that profess the tenets of liberalism. The failure of government perspective implies conceiving political failure as collapse of the asymmetry that guarantees the requisite alignment necessary for institutions of governance, especially state bureaucracy, to function. From the perspective of public culture, political failure is a situation where the self-understanding of a people is in deep crisis and hence is not able to ensure cohesion among the polity, provide meaning for ideology, or enable the imagination of a new utopia that responds adequately to new experiences they are attempting to conceptualize and overcome.

Although the first and second senses of political failure (failure of politics and failure of government) present serious challenges to countries, the third sense (failure of public culture) is the most devastating. When a people's self-understanding is in deep crisis and unable to give meaning to ideology, ensure cohesion, and enable contemplation of a new utopia, the result is loss of a reference point for articulating meaning. Should this occur, experiences will become merely the aggregation of events that occur randomly, and politics will be transformed into a permanent state of responding to everyday emergencies. The sense of teleology will be lost, and a crippling feeling of inertia overtakes the agency of people in the sphere of politics. The crisis of self-understanding is therefore a totalizing form of political failure because where it occurs, there will be uncertainty regarding how to conceive the good life and, subsequently, a well-ordered society that will constitute the end of social and political pursuits.

It is the third sense of political failure that I am concerned about in the inquiry to follow. The challenge of political failure as a failure of public culture in Africa demands a different approach to conceiving solutions to political problems. It requires us to first acknowledge that we cannot proceed by seeking to find out the cause of the problem in order to propose a solution. The challenge posed by the phenomenon of political failure in this sense requires us to contemplate the possibility of developing a new form of political philosophy. This means to conceive an approach to reconstruct a sense of self-understanding that will provide a reference point for a political culture in the African context. As we have seen, perspectives that explain African political experience through recourse to the problem-solution paradigm miss this point. Perhaps African philosophers have an answer that is viable and systematically justified? It is to their analysis that we turn for an answer in the next chapter.

AFRICAN POLITICAL THOUGHT

Theory through Conceptual Retrieval

ONE OF THE MOST CRITICAL voices in African philosophy, Olusegun Oladipo (2000, 100), expressed eloquently his discontent with the field by noting that "while African intellectual-politicians . . . were busy fashioning political philosophies (or ideologies) for the newly independent African states . . . African (professional) philosophers were busy posing, and philosophically addressing, the question of whether there was an African philosophy." This observation is a serious indictment of African philosophers that needs further probing. To understand the discussion regarding the nature and significance of the experience of political failure, we need to examine the disciplinary context that shapes intellectual pursuits in African political thought. Why does Oladipo level this charge, and how is his claim borne out by the history of African political thought? This is the question I aim to answer in this chapter. I argue that inherent in African political thought is a normative deficit that must be tackled in the interest of finding answers to novel challenges. To make conceptual resources in African political thought capable of informing answers to current political challenges, we must make them fit again for the normative theorizing demanded by current challenges. Getting to this point requires us to consider how African political theorists have attempted to conceptualize the continent's political experience and the normative deficit inherent in the attempts.

Oladipo is certainly not worried that African philosophers are doing bad philosophy. His concern is not that debates about the existence of African philosophy is neither interesting nor useful. In the passage cited above, he is pointing to a fundamental concern—namely, that, given the reality they face, the question thought relevant by African philosophers is problematic. The point Oladipo is making should become clearer in his suggestion that, as scholars, philosophers have a social responsibility determined by the environment in which they exist and engage in their activity of intellection. He makes the argument buttressing this claim in two stages. First, he links scholarship to societal pursuits to show why it is correct to assert that scholars have a social responsibility. Secondly, he leverages the implications of the ties between scholarship and the pursuit of the good life to argue that African philosophers have a social responsibility to their context.

The first stage of Oladipo's argument is to demonstrate that there is plausibility to the thought that scholars owe their societies certain duties. He makes this case by pointing out, first, that scholars are part of a human society, a rather incontrovertible point. In addition, he contends that scholarship thrives within a context—namely, in societies that have concrete realities that are shaped by specific concerns. This could mean good or bad for scholarship. Should a society create an environment that is supportive of scholarship, then, scholars can thrive. When this happens, scholars enter into a relationship of reciprocity with their society because they make demands on the society to create conditions conducive to scholarship.

By making the intellectual pursuits of scholars possible, societies establish the ground for reciprocity on the part of scholars. Taking this expectation of reciprocity as a legitimate social responsibility, Oladipo (2000, 94) argues that reciprocity on the part of scholars "becomes more pressing in African societies where the struggle for survival, as Nigerians would put it, has become so severe that the difference between a commitment to human interests in the society and indifference to them, translates easily to a preference for life or death." The main point of the first stage of Oladipo's argument is to show that two things impinge on scholars' activities. One is the fact that they belong to specific societies. The other is that they thrive on the basis of the demand that society should create conditions conducive to scholarship. If we take these two points together, what they amount to, in Oladipo's view, is justification of the claim that scholars have a social responsibility to their societies.

The second stage of Oladipo's argument links scholarship to the pursuit of the good life, the goal being to demonstrate that this constitutes a challenge for African philosophers. We find this linkage in the unity of knowledge and the good life. Knowledge, he says, is an effort on the part of human beings to harness nature to their advantage. Thus, scholarship has a teleology. It is not itself an *end*. Scholarship, he argues, serves the fundamental purpose of enabling people to realize improvements of living conditions that enhance overall well-being. To this end, "the commitment of a scholar cannot be to the pursuit of knowledge for its own sake. Rather it would be to the human interests of the community in which he functions as a scholar" (2000, 95).

What is hereby established is that intellectual commitment must be to furtherance of the good life. Another way to say this is to propose that the ethics of scholarship is located in the context of the response scholars offer to address the challenge of realizing the good life. Should a scholar not show commitment to the pursuit of the good life but to an abstract notion of scholarship for its own sake, we can infer a dereliction of duty on the part of the scholar. For African scholars, the direct consequence is clear: they ought "to be committed to Africa, its problems, hopes and aspirations," meaning that African scholars "would have to put whatever intellectual skills [they have] to the service of the African quest for growth, development, justice and freedom" (Oladipo 2000, 96). Taking this point seriously would lead African scholars to be very attentive to the practical dimensions of scholarship.

AFRICAN PHILOSOPHERS AND THEIR DUTY TO AFRICA

How does this claim relate to African philosophers? The straightforward, descriptive answer is that an African engaged in scholarship is an African scholar. As such, African philosophers are first of all African scholars. Beyond this descriptive answer, however, there is a deeper sense in which the foregoing is relevant to African philosophers. This has to do with the fact that African philosophers spent most of their time in the postcolonial period debating whether African philosophy exists.

As already noted, Oladipo's view is that the unity of scholarship and the good life sets the agenda for the conception of the questions that should guide African scholars. His proposal is that African scholars should be guided by questions about the relevance of investigations in their disciplines for the attainment of the good life. This is the reason Oladipo believes that it is simply pointless—in fact, dangerous—to be so obsessed with questions regarding the existence or otherwise of African philosophy, as African philosophers were during the first few decades after independence. As Oladipo (2000, 97) argues, "what would be the point of abstract definitions and classifications in a human community where, at the dawn of the 21st century, the realization of any meaningful development programme is still elusive and life (for the majority at least) is becoming increasingly 'nasty, brutish and short'?"

Although we can infer different conclusions from Oladipo's charge of dereliction of duty on the part of African philosophers (Oladipo 2000, 100), I will focus on explicating one conclusion. Seen in context, his observation that indifference by African philosophers to their situation could mean a preference for life or death shows that scholarship in African academia is bound to always involve an ethical concern. African scholars have a responsibility to contribute to the realization of human well-being. In Oladipo's view, this means they ought to pay attention to how their inquiry can be relevant to Africa. Thus, the duty he has in mind is the sort of duty one can only ignore due to a serious constraint. Such constraint would require an acceptable justification that must show, among other things, that the scholar unable to carry out the duty is at least not indifferent to the condition of society. The justification must demonstrate that there are reasons why the scholar in question cannot fulfill the envisaged social responsibility and why regardless of this constraint, scholars can continue to make demands on their society to provide an environment conducive to scholarship.

Although African philosophers agree that—as African scholars—they should theorize the conditions of existence in Africa, understandings of the path to this goal differ. Disagreements about the nature of African philosophy thus do not just indicate anxiety about the universality of philosophy, especially in the Western tradition. It is a response to the ethical aspect of scholarship in Africa. What should African philosophers do in response to the situation of the continent? How should they respond to the claim that they have a social responsibility in relation to the conditio humana in Africa, without pretending to be able to deliver more than they really can deliver? This is the disciplinary context that shaped engagements with African philosophy at the time of its emergence as a field of inquiry in postcolonial African universities.

It is important to note that Oladipo's discussion of the challenge of relevance faces a shortcoming. He fails to distinguish between two aspects of the problem of relevance he raised. In fact, his charge that African scholars and, by extension, African philosophers should be attentive to the issue of relevance implies two things. Firstly, it implies there are one or more compelling, context-specific reasons that make attentiveness to context desirable. Second, it entails that African philosophers do not as yet pay sufficient attention to the demands of relevance. Although exploration of the former implication might be related to issues that lie at the heart of the latter, it is mistaken to assume that the two issues are the same. Arguing that a duty expected of an agent is imperative and desirable cannot surely be equated with accounting for the reasons the agent has neglected to perform the desired duty.

In other words, showing that African philosophers have a duty to pay attention to how their work can be relevant to their context does not tell us why they have not been attentive to the demand. Oladipo's discussion of the problem of relevance, which he sees as confronting African philosophers as African scholars, is a case for the imperativeness and desirability of relevance. The problem, however, is that we cannot evaluate the claim, which suggests that African philosophers should ensure their intellectual musings are relevant to their context, without knowing if indeed it is the case that African philosophers are inattentive to context. Evaluating the cogency of Oladipo's proposition that African philosophers owe their society a social responsibility is contingent on knowing if and why African philosophers have neglected this duty.

Henri Maurier (1984) provides a perspective on why African philosophers have not paid attention to the duty Oladipo suggests. For Maurier, African philosophers cannot produce what might be called genuine African philosophy because they lack a conceptual scheme that will make such an endeavor possible. The ideas of an African philosopher "will become truly African when his philosophy is finally thought through a conceptual framework properly African, adapted to African realities" (1984, 31). The absence of such a conceptual framework explains why African philosophers may well not be fulfilling the social responsibility Oladipo postulated. We can see why this thought is important if we recall that the imposition of foreign conceptual frameworks on African reality is the easiest route to explain African experience "by posing all sorts of false problems and giving them pseudosolutions" (31). For African philosophers to philosophize in ways that are attentive to context, they need first to develop the tools suited for the proper apprehension of African realities, so the claim goes.

Regardless of the value of conceptual frameworks for the task of apprehending African realities, Maurier, it seems to me, is incorrect to assume that African philosophers ought to first develop an African conceptual framework before they can create a tradition of philosophy genuinely African. My point is not that conceptual frameworks are unimportant. My claim is that Maurier is proposing a sequence of events that neither obtains nor is informed by the sort of necessity he implies. Wherever there is a thriving tradition of philosophy, fully developed conceptual frameworks usually emerge due to a sustained dialogue among the philosophers working in that tradition.

It is usually not the case that philosophers first have to step back to develop a conceptual framework before their work can become genuinely part of a tradition. By suggesting that developing an African tradition of philosophy demands a prior task of conceiving a conceptual framework that is duly African, Maurier is putting forward a false sequence of order. It is invalid to claim that developing a conceptual framework is a condition for the creation of a body of work that make up a genuine tradition of thought. Rather than being prior, conceptual frameworks emerge from the very activity of philosophizing about the *human condition* in specific places and epochs. Thus, there is neither necessity nor cogency to Maurier's attempts to postulate a relationship of priority between developing a conceptual framework and the emergence of a genuine African tradition of philosophy that can be useful to its context.

There are a number of other reasons that are worth exploring if we want to explain why African philosophers neglected their social responsibility, as Oladipo has alleged. These reasons include issues related to institutional context that shaped the emergence of philosophy as a field of inquiry in postcolonial African societies, the impact of history on the education of the first cohort of African philosophers, and the lack of structures necessary to encourage research in African philosophy. These are practical challenges that could only be resolved with time. Thus, although these challenges were cogent explanations for the slow take-off of the sort of philosophical activity in African universities that is relevant to its context, they have lost the force of their validity in the present decade (Okeja 2012).

The practical concerns first generation African philosophers confronted cannot be invoked in the present century to explain why African philosophers might choose to not engage with African realities. There are now institutional frameworks for the advancement of the pursuit of philosophy in a way that is attentive to African realities. In many places, courses on African philosophy now constitute an essential part of the philosophy curriculum. Even in universities in South Africa, where this was not the case a little less than a decade ago, things are changing rapidly as serious efforts are underway to review the philosophy curriculum in most of the universities there.

The history of the events that shaped modern African philosophy are connected to the problem of relevance (Bodunrin 1985, viii; 1992, 18; Sogolo 1988; 1990, 15). This issue is reflected in debates about what it means to do philosophy in a way that is responsive to the environment in which the philosopher finds herself or himself (Janz 2009; Jones 2006; Jones and Metz 2015). Regarding the African trained in philosophy, the demand of relevance is that she or he should practice philosophy in a way that is responsive to Africa—that is, in a manner that takes insights embedded in the experience and *Lebenswelt* of Africans as its starting point. Thus, the way we conceive the starting point of our philosophical reflection is an ethical issue.

In this light, we can say that the debate on the existence of African philosophy was an ethical matter in two senses—namely, concerning *choice* and *attitude*. The polemics in the debate on African philosophy became necessary because it was assumed that the attitude expressed toward the work of an African philosopher is a form of moral judgment about the professional ethics of the philosopher in question. One whose work was perceived to exemplify or promote ethnophilosophy was in a sense charged with professional dishonesty. And one whose work was labeled neopositivist was in effect charged with dereliction of an important professional responsibility. This is why understanding the debate on the existence of African philosophy from the viewpoint of ethics is relevant for the attempt here to explore the response of African political philosophy to the challenge of political failure, which is the main feature that defines postcolonial African experience.

Taking the observations about the narratives that shaped the emergence of the field of African philosophy as the starting point of this chapter provides a background to understand African political philosophy as an academic field. The ethical dimension of the debate on the nature of African philosophy matters because it provides a suitable framework through which we can evaluate the theories of African political philosophers. Understanding the ethical concerns relating to the field of African philosophy therefore sets us on a good path to make sense of the pace of progress in the field of African political philosophy. Beginning the inquiry in this chapter with a brief assessment of the historical debate that shaped the field of African philosophy enables us to be attentive to assumptions that are central to concerns about canon formation—that is, concerns about what belongs to the domain of African political philosophy proper and what is closely related to broader concerns in African thought that are rather more a part of postcolonial theory, development studies, or even political anthropology of Africa.

AFRICAN POLITICAL THEORISTS AND EXPERIENCE OF POLITICAL FAILURE

Let us now turn to the issue of political failure. The question to ask is whether African political theorists fare better than their Africanist counterparts in understanding and responding to this phenomenon, given the history of African philosophy. How did African political philosophers conceptualize and attempt to resolve the challenge posed by political failure? Said differently, what are the theories about the challenge of African political experience developed by African philosophers? To consider these questions, I think it is reasonable to begin with a description of the concerns that shaped the works of postcolonial African philosophers, starting from the period of anticolonial struggle until the present decade. The focus in the description will be on the political thought of leaders of anticolonial struggle who fall into the category of sub-Saharan pan-Africanism, as Mazrui called them. In this chapter, I focus on this brand of pan-Africanists, but the discussion will continue in chapter 3 with examination of ideas of professional African philosophers.

The aim of the present chapter and the next is therefore to examine the viability of the major ideas offered by African political theorists on the phenomenon of political failure. I argue, partly in this chapter but more fully in the next chapter, that more systematic thinking is needed to conceive a political philosophy not only informed by contemporary experience of political failure but one that can address the problem posed by this experience. Conceiving such a philosophy will only be possible if it is premised on a new normative orientation in African political philosophy, something yet to be developed. This explains why the deliberation-based account of contemporary African political philosophy I articulate is preceded by explication of the method of conceptual creativity as a new orientation in African political philosophy. I turn to these tasks in chapter 6. In the meantime, we shall proceed with an exploration of attempts by African political theorists to deal with the continent's political experience.

The literature on African political philosophy offers diverse responses to issues related to African experience in the postcolonial era. The texts address wide-ranging questions, such as negritude, African socialism, critical modernity, theories of democracy, African personality, and colonial mentality. Although African philosophers seem to agree with Oladipo that African scholars, especially philosophers, must be attentive to their social responsibility, the ideas they offer revolve around concerns similar to their Africanist counterparts. Before arguing this point, I would like to explore the views they propound to explain postcolonial experiences in the continent. I undertake this task as a way to provide a systematic analysis. To this end, I consider the main concerns of African political philosophers from the era of anticolonial struggle until the present decade. The aim is to show how questions raised at different times in the history of this tradition of political philosophy constitute attempts to respond to the experience of political failure.

Edward Blyden coined the concept African personality in 1893 to convey his thoughts about the common experience and aspirations of Negros everywhere. The concept inspired Africans in their nationalist struggles, especially for freedom in the sense of independence and self-rule (Smet 1984, 83). Although it is contested in what sense it can be assumed that pan-Africanism is a coherent body of thought, it can nonetheless be affirmed that the concept was important to people committed to the emancipation of Africans everywhere. The concept of pan-Africanism may be opaque when viewed as the global nationalism of Black people in the quest to restore their dignity. Mazrui (2001, 108) has aptly noted the difficulty involved in stipulating the sense "Africans and the diaspora in the Americas, but also black people in Europe, the Arab world, and even the aborigines of Australia and the people of Papua New Guinea . . . would be searching for a sense of shared nationhood." In the absence of a rational basis to postulate a shared nationhood as the core of pan-Africanism, it would be reasonable to assume there is more to the concept beyond nationalism. But this cannot be deciphered if one does not distinguish between different senses of the concept.

Mazrui (2001) proposed that there are at least five strands of pan-Africanism: sub-Saharan pan-Africanism, transatlantic pan-Africanism, trans-Saharan pan-Africanism, trans-American pan-Africanism, and global pan-Africanism. At the foundation of various forms of pan-Africanism lie the solidarity of people of African descent across geographical spaces. Thus, sub-Saharan pan-Africanism is the strand of solidarity among sub-Saharan Africans, while transatlantic pan-Africanism refers to a similar form of solidarity that obtains among African descendants in Africa and the West. The trans-Saharan form of pan-Africanism would then be the solidarity of Africans extending across the Sahara. The solidarity of Black people in North America, Latin America and the Caribbean, is designated by Mazrui as trans-American pan-Africanism. And, to round it off, global pan-Africanism is the solidarity of Black people everywhere in the world.

Discussing the responses of African philosophers to postcolonial African experiences does not require us to examine in detail all the strands of pan-Africanism. It should suffice to focus on the sub-Saharan strand because what is important is the understanding of the way the evolution of this movement shaped the thoughts of the major figures of anticolonial struggle. The aim therefore is to inquire into pan-Africanism as a broad category that offered anticolonial figures a framework to understand African experience. We learn from J. T. Erumeva (1985, 190) that in sub-Saharan pan-Africanist movements "it is widely recognized that the formation of a strong and virile political union by emergent African states is the fundamental guarantee for true development and progress in the African continent. As long as individual African states continue to ignore their joint potential, each one struggling separately for progress, not only are their efforts doomed to fail, the task of freeing themselves from outside exploitation would be extremely difficult if not altogether impossible." This is a clear synopsis of the ideas of sub-Saharan pan-Africanists on the African condition. African solidarity at the sub-Saharan level was considered essential because it enabled the realization of aspirations like development, political progress, and freedom.

Although this is true of major figures of sub-Saharan pan-Africanism, the ways their ideas at the individual level reflected this understanding varies. Also, proposals for the realization of the goals enabled by pan-Africanism bear marks of differences worth taking seriously. This implies that it is necessary to look closely at the manner in which pan-Africanists understood the continent's experiences and the proposals made on this basis regarding what an adequate response would entail. Due to the expansive nature of the literature on pan-Africanism, I will review the ideas of only a few representative figures in the movement.

Although I cannot justify the choice of the figures discussed, it is important to note that my aim is to pay attention to the influence of each figure beyond the local context in which they worked. The figures I will discuss include Kwame Nkrumah, Julius Nyerere, Nnamdi Azikiwe, Amilcar Cabral, and Leopold Senghor. My aim is to explain their contributions to understanding and resolving the challenges posed by the African political experience. This means that I will be less interested in interpreting the tenets of pan-Africanism. Instead, I will focus on distilling from the works of these pan-Africanists an understanding of African experience to consider the viability of the ideas they offer on the phenomenon of political failure.

KWAME NKRUMAH

Kwame Nkrumah was prominent in sub-Saharan pan-Africanism for many reasons. Not only was his country, Ghana, the first to gain political independence, but he was also one of the few African participants, as opposed to those from the Diaspora, at the fifth congress of pan-Africanists in Manchester in 1945. Throughout his political career, especially prior to the toppling of his government by the military in 1967, he devoted his energy and sagacity to the project of envisioning a path that could lead Africans to freedom and prosperity.

He invested so much confidence in his belief in African unity that he accepted that Ghana should be ready to surrender her sovereignty if doing so would advance the interests of a united Africa. Although convinced still in later years of the necessity of African unity as a path to achieve a better future for Africa, Nkrumah's understanding of what the pursuit requires changed due to his concerns about neocolonialism. Whereas he was initially convinced about the efficacy of political unity in bringing about the desired unity of Africa, he abandoned this view to affirm another path to African unity—namely, establishing a unity of African peoples and not African governments.

His pan-Africanist vision required the development of a social and political philosophy that would ensure its realization and assessment. Said differently, Nkrumah was convinced that a philosophically grounded ideology was required to guarantee the orientation and means to pursue and regulate the ideals of pan-Africanism. He addressed this task in his study of the problem of freedom and economic prosperity in Africa. In *Consciencism: Philosophy and Ideology for Decolonization and Development with Particular Reference to the African Revolution*, Nkrumah (1965) proposed a materialist philosophy he says avoids the pitfalls of rationalism and empirical idealism. The philosophy in his view offers a foundation of an egalitarian society founded on a materialist ontology. Certainly, to say Nkrumah offered a foundation for the social and political change he envisioned for Africa does not amount to asserting that there is homogeneity to the entirety of Nkrumah's works.

Like Paulin Hountondji (1983) has noted, reading Nkrumah's work demands approaching it from a historical angle. Adopting such a perspective enables us to "rediscover the unfinished text of a thought in search of itself beneath the system in which it has been trapped, willingly, for a while." Reading Nkrumah requires that we "restore to the work its hesitations, its internal contradictions, its life" (Hountondji 1983, 134). This means we must distinguish between earlier and later phases of Nkrumah's works. While a study of the earlier phase focuses on elaborating the concepts and arguments he employed in his push for the realization of independence from colonial rule, the latter phase is directed more toward analyzing the way he dealt with the complex challenges of freedom under neocolonial conditions. The point of the distinction between the two phases of Nkrumah's work is that some of the ideas he advanced during the first phase would come into tension or contradict what he proposed in the latter phase of his work. Thus, by looking at his oeuvre as a historically situated attempt to make sense of reality in Africa, we can see the sense in which Nkrumah's ideas are a stream of an ever-evolving reflection on the human condition in Africa.

Nkrumah aimed to construct an African socialism through a framework of Marxist philosophy and the analysis of social life in traditional African society. In *Consciencism*, he relied on dialectical materialism and categorial conversion to construct the foundation upon which a plausible system of values for postcolonial Africa could be premised. He believed class struggle cannot account for the basic structure of precolonial African societies because of its idealist presupposition. He held that a form of materialism constitutes the foundation of traditional African reality, making Africa predisposed for successful implementation of the principles of egalitarianism.

Nkrumah proposed that there is a crisis of conscience in Africa. He interpreted this crisis to be indicative of the continent's loss of identity. This crisis is schizophrenic and arises from the incompatibility of traditional African values and the values of two religions exerting far-reaching influence in Africa: Christianity and Islam. Nkrumah's diagnosis of the challenge of postcolonial African experience is that decolonization is necessary to restore the dignity of Africans. Resolving postcolonial challenges would be possible only if we develop a conception of the necessary transitions African societies need to make to reap the fruits of the advantages of self-rule.

It is against the background of this diagnosis that Nkrumah insisted in *Consciencism* that the transition Africa must make after decolonization is to reestablish values that align with the materialist ontology of traditional Africa—that is, to reconstruct the socialist values that informed life in traditional African societies. Egalitarianism for him coheres with the ontological foundations of African societies, just as socialism is a better way for postcolonial Africa. This is because "the condition for optimum development which shall be humanist is socialist through and through" (1968, 114). To this end, Nkrumah's argument is that socialism is not just the foundation of social life in precolonial Africa; the modified version he offers is essential for the establishment of a form of development that is desirable and fitting for Africans.

Given the humanistic outlook of traditional African societies, the value they embody can be reestablished by conceptualizing and implementing a socialist system. Nkrumah (1968, 114) goes further to suggest that his socialist formula summarizes "a number of weighty truths, namely, that there is socialism if and only if there is the conjoint presence of philosophical materialism, philosophical consciencism, dialectic and national unity in a liberated territory." By this means, Nkrumah supplies through his theory of consciencism what the basic structure of traditional African society lacked.

We can, to this end, say with Diana E. Axelsen (1984, 233–234) that Nkrumah's attempts to come to grips with the African condition led him to emphasize "the socialist ideals of equality and human integrity, on the basis of his dialectical materialism and his doctrine of categorial conversion. His application of materialism leads him, too, to a Marxist treatment of class struggle, but with a profound difference; he acknowledges the centrality of racial and national liberation, and thus develops the doctrine of Pan-Africanism."

A prominent critique of Nkrumah's ideas came from Hountondji, who argued that Nkrumah's attempt to resolve the crisis in African conscience is spurious. Hountondji (1983) asserted that an attempt like Nkrumah's to resolve the challenge of pluralism in Africa through a synthesis that reduces to collectivism does not stand up to scrutiny. The "ideological unity" Nkrumah advances in his solution to the so-called African crisis of conscience is disappointing because it is an "unanimist illusion," which is tantamount to endorsing the view that politics is only possible when it is firmly established on an ontological foundation. This is not evidently true, Hountondji points out, because the "political as a level of discourse" has its own autonomy. As such, it is "unnecessary" for Nkrumah to attempt to anchor his political discourse on a "discursive authority"—namely, the ontological materialism he attributes to African societies (1983, 154).

Katrin Flikschuh (2017) responds to Hountondji's criticism by arguing that it is not clear the sense in which a socially engaged philosophy of the sort John Rawls and Nkrumah developed can maintain a clear-cut separation between ideology and philosophy. Besides Hountondji, a number of African philosophers argued against the shortcomings of Nkrumah's diagnosis and response to the African condition. What is at issue for these discussions relates to the difficulties associated with the relationship of socialism and authoritarianism, especially in the guise of the one-party state whose socialist dreams injured the quest for lasting solutions to political challenges in Africa. I evaluate Nkrumah's propositions toward the end of this chapter when I make a case for a new normative orientation in African political philosophy. In the meantime, let us consider another philosopher-politician, Julius Nyerere, to understand his perspective on African political experience.

Like Nkrumah, Nyerere was also invested in developing solutions to the challenge of freedom and governance in postcolonial Africa. Focusing on political independence, Nyerere envisioned freedom for African people on the basis of social and political strategies aimed at overthrowing colonial rule and establishing a system of governance that is true to African values and aspirations. In this discussion of his comprehension of the African political condition, I focus mainly on exploring his notion of Ujamaa, which now is a popular shorthand for his political thought. The background to Nyerere's philosophy of Ujamaa is his conviction that the challenge of postcolonial Africa is essentially about the mind. He considers the mental disposition of Africans as a vital battleground. The major challenge is to reclaim the African mind from distortions introduced by colonization. This conviction is at the center of Nyerere's development of Ujamaa philosophy.

JULIUS NYERERE

In his initial description of Ujamaa, Nyerere (1968) pointed out the linkages between systems of political rule and mental attitudes. By beginning the explication of the principle of Ujamaa in this way, what Nyerere aimed to achieve was to show that there are good reasons to adopt the system he advocates. His philosophy of Ujamaa unfolds as a linkage of four basic issues that culminate in one grand system. These four issues are the connection between political systems and mental attitudes, the contrast of the different states of mind and the system they may logically produce, inferences about the cogency of mental attitudes in traditional Africa and the socialist system it produced, and finally, explanation of the steps necessary to build a desirable socialist system for postcolonial Africa.

Given that socialism is an attitude of mind, a socialist system cannot produce citizens who exhibit certain forms of social, economic, and political proclivities. Looking on the socialist attitude of mind as the central feature of traditional African societies enables us to see why the reestablishment of African socialism is vital for the resolution of postcolonial challenges in Africa. Not only will this move help to stem the evils of unsocialist systems and the corruption of social and political virtues introduced by colonialization; it will contribute positively by accelerating development. This is because it activates African values.

For Nyerere (1968, 12), the path postcolonial Africa should follow to secure a better future is in fact self-evident, for, as he noted, "we, in Africa, have no more need of being 'converted' to socialism than we have of being 'taught' democracy. Both are rooted in our own past—in the traditional society which produced us." Nyerere's insistence that ideas of traditional Africa should be reconceptualized as foundation of politics in postcolonial Africa is similar to Nkrumah's assertion that, when it comes to using indigenous African knowledge, the important issue is not to determine whether Africans have a written tradition. The focus should instead be on the very existence of thought in traditional Africa. Given that the thought informing social and political values in traditional Africa can be recaptured, what is needed is to determine the framework that will make these values useable again after colonial interruption.

Although one may be tempted to think this is a naive approach to tackling the effects of colonization and nation building, I think Nyerere is neither naive nor uninformed. It is evident that what he is advocating is a reconstruction of the very conditions of social and political life in postcolonial Africa. Understood as the embodiment of social and political virtues, the principle of Ujamaa he proposed is meant to recapture the very possibility of politics in a society whose reference point, regarding social and political values, has been shattered. Nyerere should be understood as providing, through his idea of Ujamaa, an indispensable reference point for the values that should constitute the basis upon which political orientation, in the sense of political culture, can be premised.

The form of African socialism Nyerere (1968, 2) proposes is opposed to capitalism, not because the end of the former is good as opposed to the end of the latter. The opposition between these two ideas of social and political organization arises due to the means they employ. Here we see an indication of the reason a reconstruction of a foundation for a new political culture is essential for Nyerere. Due to the widespread perception that the material progress that is closely tied to capitalism is an end that must be pursued, regardless of the means employed, Nyerere attempts, through his idea of Ujamaa, to demonstrate that the means matter just as much as the end in the functioning of any legitimate and justified political system.

The values that emerge from Ujamaa commend themselves to a people who, at the demise of an exploitative system, want to build a just society. The implication of this is that the foundation of politics in such a society must be attentive to the primacy of politics over economic reason. This is the reason Nyerere emphasizes the importance of ensuring that, in the emerging new states in postcolonial Africa, a symmetry is established between political and economic rationality so that economic calculations do not become totalizing—in the sense of eclipsing every other thing.

According to Nyerere, the values of socialism premised on the principle of Ujamaa are as follows: value of work and solidarity based on justice and the value of community. Nyerere proposed that valuing work is indispensable for socialism because work secures livelihood. By participating in the collective creation of the wealth of the community, individuals establish the basis of their entitlements from the community. Solidarity based on justice requires that every member of the community should be protected from starving. Whereas the value of work establishes the grounds of security of livelihood in a socialist society, a sense of justice informed by solidarity guarantees the even distribution of wealth in such a society.

For these two things to obtain, there needs to be an overarching political self-understanding that justifies the commitments—there needs to be a collectively shared frame of reference. Nyerere sees the value of community as a frame of reference for his version of African socialism because it is by taking care of the community that we make it possible for the community to take care of us. Thus, the ideal African socialism is a form of extended family. It is a society in which the creation and distribution of wealth is organized in a manner that makes domination impossible, or at least avoidable in many respects. In such a society, commitment is not to one's class—a category Nyerere considers absent in traditional African societies—but to the whole of humankind. In Nyerere's (1968, 12) vision of African socialism, people ought to have as their creed a belief in "human brotherhood and the unity of Africa."

A criticism leveled against Nyerere's understanding of postcolonial African condition is that his views are idealistic (Ibhawoh and Dibua 2003). The claim of the criticism is that his desired egalitarian society is unrealistic. His restructuring of his country into groups engaged in corporative production, known otherwise as villagization, is considered by scholars as a classic case of an ill-advised utopia that was bound to end in failure and avoidable impoverishment. Besides this criticism, there are other points of disagreement about Nyerere's conception and implementation of Ujamaa in Tanzania. For some, Ujamaa is not socialist enough because it does not recognize the place of class struggle in the socialist equation. For others Nyerere's views are perplexing because they fail to come to grips with the complexities of the modern state.

Although I certainly cannot claim to be able to consider all the engagements with his work, I think the essential point to underscore is that, whereas some of the criticisms "are based on reasoned empirical research and analysis of the Tanzanian experience, many others merely border on the speculative, conforming to a pattern that Fredrick Cooper has described as 'Africa bashing'" (Ibhawoh and Dibua 2003, 60). Discernment is therefore needed to evaluate criticisms of the various strands of socialism proposed by African scholar-statesmen, such as Nyerere. I return later to considerations of the shortcomings of Nyerere's socialism in the discussion of the importance of a new normative orientation in African political philosophy. I continue presently with exploration of attempts by Nnamdi Azikiwe to make sense of African political experience in the postcolonial era.

NNAMDI AZIKIWE

Nnamdi Azikiwe's influence on generations of African nationalists is best reflected in the remarks of his ardent follower, Nwafor Orizu (1944), who said that Azikiwe's ideas as expressed in his book, *Renascent Africa*, constitute the "Bible of West African Youth." Another believer in Azikiwe's philosophy of Zikism, Ikenna Nzimiro (1978, 282), opined that the "philosophy contained ideas aimed at decolonizing the minds of young Africans so as to fit them for battle against the Old Africa, the old in mind because of colonial mentality and brain washing." It is natural to wonder what constitutes the basis of the confidence posed in Azikiwe's philosophy. This is especially the case when we note that he had the following to say about African philosophy: "African philosophy and life, in the past up till the contact of the African with the West, has been based on materialism. The concept of food, shelter, and clothing has made Africans materially deterministic that in certain vital respects, they have been under-developed from the neck up" (Azikiwe 1968, 139).

Although he thought materialism was the foundation of the African ontological outlook, Azikiwe was not in doubt about how far he wanted to go with the notion of a glorious African past. In this regard, it is pertinent to ask what the philosophy of Azikiwe consists of, especially his political thought that aimed to imagine the African predicament and the future society the continent should aspire to establish after independence from colonialization. The basis of his philosophy can be seen in the central influences on his personal and political development.

Before digging deeper in that direction, let us consider, as a prelude, aspects of Azikiwe's framing of the African experience and his ideas about what needs to be done to conceptualize solutions to the challenge. Like other sub-Saharan pan-Africanists and latter-day nationalists, Azikiwe believed in the necessity of the struggle for independence as the fulcrum for the imagination of African political thought. His political thought, as a result, dealt with two major concerns: the articulation of a path to decolonization, in the form of political independence; and the stipulation of the ideological foundations of self-rule that should be established when independence is attained. His engagement with these two issues should, however, not be interpreted to mean that there is a sharp line dividing his ideas into two so that one part may be said to constitute his theory of decolonization and the other his theory of ideology of self-rule in postindependence Africa. Doing that will decontextualize his thought, certainly. This is because Azikiwe was aware of the fact that emancipation, be it from colonial rule or other factors operating to enslave Africans, remains a work in progress.

We see this in the strong evolutionary apprehension of reality that was central for the development of his social and political thought. Michael Echeruo (1974, 254) has correctly observed that an evolutionary idea permeated Azikiwe's thinking "throughout his career." This mode of thought, Echeruo informs, became part of Azikiwe's consciousness due to his engagements with the ideas of the missionary and intellectual, James Emman Kwegyir Aggrey, most importantly Aggrey's "idea of an African potential in need of release and nurture." The idea here is that, "given time, the negro race would develop its potential, and thereby make itself equal (in fact, as well as in principle) to other races, who would then acknowledge the change by their open admiration and respect of the black man" (Echeruo 1974, 254).

Azikiwe's understanding of the African political condition, which became very influential in the 1940s, developing an even larger following in the period leading to the political independence of his country, Nigeria, relied on an evolutionary insight. In *Renascent Africa*, for instance, he put forward the argument that "life revolves around one axis. This axis has two poles—the forces of good and evil. Both poles are continually at war with themselves. Between the two poles is the equator—the ethical norm. Its warmth helps to disentangle humanity from the frigidity of any vice or virtue" (Azikiwe 1968, 211).

His belief in a unitary reality, which is composed of opposing forces, finds expression in his understanding of the African experience of domination. Africa, in Azikiwe's view, is where it finds itself due to the stranglehold of Old Africa on New Africa. The battle is between these two opposed visions of life, a fierce opposition around which everything revolves. As he argues, "people who are strangers to one another cannot experience mental emancipation, much more economic emancipation. If the New Africa must be realized, then the Old Africa must be destroyed because it is at death-grips with the New Africa, which should guarantee to Renascent Africans the enjoyment of life more abundantly" (Azikiwe 1968, 18). The issue that brings to light Azikiwe's understanding of the African condition is the oppressive domination of New Africa by Old Africa.

Old Africa represents factors and forces of history that enslave people by forcing them to remain in relations of domination by forces of nature and other people. The old, in his view, represents a way of seeing the world that is retrogressive and opposed to good. He says that "were it not for the old, youths of Africa and youths of Europe would have understood one another better. But the old heads continued to pollute young minds with their old prejudices, hence the present dilemma" (Azikiwe 1968, 20). He couches this opposition of old and young in a language of human nature to point out not only how the two differ but also how the old is undesirable and embodies the current African predicament. The old is a passing "phase" of human nature, a "lake," which cannot flow. The young is a new dawn, a "spark" that enables the river to flow. In short, the young is the "river" that flows (Azikiwe 1968, 19). The young is the New Africa that, in its renascence, restores dignity and purpose to the African world. The old or young refer here to an attitude of mind. This means it is the old in mind or vice versa that is addressed, for an old person may be young in the mind.

To overcome its predicament, Africa needs to turn to renascence to reestablish itself through political independence and economic prosperity. Zikism is the philosophy derived from Azikiwe's political thought by his followers, most especially Nwafor Orizu and Mbonu Ojike, who wrote the most important works on aspects of this philosophy (Ojike 1946; Orizu 1944). At the center of this philosophy was the necessity of decolonization, premised on the philosophy for a New Africa that was put forward by Azikiwe in *Renascent Africa*. In Azikiwe's (1968, 24) view, the fundamental bases of the philosophy are cultivation of spiritual balance, experience of social regeneration, realization of economic determinism, creation of mental emancipation, and expectation of political resurgence.

Spiritual balance expresses the value of deliberation. It enjoins renascent Africans to listen to and respect each other's opinions. Social regeneration proposes recognition of the unity of Africans, regardless of particular identity. Economic determinism underscores the need for economic self-sufficiency, while mental emancipation requires renascent Africans to throw away complexes that prevent self-realization. It enjoins them to embody the self-knowledge proposed by Socrates—to know oneself. Finally, political resurgence expresses the importance of seeking political and social emancipation.

Azikiwe was not in doubt that the means to realizing a New Africa could mean paying with one's life. It is not something anyone can do for Africans or something that can be masked by talks about peace. As Azikiwe (1968, 283) asked, "Why proclaim from the pulpit of Africa, of goodwill to mankind, when the only goodwill Africans and their children had known through the centuries, is nothing but a baptism by rifle bullet fire, confirmation by machine gun fire, and communion by Ordinances and Regulations and Orders-in-Councils?"

When it comes to questions about the ideology of organization that enables the attainment of the ideal republic Azikiwe (1979, xi) envisages, the path must be to develop a system where socialism, capitalism, and welfarism are synthesized, for "in the light of experience and reason, neither capitalism nor socialism or welfarism has been practicable, in the sense of guaranteeing to humanity political freedom, social equality and economic security." This implies that pragmatism must be the basis of the path chosen because whatever is considered to be an ideology of a modern African society must also be practicable. This point comes out clearly in his attempt later in his political career to show the way in which the problem of tribalism, which posed a critical challenge to social cohesion as it became the foundation for intolerant politics, could be resolved.

Azikiwe (1978, 279) sought to show that it is possible to conceive of tribalism as an integrative factor in postcolonial politics if a federal system is put in place to ensure "de jure equality and de facto inequality" of regions that coincide with the tribal divisions of the country. By de jure equality, he refers to formal equality of the groups within the country, while with de facto inequality, he points to natural differences in size, means, and capabilities. When these two principles are taken as foundational principles for the distribution of resources, a sort of fairness that is not oblivious of the general interests of a nation and the challenges of distinct groups that make up the nation will be guaranteed.

It was misguided in Azikiwe's view to seek an ideology for his country, Nigeria, and, by extension, any postcolonial African country because such a quest presupposes in the first instance that these societies had no ideology. What is needed is not to develop an ideology that could be imposed on postcolonial African societies but rather to reorient the ideologies embedded in the cultures of these societies. When he looked to capitalism, socialism, and even African traditional ideologies and considered them in the light of their evils, Azikiwe found that neowelfarism was what would lead to a better society.

However, to realize the ideal of neowelfarism, there needed to be entrenched in the society "basic freedoms and fundamental rights without any provisos. In addition, basic needs must be satisfied beyond 'the minimum subsistence level'" (Azikiwe 1979, 125). A neowelfarist society would thus be eclectic, combining the best and most desirable elements of socialism and capitalism. The ideal of a neowelfarist society is pragmatic because it pays attention to the necessity of developing a practicable idea.

Echeruo (1974, 262) criticized Azikiwe's political view in an important area. Although he recognized that "Azikiwe's philosophy . . . pushed Nigerian thinking on a subject of regeneration into the pan-Negro groove," Echeruo wasn't convinced about important details. Echeruo was convinced that Azikiwe "did not lay new foundation for Nigeria's intellectual growth" (263). He argues that there is a serious flaw in the evolutionary approach to understanding the problems and solutions to the African challenge that Azikiwe carried forward from one of his major influences, Aggrey (253).

What the evolutionary approach meant was that the response of Africans to their predicament was directed toward demonstrations to the colonizers that they too were capable of aspiring and realizing the colonizers' ideals rather than simply pursuing the goals that were in their true interest. I do not make any judgment about the plausibility of this criticism because my goal here is mainly expository. I should underscore however that there are disagreements about Azikiwe's ideas from perspectives unconnected to the arguments against his evolutionary approach. With this in mind, we turn to consideration of the last two scholar-politicians that proposed versions of African ideologies of decolonization and self-rule as ways to explain and deal with Africa's political experience.

AMILCAR CABRAL

Amilcar Cabral, the leader of the struggle for the liberation of Guinea-Bissau and Cape Verde Islands, was a vanguard Marxist thinker in Africa. Although influenced by Marxism, Cabral did not just set out to apply Marxism to the conditions in Guinea-Bissau. Rather, he attempted to reconstruct, through a prism of Marxism, a cultural basis of politics. African culture was for him an important dimension of the struggle for freedom. This is the reason he observed that "whenever Goebbels, the brain behind Nazi propaganda, heard anyone speak of culture, he pulled out his pistol. That goes to show that the Nazis . . . had a clear idea of the value of culture as a factor in the resistance of foreign domination" (Cabral 1974, 12).

Cultural contexts matter for any attempts to understand the prerequisites of resistance. Nonetheless, the centrality of culture in Cabral's conception of the challenge posed by African political experience, especially under colonialism, does not imply a universal image of culture—in the sense of cultural hegemony. The cultural imperative, he avers, is central because "it is generally in culture that the seed of protest, leading to the emergence and development of the liberation movement, is found" (Cabral 1974, 13). And given that colonization did not last long enough in Africa to destroy the essential aspects of the people's culture (1973, 60), there exists a basis to articulate a revolutionary struggle for freedom and a vision of the future society that is desirable.

Cabral was convinced that Africans will have a chance to reenter history by asserting their cultural personality. This means reentering a universal process they were excluded from by domination (Cabral 1969, 102). With his Leninist conviction that "nobody has yet made a successful revolution without a revolutionary theory" (93), Cabral felt careful attention must be paid to both theoretical and practical dimensions of the revolution envisaged. The reason is that "people are not fighting for ideas, for the things in one's head. They are fighting to win material benefits, to live better and in peace, to see their lives go forward, to guarantee the future of their children" (86).

Put in context, it could be surmised that Cabral's perspective on the political condition in Africa emerges from his understanding of the nature of African personality, how it has been affected by forces of history, and what needs to be done to restore it. Viewed in this light, his view demands a holistic perspective to the African challenge. Thus, Pablo Idahosa (2002, 31) was on point in his assertion that "the interaction of class, production and culture was an enduring theme of Cabral's political thought and practice." It is for this reason that Cabral conceived of national liberation as the means that will guarantee welfare for the disposed and dominated people of Africa. To achieve a liberation that is based on an understanding of local conditions and culture, a form of socialism is inevitable as the system of organization in postcolonial Africa.

The question that arises for Cabral's perspective on the political condition in Africa is how to understand the consequence of foreign domination. What are the consequences of the suppression of a "subject people's" (Cabral 1973, 60) culture during colonization, especially in relation to the possibility of emancipation? Cabral attempted to find an answer through recourse to the idea of return to culture, a notion he used to describe how indigenous petite bourgeoisie deal with their frustration complex. In his view, the experience of colonization created in Africa a class of petite bourgeoisie. This class, although aspiring to the lifestyle and values of colonial elite, are often frustrated by the system. They can hardly advance beyond a certain point.

However, because the integration of this class, no matter how partial it might be, into the colonial system alienates them from their roots, they inevitably fall into a crisis of identity, for they are neither fully part of the colonial elite nor rooted in their cultural values and ethnic ties. Thus, Cabral's approach to resolving the consequence of the experience of the suppression of a subject people's culture through colonization is to first locate the problem in its proper context. And he achieves this by arguing that the masses of the people who lived mostly in the rural parts of colonial Africa were untouched by the colonial imposition of values. Thus, they did not struggle with identity crisis because their culture always provided a source of identity formation and, hence, the foundation for resistance. This was not the case for native elites, the so-called petite bourgeoisie. This class of urban Africans alienated themselves in the quest to integrate into the colonial system. The sad story though is that the more they tried, the more they were prevented by the system.

What this means for them is that they have become a marginal or marginalized class. The consequence of the complicated position of the petite bourgeoisies in the colonial system is that, to be liberated, they have to first deal with their social and cultural contradictions. For Cabral, the penchant of this class to approach the situation through "return to the source" must go beyond affirming indigenous African culture. It must include a rejection of the "pretended supremacy of the culture of the dominant power over that of the dominated people" (Cabral 1973, 63). And the rejection must translate into a movement for them to transform their struggle against the contradiction of their lives into a struggle for liberation from colonial domination.

Cabral (1973, 63–64) noted that, among the petite bourgeoisie, there are three groups. The first is a minority that attaches itself to colonialists, despite their interest in living in a society that is free from domination. The second is a group of those who are "hesitant and indecisive." The third is another minority who identify with the aims and activities of the masses engaged in liberation struggle. Those who fall into the third group constitute the fraction of the petite bourgeoisie who are useful in the struggle for liberation. Essentially, the petite bourgeoisie is a group from which the first step toward liberation arises because, although it is a class created by colonialism, the members are aware of their own humiliating encounters with the system, just as they are aware of the deprivations and injustices suffered by the masses of their society.

In a chat with African Americans during a visit to the United States in 1972, Cabral, in a response to a question posed by a member of the audience, expressed his views about the future African state that is worth striving for. Asked to comment on the sort of law he wished to see established in his country, Cabral replied by stating that he was in favor of expunging all the vestiges of the colonial system. His conviction, he said, was that "it is necessary to totally destroy, to break, to reduce to ash all aspects of the colonial state" to make a new beginning for his country possible (Cabral 1973, 83). His thought was that replacing colonial administrators with Africans would not lead to or give meaning to the type of society that would make the hard-won liberation satisfactory. The postcolonial state must aspire to build a different kind of state, one in which the masses of people would be the focus of government. It must do so if it wants to succeed. In the future African state, colonial palaces should become a center of culture for the people, in Cabral's view, to give them the sense that they defeated their oppressors.

The main point Cabral (1973, 84) wished to make by articulating the need to break clean with the colonial system is that "the nature of the state created after independence is perhaps the secret of the failure of African independence." The widespread discontentment in postcolonial Africa decades after independence shows the depth of Cabral's insight. Indeed, it has been argued that the problem of Africa in the postcolonial era has to do with the constitution of the postcolonial state. Crawford Young (1994), a respected scholar of African politics, has shown in a number of works how Cabral's ideas about the link between colonial state and political failure explains a lot of what is going on. We return anon to consideration of the evaluation of Cabral's ideas in relation to the political failure that is the core of current African political experience.

LEOPOLD SENGHOR

Leopold Senghor, of Senegal, approached the explanation of the African predicament from the perspective of culture. As a leading light in the struggle for independence in the continent, Senghor confronted similar problems faced by other sub-Saharan pan-Africanists. His insights about the experience of colonialization are encapsulated in his theory of negritude. Negritude is a conceptual apparatus through which he articulated a cultural response to the problem of domination that shaped the modern history of Africans everywhere in the world. As Abiola Irele (1964, 9) has argued, "negritude was in the beginning a movement of black solidarity." The concept differs from "class solidarity" because it embodies a form of "racial consciousness." It is for this reason that negritude is perceived as more than an empty, aimless slogan. Its goal is to enable the dominated people of African descent to assert their humanity through the projection of a "healthier image of their race."

Considered alongside Leon Damas and Aime Cesaire as the most important figures in the development of the theory of negritude, Senghor's greatest contribution are his theoretical inputs into the fashioning of this idea as a sociopolitical and literary movement. Negritude has attracted many commentaries over the last two decades. Although it emerged through the intellectual, social, and political engagements of people of African descent who had converged in the colonial metropolis of Paris for the purpose of education in the 1930s, the ideas and vision encapsulated in the concept and the movement it inspired gained currency for many reasons.

Its influence on African scholars and the political orientation they endorsed was restricted to so-called francophone Africa and the African Diaspora initially. But gradually the theory became a preoccupation of the so-called anglophone Africans. The catalyst for the broadening of interest in negritude was not just the attraction of what it stood for but also due to the severe criticism it attracted in the 1960s from prominent postcolonial African scholars, such as Wole Soyinka. Given the widespread influence exerted by negritude, it will be useful to ask questions about the core of the idea and how it framed African political experience in recent history.

As would be expected, there are different approaches to understanding the concept because the intellectuals that contributed to its articulation were diverse and had different interests. Besides, the diversity of perspective is to be expected due to the eclectic nature of the currents of intellectual influence on the movement. Still, it can be inferred from the literature that the following are central to the idea of negritude: rejection of assimilation, affirmation of the humanity of Black individuals, rejection of the superiority claims of Western imperialism and colonization, and liberation of Black individuals from oppression everywhere in the world. To understand Senghor's perspective on negritude, it is important to take note of the background from which he embraced this movement.

As Senghor (1998, 438) recounted in *Negritude and African Socialism*, the text of a lecture delivered in 1961 at St. Anthony's College, University of Oxford, alongside other Africans who had received elite educations in French schools, he was taught that he had no history, "having been left off the list of guests at the Banquet of the universal." To explain negritude, Senghor goes on a long journey in intellectual history, albeit his own intellectual history. He does this to narrate how his experience of France became a catalyst for his quest for the sort of self-understanding that became a basis for the negritude movement. The experiences that set him on the journey that eventually produced negritude include the imposition of an assimilation policy by France. Knowing that, regardless of how much he assimilated "mathematics or the French language," it was impossible to shed off blackness (439), Senghor and the founders of the negritude movement were compelled by the situation to seek their "collective soul," their essence as Black people of African descent.

For Senghor (1998, 440), "negritude is *the whole complex of civilized values—cultural, economic, social and political—which characterize the black people* (emphasis in original), or, more precisely, the Negro-African world." The central principle of these values, Senghor claims, is intuitive reason. The fact that negritude rejected negative ideas about Black people does not mean Senghor opposed everything of European origin. For him, "the balance sheet of colonization is positive rather than negative" (445). Notwithstanding that the domination experienced by Africans demanded agitation for emancipation in the form of political independence, it does not follow that everything put in place by colonization should be thrown away. This is why Senghor proposed that attaining independence inaugurated for him and his compatriots the task of attempting "to eliminate the flaws of colonial rule while preserving its positive contributions, such as the economic and technical infrastructure and the teaching of the French language" (445).

READING THE IDEAS OF SUB-SAHARAN PAN-AFRICANISTS

Having reconstructed the ideas of sub-Saharan pan-Africanist political thinkers, we need to ask if their thoughts on the African political predicament amount to political philosophy or political theories and if the ideas they offer suffice to tackle the challenge of political failure. In other words, do the ideas considered so far provide adequate responses to the problem of political failure that is characteristic of contemporary African experience? To begin answering these two questions, I should note that the broad overview offered here is not exhaustive. For one, the brevity of engagement with each of the figures considered indicates the overview cannot claim to be a comprehensive treatment of these theories. In addition, it must be noted that theoretical distinctions that may prove useful for a fine-grained analysis are absent in large parts in my reconstruction of these ideas. What I have presented is merely a broad picture of the ideas espoused by these figures. Thus, my claim is not that what is reconstructed encompasses all that can be said about the views of each of the figures considered.

My focus is on how each scholar-politician explained African political experience and the ideas they developed to address the challenges thereof. From what we have considered to this point, it could be said that a form of retrieval of the past was central for these forerunners of African political thought. Even the self-proclaimed pragmatist, Azikiwe, looked to the past for guidance in articulating his ideology on the African condition. However, they did not just seek to reconstruct the past blindly. They creatively used the past to speak to the present, and the main purpose was to produce a sketch of a desirable future. They did this in the interest of constructing perspectives that were fitting for the epoch in which they lived. But what sort of theory did they offer? Do their thoughts amount to political philosophy or political theory?

The question pertaining to whether the ideas of these thinkers are political theories or political philosophy demands that we establish what it means to say that a body of thought is the sort of thing we may regard as either of the two. This obviously raises anew the question of boundary, just like we find in the debate on African philosophy. How do we determine that an African thinker is propounding a political theory or philosophy? Do we resort, in making this determination, to conventions in of the Western tradition so that we can say, for instance, that an African is doing political philosophy if she or he engages the sort of questions emphasized by canonical Western philosophers? Can we say that, if an African thinker explores the sort of questions about politics that preoccupied Plato, Aristotle, and the thinkers of the Enlightenment, leading up to contemporary Western greats, such as Jürgen Habermas and Rawls, then, she or he is doing political philosophy? It should be evident that consideration of this sort is another shortcut to raising the question about the universality of philosophy that was at the center of the discourse on the nature of African philosophy.

I do not think that the question whether the thinkers considered were doing political philosophy or political theory carries any weight. I do not grant this concern any cogency due to the fact that political philosophy and political theory both imply a form of thinking about the political. Given that engagement with core questions about politics is always conceivable within particular contexts or relations, political theory or philosophy in any context is bound to reflect particularistic concerns, even as they aspire to articulate something that does not as yet obtain. In this sense, political philosophy and political theory both are methods of thinking about questions pertaining to how we should live together in a community. They are imaginations of a future society that may not yet exist but is nonetheless desirable. But thinking about how we should live together implies thinking about how we should think about the phenomenon of living together. By this I mean there is always a meta-level dimension to the sort of thinking we call political philosophy or political theory.

From the above, it is reasonable to assert that the sort of thinking designated as political theory or political philosophy incorporates reflection on categories and concepts we employ in thinking about political phenomena. In deploying these categories, we reflect on what it is we do when we engage questions pertaining to coexistence. Therefore, political philosophy or political theory can refer to a history of political ideas, reflection on the organization of collective life in a given context, or analysis of the concepts employed in political practice. Although we do political philosophy or political theory when we engage any of these three things, all three tasks are connected in some ways.

What binds all three are the history of political ideas that provides resources we employ in reflecting on the organization of collective life in a given context, the consideration of the way political concepts evolve, and the implication of this evolution for how we think about political questions. In light of this, it should be possible to point out the sense in which the thoughts of sub-Saharan pan-Africanist thinkers constitute a form of political theory, or, if one prefers, political philosophy.

An issue that beclouds the judgment regarding the fittingness of the political ideas of African scholar-statesmen as political philosophy relates to how we should understand the intersection of ideology and philosophy. For some, ideas proposed by African politicians are wanting as political philosophy. Proponents of this view argue that an appropriate description of the ideas of African political thinkers is to regard them as political ideologies. The reason for this is the suspicion that ideology is opposed to political philosophy. Unlike the latter, the former discounts with reasoned justification. In contrast to the reasoned justification political philosophy offers, political ideologies rely on a mixture of propaganda, manipulated consent, and authoritarianism. As we saw in the critique Hountondji advanced against Nkrumah, the challenge of distinguishing ideology and political philosophy is not a superficial concern.

Besides the matter of theoretical distinction, there is also the issue of the connection between theory and praxis that propels the reluctance to consider the political ideas of African scholar-statesmen as political philosophy. In an insightful consideration of this point, Olufemi Taiwo (2004) has noted that the failure of an idea in practice is often taken to mean a failure of the idea itself. He says, "If, for example, Kwame Nkrumah's ideas informed his statecraft at Ghana's helm, then given the failure of his practice, it follows that the ideas could not have been good to state with" (Taiwo 2004, 243). This conclusion is erroneous, notwithstanding that the empirical fact it relies on may be true. Taiwo is correct to suggest that ideas may fail in practice regardless of their soundness as theories. This may happen, as Taiwo has correctly pointed out, due to timing, execution, and other random factors.

Mazrui (1963) was surely perceptive when, in attempting to make sense of the revolution in Congo, he proposed that there are five ways of approaching political theory. One possibility is to see it as a pure intellectual exercise. The second is to consider political theory as a source of "practical philosophy for oneself." The third is to view it from a historical angle—that is, as a way to understand a historical period. Fourthly, it may be approached from the perspective of intellectual history and, fifthly, from the perspective of its application. This last possibility involves putting the theory to use in a context that lies outside its milieu or history to see how it could explain a situation or if the situation could help develop the theory further (Mazrui 1963, 3). Although he did not explicitly state this point, Mazrui seems to have arrived at the distinctions regarding the five approaches to political theory due to the challenges posed by the question we are attempting to answer. When we contextualize the thoughts of the intellectual politicians we have considered, their understanding that contemporary political challenges in Africa are informed by one or more of the approaches to political theory proposed by Mazrui becomes apparent.

The ideas of sub-Saharan pan-Africanists can be regarded as political philosophy or theory, and I explain why this is the case. But before doing so, it is pertinent to consider the distinctions to be made more generally between political theory and political philosophy. Notwithstanding that I have so far used the two concepts in a manner that suggests they are interchangeable, they are not conceptual equivalents. Whereas political philosophy is a part of political theory, the reverse is not true. Political philosophy is normative in the sense that it attempts to explore what should be the case about coexistence in a society. This is to say that it engages questions about coexistence from the perspective of nonempirical evaluation. Even where use is made of empirical resources, political philosophy generally does not arrive at its conclusions from the point of view of empirical inferences.

Political theory, on the other hand, might employ the means of political philosophy to analyze political phenomena. But it could also employ other means, such as purely empirical procedures that can yield plausible inferences about, say, the behavior of electorates in certain situations. This, however, does not mean that political philosophy is a rational and abstract discipline and political theory is its opposite. The point is, rather, that we can consider political theory as encompassing political philosophy, in the sense of it being a broader inquiry about politics. I make this distinction to underscore that the ideas of the sub-Saharan pan-Africanists we have considered cannot be evaluated by asking if they conform to the norms of disciplinary conventions in political philosophy. That would be an unfair, reductive view of what these thinkers aimed to achieve. Thus, arguing that the thinkers were not professional philosophers does not suffice to downgrade their ideas, as Taiwo (2004, 243) rightly argued.

Having established how to classify the views we have so far considered, the question to ask is how to evaluate these ideas as responses to the phenomenon of political failure. Are the ideas of African scholar-statesmen sufficient to address the main challenge of political thought in contemporary Africa—namely, the phenomenon of political failure? Considered in light of the challenge of political failure, the most these views can offer is a perspective on who or what to blame for the African political condition. Generally, the strategy is to point out what ails Africa and proceed on the basis of this stipulation to conceive a response that will solve the problem. Thus, some of these thinkers, like Senghor, proposed that dehumanization wrought by colonialism and the slave trade explains the African political experience.

To tackle the problems these experiences pose, the response articulated was the conception of an African personality that rejected Europe to affirm the dignity and humanity of the African person. Others, like Azikiwe, argued that the combination of internal factors of backwardness and external forces of domination is to blame for the African predicament. Expectedly, the proper response to the challenge from this perspective was to conceive an ideology that allowed a release of the dormant African ingenuity in a bid to not only defeat colonialism but also to earn admiration and respect for Africans. Nkrumah and a number of thinkers who subscribe to his thought proposed further that a crisis traceable to the competition of the African worldview against two others—the Christian and Islamic worldviews—explained the political dilemma in Africa. Thus, the solution was to reach back to the traditional African past to retrieve relevant resources that could be developed, using the fitting conceptual categories drawn from Marxism, to articulate societal organizational principles suitable to postcolonial African.

I do not think that the approach of establishing a cause and reaching back to the past to draw inspiration in crafting a solution is viable today, where the major challenge of African political philosophy is not contention with alien rule but reflection on the phenomenon of political failure. Asking what is to blame for the African predicament, although therapeutic, does not suffice if we wish to raise the morally relevant question that will lead to the discovery of what must be done today to bring about a better future for the continent and its people. It is essential to go beyond this approach to consider the orientation that makes possible the articulation of a modern African political philosophy capable of solving the challenge of political failure.

Instead of remaining in the dark alleys of questioning what caused Africa's problems, what ought to be done is to reorient African political philosophy by considering how to understand the historical experience of the continent and harness its criteriology in light of that reality. This is what will make future aspirations possible. This approach is an empowering response to the situation because it does not begin with a premise that calls the agency of Africans into question. Instead, it affirms that Africans are agents capable of dealing with experiences in different epochs of history, using creatively their conceptual resources.

Reorienting African political philosophy in this manner will enable us to direct our attention to an analysis of fundamental questions about collective life under the current conditions in Africa. It enables reflection on numerous central questions of African political philosophy today: What impact does it have on politics that there are now generations of Africans who have lived or must live out their entire adult existence in societies that lack imagination about how to coexist, govern themselves, and succeed collectively? What sort of political imagination is acceptable in a context where economics, in the sense of ideology of development, has either failed to emerge or is severely deficient? What is the good life for a person in a failed political community—that is, someone for whom the basic foundation for the pursuit of meaning has collapsed completely? In what way does thinking about the political make sense for a person who has basically become a prisoner of freedom, one condemned to an existence in a geographical space that is constraining and itself is constrained by global anti-immigration laws and sentiments? What is the nature of justice in such a society, and how, in fact, is justice possible in a context characterized not just by political failure but by a situation where talk of a social contract as the starting point of political imagination is a meaningless idiocy?

Answering these questions requires a normative standpoint that cannot emerge from the political thought of sub-Saharan pan-Africanist political thinkers. The normative deficit their theories embody does not arise because of what they did not consider but rather due to the way they considered what they explored. In their bid to solve the challenge of postcolonial Africa, they retrieved concepts and ideas from the traditional African past without offering a sufficient refashioning of these concepts and ideas. What is required, however, is the exercise of greater conceptual creativity. I return in the next chapter to the consideration of this normative deficit because it plays a crucial role for the professional philosophers whose ideas I consider there. In the meantime, it is useful to note that this normative deficit necessitates a new orientation in African political philosophy, a task I attempt to accomplish in the last three chapters of the book.

THREE

—ɯ—

NORMATIVE DEFICIT

Toward a New Orientation in African Political Philosophy

KOLE OMOTOSO (1998) MADE AN interesting remark on the fate of the theoretical exertions of African scholars. He observed that it is not clear who composes the audience being addressed. Although African scholars write about European ideas, evidence shows their works to be inconsequential for Europeans and Africans. Thus, if what African scholars "are saying does not matter to the French and it does not matter to Africans, to whom does it matter?" (Omotoso 1998, 77). The concern raised by Omotoso resonates with the issue discussed in the preceding chapter, which is amplified by Kwasi Wiredu's (1996, 145) remark that "the post-colonial era in African philosophy is the era of professionalism. Yet paradoxically, in this same period philosophical doctrines have been propounded by non-professionals more than by professionals.... The philosophies produced by the non-professionals have shaped the destinies of millions of Africans since independence." The main question raised by both Omotoso and Wiredu relates to the relevance of the theories African scholars churn out in their intellectual odysseys. Applying this logic more narrowly to African political philosophy, the question translates into a concern about the role the field should play in the affairs of Africans, especially in light of the current challenges facing the continent. As noted in the preceding chapter, questions about relevance relate to the ethics of scholarship.

In this chapter, I discuss the response of African philosophers to the challenge of postcolonial African experience. I will argue that inherent in the theories they offer is a normative deficiency that must be remedied in the interest of progress in African political philosophy. I propose that an urgent task facing African political thought is to articulate a new approach to the analysis of African experience. The new orientation I suggest, which will be discussed in detail in chapter 6, proposes moving from the approach of conceptual retrieval, currently dominant in analysis of African experience, to conceptual creativity. Making this move implies relying on a new normative theorizing in African political philosophy to develop a new conception of politics, one that is capable of offering new meaning and imagination about the experience of political failure.

The outline of the chapter is as follows. I begin with a reconstruction of the major political thoughts of postcolonial African philosophers. The aim is to show how they construe African experience in the present century. In the next step, I examine the viability of these ideas as responses to the phenomenon of political failure, which constitutes the core of contemporary African experience. Going forward, I discuss the normative deficit inherent in the theories of African philosophers and point out why this constitutes a demand for the reorientation of African political philosophy. My proposal is that African political philosophy should be approached from a perspective that allows the analysis of pertinent questions through the creative use of concepts.

RECONSTRUCTING POSTCOLONIAL
AFRICAN POLITICAL PHILOSOPHY

Many professional African philosophers can be seen as leading lights of political philosophy in this tradition. Prominent names include Kwasi Wiredu, Ifeanyi Menkiti, Kwame Gyekye, Emmanuel Eze, Dismas Masolo, Olufemi Taiwo, Kwame Appiah, Ajume Wingo, Teodros Kiros, Souleymane Bachir Diagne, Jean-Godefroy Bidima, and Olusegun Oladipo. In addition, Katrin Flikschuh, Thaddeus Metz, and Barry Hallen have also contributed vital insights to the field. This is an extensive list, meaning that an entire book could be written on the exposition and evaluation of the ideas of these philosophers. Since I cannot engage all their theories, for obvious reasons of space and the focus, I will cut through the differences among these works. To this end, I will analyze the contributions of these scholars to the quest for answers to central questions in African political philosophy.

Let me begin by pointing out the questions at the center of African political philosophy and reconstruct the perspectives offered to address them. People familiar with discussions in the field will agree that the relationship of persons and community, the opposition of tradition and modernity, and the nature of traditional consensual politics and conceptual decolonization are some of the central questions in African political philosophy. The question to ask is how the analyses of these questions tackle the challenge of political failure, which is the core of current African experience. Relatedly, it is worth considering whether the ideas of African philosophers, when considered individually, constitute a viable response to the problem of political failure. Analyzing these questions will put us in a position to address the normative deficit mentioned earlier and conceptualize how the method of conceptual creativity presents a promising way forward.

The problem regarding the relationship between individuals and community in postcolonial African philosophy originates from a seminal publication of Ifeanyi Menkiti in 1984. Menkiti reconstructed in the paper an idea of personhood and sought to determine the nature of the relationship between persons and community. The discourse on personhood is essential for understanding the nature of political community. This point should be apparent when we consider the role debates about the ontological primacy of the community over the individual, a debate that is now a distinctive feature of African thought, plays in conceptualizing the nature of political community. Who is borne in mind in the talk about *we the people*? To understand the sense of what "the people" designates in African political thought, our inevitable starting point is to determine the nature and constitution of personhood. This is to say that, for the African context (at least as we find in the works of major African philosophers), to know how the political community should be constituted, we must first answer a question: What is a person?

Menkiti (1984) answers this question by drawing parallels between traditional African thought and Western philosophy. He notes that the abstract idea of the person, located in the isolated features of the individual according to the Western approach to defining a person, does not obtain in African thought. The African approach takes community as a starting point in defining personhood. In explaining his view, Menkiti makes three claims. The first claim is that "the reality of the community takes precedence over the reality of the individual histories, whatever these may be." This is true "ontologically" and "in regard to epistemic accessibility" (171). Menkiti's view is that personhood entails that individuals have roots in the community. Put differently, one is not a person due merely to the attribution of "some isolated quality of rationality, will, or memory" but because of belonginess in community (172).

The second claim Menkiti (172) makes is that the nature of being is "processual." In other words, a process of "incorporation" precedes the attribution of personhood to human beings. Without undergoing the process of incorporation into a community, an individual does not become fully a person. Personhood is achieved; it is not something one acquires just because one is human in the biological sense. Through a process of incorporation, human individuals acquire "excellencies" necessary to become full, adult members of a community. The means to acquiring these excellencies is "social and ritual transformation" (172). From these observations, Menkiti infers a third claim—namely, that personhood is something a human being can fail to attain. Personhood is thus a journey in which the individual must demonstrate commitment, tact, and ability; it is not a given that ensues merely because one is biologically human (176).

What is described by Menkiti is the idea of "full personhood" (173). Thus, the objection that his theory is unfair to children because it denies them something they have not acquired due to their limited chance of being incorporated into a community is forestalled. The reason is that the degrees of excellencies expected at different stages of the progression to full personhood are clear. Although young and inexperienced members of a community possess degrees of personhood, acquisition of full personhood is something that comes with age and maturity. Thus, Menkiti (1984, 173) argued that "a qualitative difference exists between old and young" and also that there occurs an "ontological progression between infancy and ripening old age."

Because Menkiti wants to present his ideas in a manner that is comprehensible to non-Africans and Africans alike, he makes recourse to "it" in referring to a child. He notes in this connection the remarks by anthropologists that there is an "absence of ritualized grief" (174) when a child dies in African societies. This way, he can underscore how the ontological progression, from one it (as a child) to another it (as a nameless ancestor), and the journey implied therein are not unfounded assumptions in the African worldview. The absence of incorporation, in the sense of being "nameless" and "lacking moral functions" (175) is the defining feature of the starting point and end phase of the journey toward personhood.

Many scholars have discussed Menkiti's ideas from a variety of perspectives. As such, it is impossible to consider all the engagement with his ideas on personhood. I therefore limit further exploration of Menkiti's understanding of personhood to two interventions. The Ghanaian philosopher Kwame Gyekye's discussion (the older of the two in terms of publication) is a major source of disagreements in relation to Menkiti's thought on personhood. More recently, Katrin Flikschuh's comparative exploration of the ideas of Menkiti and Kant has marked an emerging critical engagement with Menkiti's ideas beyond African philosophy.

Before discussing the responses by Gyekye and Flikschuh, let me consider the context of Menkiti's ideas. By context here I mean the oral basis of African thought. In his discussion of the impact of orality on philosophy, Wiredu (2009) argues that we can understand why Menkiti's reconstruction of personhood is correct when we evaluate it from the perspective of the impact of orality on philosophy. Wiredu considers orality the reason some propositions or concepts become unintelligible when extrapolated from one language context to another. Orality does not only inflect the meaning of concepts but matters in our conceptions of phenomena. In this regard, Wiredu notes the absence of dichotomies in African languages and its implication for inferences we make about the normative significance of concepts. For instance, he has pointed out that, because existence is often spatially imagined by Africans, it will be incomprehensible to infer from the African conceptual designation of "to exist" a nonspatial, spiritual existence. The impact of orality is further accentuated by the question of what it means to be a person.

Commenting on why he agrees with Menkiti's outline of personhood, Wiredu (2009) relates personhood to the conventional use of language, such as the widespread practice of referring to a person as "not human." Wiredu argues that "the corresponding concept of a person" to infer from communalism is that a person is "a morally sound adult who has demonstrated in practice a sense of responsibility to household, lineage and society at large" (16). Wiredu asserts with Menkiti that personhood is acquired. Thus, it is something we can fail to attain. But Wiredu adds another point—namely, that personhood "is something we can gain and later lose" (16). He notes that the "discomfort" people feel about the normative sense of personhood Menkiti articulated has to do with "a clash of oral intuitions reflecting the deep differences between African communalism and Western individualism" (16).

In Gyekye's (2004) engagement with Menkiti, several points of disagreement emerge. Gyekye is not convinced by Menkiti's normative personhood. His arguments center on what we can infer from the primacy of the community over individuals. He disagrees with Menkiti that we can infer from the primacy of community over individuals that the community, rather than some abstract notion or quality, "defines the person as person" (103). Further, Gyekye (2004, 106–107) argues that Menkiti's conclusion that personhood is acquired and that it is something human beings can fail to attain is erroneous. Gyekye considers the idea of "ontological progression," which Menkiti says is useful in acquiring personhood, a wrong interpretation of the traditional African worldview. Gyekye's concerns reduce to the inaccuracies embedded in Menkiti's normative personhood. Thus, rather than argue that Menkiti's view should be discarded entirely, Gyekye is interested mostly in conceiving ways to remedy the deficiencies of Menkiti's proposal. His view amounts to what he calls "moderate communitarianism," which is a theory of personhood in which individuals are guaranteed rights and independence.

Flikschuh (2016) recently brought Menkiti's discussion of personhood into dialogue with Kant. Flikschuh's efforts mark a refreshing engagement with an important issue in African philosophy beyond the field. Her comparison was not aimed at demonstrating that Menkiti's views live up to a standard set by the primogeniture of European philosophy. She aimed to show how the two perspectives display an unexpected affinity that illuminates what it means to be a person. The affinity relates to the reasons both theories are moderately anti-Cartesian. Flikschuh notes: "Kant's rejection of introspective self-knowledge moderates his individualism, Menkiti's endorsement of reflexive self-awareness moderates his communitarianism" (438).

PERSONHOOD

Recall that it was noted in the preceding chapter that proponents of African socialism offered arguments about the political organization that best reflects the traditional views of Africans. Based on the thought that the African world-view supports communalism, they endorsed African socialism or some strand of Marxist-inspired socialism. They argued that an updated conception of socialism would be a good successor to the traditional practice of the ideology. The point for them is that personhood, especially the way it frames interconnections between the individual and the community, has had an enormous impact on political thought.

The relevance of conceptions of personhood to African political thought is not limited to its role in shaping the imagination of suitable structures of political order. Personhood is also vital because it was taken to provide a foundation for the justification of institutions of governance. To see why African scholar-statesmen thought this was true, one needs to look at how personhood was taken as the foundational inspiration for a one-party system, which became a widespread form of governance in postindependence Africa. The proponents of the one-party state argued that the community is *the* proper site of politics because, as communal beings, persons depend on the community for the cultivation of qualities required to realize their nature.

As the primary site of politics, the community eschews adversarial politics because this sort of politics advances the pursuit of selfish interests over collective interests. Adversarial politics must therefore be jettisoned because it does not conduce to the advancement of community. The community must collectively agree on the desired course of action if it is to survive. The decisions that advance community must, however, be arrived at unanimously in the spirit of communal living. Based on this view of the relationship between individuals and community, postcolonial politicians argued for the cogency of one-party states. Only a one-party state, they proclaimed, would guarantee genuine national democracy.

In a lecture at the University of Chicago, Menkiti recently explored the political implication of his theory of personhood. He sought to show the implication of personhood, conceived in communitarian terms, for the linkages between the concept of a person and that of a citizen, the role of states, and the causes of normative instability. Menkiti (2017) proposes that the "conceptual divide" between citizen and person aside, the idea of citizen harbors assumptions about personhood. The sense of this observation, he says, is that the moral foundation for the rights said to be entitlements of citizens derives from the concept of personhood. Menkiti proposes that the concept of citizenship introduced new ways of meaning making that involve a transience that is at variance with personhood.

It is problematic to replace the idea of personhood with that of citizenship, the reason being that the notion of citizenship cannot carry the burdens shouldered by personhood. The idea of a citizen "does not, cannot, encompass the full range of a person's dignity" (Menkiti 2017, 11). The idea that the citizen is at the center of "effective political action" (11) makes sense because it embodies political agency. Still, Menkiti asserts that we must pay attention to the differences between the story of a person and that of a citizen because the two stories create different kinds of connection between people. To think that the citizen is paramount in the scheme of everything political is wrong. According to Menkiti, in the absence of the story of personhood, it will be impossible to make a connection between freedom and community. Basically, "the citizen may come and go, but the person is here always with us" (16). This is why it is necessary to always reexamine the basis of governance in light of the specialness of personhood.

Although certain consequences for politics emerge from the discourse on personhood, one cannot infer from this that African philosophers provided the basis for political praxis on the continent. That would be a wrong inference, especially if it is taken to mean endorsement of a sequence in which there were first African philosophers who engaged the task of thinking and then African politicians who put into motion national systems of politics based on the ideas created by African philosophers. If any sequence of events can be supposed at all, it is the opposite. That is, African politicians first put systems of politics in place before African philosophers came along to reflect on the consequences of the systems. At any rate, I consider it implausible to think in this manner about the connection between personhood and political thought.

TRADITION AND MODERNITY

Another question debated by African philosophers that has shaped the discourse on African political philosophy is the relationship between tradition and modernity. This problem emerges due to concerns about what viable approach to adopt in retrieving and applying in the postcolonial era ideas that informed the social, economic, and political institutions in the traditional African context. Concerns about the relationship between tradition and modernity, therefore, represent a quest to demonstrate the ways in which concepts and ideas retrieved from the indigenous African past may be fruitfully put to use in fashioning systems of governance or a social, economic, and political order capable of solving current challenges in Africa.

Although this is a central point of controversy in postcolonial African philosophy, its roots go back a long way in studies of African societies by anthropologists. Writing about this issue almost six decades ago, the British anthropologist Lucy Mair (1962) clarified the trajectory of the question. By examining the place of tradition in the changing circumstances in Africa, Mair attempted to show how concerns about the opposition between tradition and modernity in the scholarship on Africa are at base a fundamental question about social change.

Mair (1962, 440) points out that the challenge of Africa after colonization was to create a new form of solidarity that would replace the one that enabled African villages to be "self-sufficient." The problem of modern Africa, she argues, is that it is no longer feasible to hold on to the idea that older forms of solidarity that obtained in African traditional society can be maintained. This implies that it is now impossible to reestablish traditions of the African past as a guide to politics in modern Africa. In the political arena, calls for a return to tradition does not amount to much in Mair's view because the political leaders espousing the rhetoric are already a people of many worlds. Besides, there is no reason to assume that authoritarianism is an Africa-specific challenge. What should be done is to conceive anew the "continuity that is somewhere in every society, no matter how rapidly it is changing" (443). Mair finds that this continuity inheres in "situations that the new order has not effectively disturbed" (443).

What Mair has in mind are the forms of social and political organization yet to be effectively brought under the control of the postcolonial African state. She refers to this as "small-scale" enclaves of patriotism, which are often resented and denigrated by Africa's new political elite as tribalism (443). By their attitude, the new African political class fail to learn the lesson that so-called tribalism teaches—namely, the value of faithfulness to tradition for politics under the conditions of postcolonialism. African elites can learn from other contexts where challenges of tradition and modernity once held sway, she suggests (443).

In sum, Mair's (1962, 443) argument is that African political elites should understand that the "national sentiment" they seek to entrench can only emerge from "the constant interaction that modern communications and common language make possible." The conclusion we can draw from this is that the central problem for modern African politics is a reflection on how social change can be mediated by tradition. In other words, the issue is how to conceive an adequate perspective on tradition as the social basis of politics in postcolonial Africa.

Recent discussions of tradition and modernity present a shift in emphasis. Instead of assuming that we know the meaning of both concepts, recent studies turn to a meta discourse to analyze the meaning of the concepts. The aim is to understand the relevance of concepts to attempts to resolve the opposition between the two phenomena. As one scholar puts it, if "tradition accuses modernity of introducing a system of governance" that is undesirable, and modernity raises the claim that tradition is "the bulwark of an obsolete" system that resists change, what we need to do is understand what both concepts mean (Orobator 1991, 273). This is because understanding the meaning of tradition and modernity as concepts will enable us to adjudicate whether it is reasonable to attribute a positive connotation to one and not the other. In this regard, the goal to pursue is conceptual clarification.

This is the reason Gyekye's perspective stands out in the literature on this topic. Gyekye turned to conceptual analysis to resolve the conflict between the two concepts. He argued that it is implausible to think of modernity as a concept devoid of tradition. Elements of tradition form an essential part of modernity. This is because modernity emerges when we build on tradition. Societal progress of the sort we call modernity comes about when people sift through the values of tradition and carry forward its useful elements. Mistaken assumptions about history partly account for why people misunderstand the connection between the two concepts. Gyekye (1997, 218) proposes that "the central, fundamental, and persistent meaning of 'traditional' is that which comes down or is inherited from the past and becomes an enduring element in the cultural life of a people." I agree with Gyekye's argument because cultures are transformed because of internal criticism—or immanent critique—and integration of the externally appropriated elements from other cultures.

The main question to ask pertains to the role tradition should play in the search for a viable modernity in Africa. Can postcolonial Africa conceive a future, be it in terms of social, political, or economic development, by look-ing to its past? Gyekye (1997, 233) identifies *sankofa*—which means "return to the past"—as the perspective that informs the work of those he calls "cultural revivalists." Cultural revivalists' belief that African tradition can be a source of cultural revival or identity is invalid according to Gyekye. Tradition, Gyekye argues, cannot be a means to mental liberation and regeneration in the present. It cannot offer a secure basis for meaningful development and nation building.

The arguments of those advancing the opposite perspective are also not convincing to Gyekye. He argues that antirevivalists, such as Marcien Towa and Paulin Hountondji, are mistaken for a variety of reasons. In the main, antirevivalists argue that the negative outlook of African cultures makes undesirable any attempt to push for cultural revival. This is due mainly to the prescientific nature and weak foundation of African culture (Gyekye 1997, 237). Gyekye (1997, 237) is right to argue that revivalists and antirevivalists are not "entirely correct in all of their arguments and criticisms." Extreme anti-revivalism is absurd in light of positive aspects of African culture documented by anthropological evidence. It is correct to say that the position lacks "histori-cal warrant" (Gyekye 1997, 239) because it contradicts our sense of the history of human progress. Extreme antirevivalism is "irrational" and will "lead to the loss of much in the past that, on rational or normative grounds, could be exploited for the benefit of the present generation" (239).

However, in rejecting antirevivalism one does not endorse the opposite perspective—namely, the view of naive revivalism. This position proposes that the African cultural past should be restored in its entirety. Gyekye disagrees because of the negative consequences of following the dictates of this view. Considering the case of development, Gyekye points to the fact that, although there may be an abstract sense of development presupposing a form of cultural logic, it is mistaken to infer from this that development requires the re-creation of tradition in the form proposed by extreme revivalists. The reason is that "the viability of a development framework is determined by, or contingent upon, the characteristics of that culture" (Gyekye 1997, 240). It is not correct to assume that the revival of tradition in its entirety is a causa sine qua non for the attain-ment of modernity because not every aspect of a culture has positive features. This is why Gyekye suggests the rigorous philosophical analysis of the foun-dations of African culture as a means to determining the shape of the future.

The problem posed by the perceived opposition of tradition and modernity continues to exercise the minds of African philosophers. It is a paradox that has serious consequences for central issues in political thought, such as the chal-lenge of pluralism and issues related to the role indigenous political institutions should play in the postcolonial era. The search for a new political order and model of governance fuels interest in the debate. Nowhere is this concern more visible than in the debates about consensus democracy and conceptual decolonization, which are two notable attempts by African philosophers to retrieve concepts from African traditions to address the challenges that besiege Africa in the present century.

CONSENSUS DEMOCRACY

Notwithstanding that many scholars refer to consensus as the core idea of governance in traditional African societies, Wiredu is the philosopher associated with the theory of consensus democracy. This is because of the analytical rigor notable in the case he made for this form of democracy as a panacea to the challenge of governance in modern Africa. For Wiredu (1996, 187), the viability of consensus democracy inheres in its nonparty character. Consensus democracy is, as such, free from the deficiencies of party-based democracy that revolves around majoritarianism.

In a consensus democracy, Wiredu explains, governance is a coalition of citizens, not a spoil of a political party that wins a majority in an election. As such, consensus democracy enables the realization of two essential forms of representation—namely, representation in council and in counsel. Wiredu's conviction is that it is essential for citizens to be represented in both senses to have a genuine democracy (186). This means that both formal and substantive representation ought to be the norm in any democracy. Assuming for now that the proposal is correct, the question is how to guarantee both kinds of representation.

According to Wiredu (1996), the answer lies in the role of deliberation in the consensual form of democracy he proposes. In such a system, deliberation is a means of decision-making because it gives value to consensus. Attaining consensus necessitates persuasive dialogue that will demonstrate to those who may disagree with an option that they can agree to a decision or course of action even if they disagree with some aspects of the decision. In this sense, what is required for the sort of consensus behind consensus democracy to obtain is that there is an agreed action without agreed notions—that is, a consensus that does not demand a "complete identity of moral or cognitive opinions" (183).

Wiredu reflected on Ashanti politics to show how this form of governance functioned. Even though the political system of the Ashanti is stratified, the substratum that provided the foundation for the general orientation of the community toward politics was the principle of deliberation and the consensus it envisages. It is thus clear for Wiredu that there are values inherent in this system that can be judiciously employed in fashioning a viable democracy for post-colonial Africa. As Wiredu (1996, 185) points out, "adherence to the principle of consensus was a premeditated option." Its basis was the belief "that ultimately the interests of all members of society are the same, although their immediate perceptions of those interests may be different" (185).

One might think that the insistence on consensus here is superfluous, at least if it is conceived as something that should apply to postcolonial Africa, whose pluralism is beyond contestation. Wiredu thinks it is exactly the pluralism that is a central aspect of contemporary African polities that makes imperative consensual democracy. If the condition for genuine political action will be guaranteed in pluralistic African polities, its basis would have to be an assurance that majority vote does not carry the day. To this end, it is necessary to ensure that democracy does not become a tyranny of a majority political party, which, as is often the case in many African countries, is ethnically based. In a consensual democracy, one can be sure that conflicts along party lines will be forestalled, for, in such a system, the winner is the people.

This raises a question about the connection between democracy and political parties. Wiredu (1996) considers his case for consensus democracy formidable because interethnic rivalry foments destructive conflicts in Africa. He argues that the pluralism of postcolonial Africa makes a nonparty system of democracy necessary. This is due to the link between the rational fear of being confined to a position of perpetual minority on the part of ethnic groups and the problem of political instability. These concerns would not exist in a consensual democracy because, in such a system, governance is "a coalition not, as in the common acceptation, of parties, but of citizens" (189).

The consensual democracy Wiredu proposed has been the subject of sustained critical attention. Beginning with the critique of Emmanuel Eze (1997), this critical reception can be found in many recent publications. I will consider Eze's critique of consensual democracy to provide a picture of the general concerns raised by African philosophers. Eze considers three problems that capture serious deficiencies in Wiredu's articulation of consensual democracy. The first is that certain important aspects about the origin of the political system upon which Wiredu's proposal is based remain unclear. Secondly, Eze does not find the understanding of political interest in Wiredu's proposal convincing. Thirdly, he disagrees with how Wiredu conceives the meaning of the concept of democracy.

According to Eze, the first problem is that Wiredu is being too optimistic to think that consensus derived from deliberation is the basis of political authority in the traditional African context he is drawing from. Eze proposes that factors like ideas of the sacred, superstitions, and related beliefs may well be the essential requirement of political legitimation, instead of rational persuasion (Eze 1997, 318). What Eze is arguing, in sum, is that Wiredu, in a bid to demonstrate that consensual democracy has a rational foundation, might have ended up alienating this system from the context that made its functioning possible. However, if this system is to function today, there needs to be certainty regarding the presuppositions that make it possible. If what made this form of governance possible in traditional Africa are myths that no longer obtain in postcolonial Africa, the implication is that there is a need to conceive new myths to make it work in the postcolonial context.

The second issue Eze raises is the nature of interests in the system proposed by Wiredu. This objection focuses on showing that Wiredu does not fully recognize the implications of individuality for questions pertaining to political interests (320). Earlier, I noted Wiredu's idea that there is a rock-bottom identity of interest that unifies the seemingly competing individual interests of people in the community. Eze does not see how this can be claimed with validity. In his view, it is an overstatement on Wiredu's part to suggest that knowing the good amounts to doing it. Thus, Eze sees the weaknesses associated with the way Wiredu conceives interests as another ground that warrants the reconceptualization of consensual democracy.

The third issue for Eze relates to issues about conceptual accuracy. Eze is concerned that, in thinking that the goal of democracy is to secure consensus, Wiredu limits the essential horizon of this political system. Making consensus a regulative ideal due to the challenge of pluralism is for Eze unwarranted. The reason, he argues, is that democracy aims at structuring disagreements by accepting them and providing the framework for contestation. Democracy's value, on this count, is to be found in the process it provides, not in its outcome (321).

One does not need to look far to see that the debate about consensual democracy is closely linked to concerns about the relationship between tradition and modernity. Consensual democracy is certainly an exemplification of the project of retrieving from traditional contexts concepts and ideas that are useful for the quest to solve important challenges besetting postcolonial Africa. One thing we can infer from Eze's disagreement with Wiredu's perspective is that the plausibility of an idea or practice retrieved from the traditional African past is often difficult to establish.

A major reason for this is that there is not a single narrative about whatever is offered as a reconstruction of the African past. Whereas one scholar might take path A to arrive at such a reconstruction and propose B as the most plausible view of an idea or concept that informed practices in traditional African society, another scholar might take path C and propose D as the most reasonable reconstruction of the same idea. The problem then becomes how to do philosophy in a context where it seems like the wheel is constantly in the process of being rediscovered—a situation, that is, where philosophical debates are reduced to quarrels about what constitutes a plausible starting point. I return to consideration of this problem in chapter 6. Let us consider in the meantime one final preoccupation that shaped African political philosophy—namely, conceptual decolonization.

CONCEPTUAL DECOLONIZATION

In a book documenting the situation of philosophy in Africa, Wiredu (1984) raised the need for conceptual decolonization. Although decolonization was a part of the social imagination after independence in many African countries due to call on Africans to free themselves from a colonial mentality, the form of decolonization proposed by Wiredu is rather specific. Noting the importance of reconstruction for intellectual progress in a society, Wiredu argues that "it is not possible to criticize or reconstruct without conceptual understanding," that philosophy in Africa will be better served if the curriculum makes conceptual decolonization a priority (34).

Wiredu (1984) identifies in this regard a challenge that must be tackled in the interest of progress—namely, that the study of African thought is mainly in foreign languages. Given that language predisposes us to think about philosophical problems and concepts in specific ways, the challenge for Africans is to devise a means that will enable them to think about philosophical questions in the spirit of African languages. In Wiredu's estimation, this will become possible if African philosophers divest their "thought of all undue influences emanating from the modes of thought" induced by colonialization (35). Wiredu understands conceptual decolonization as "the most fundamental form of decolonization" (35).

How is conceptual decolonization attained? Its possibility depends on whether Africans trained in philosophy can draw insights from their languages and cultures to evaluate the cogency and applicability of concepts they employ in thinking about reality. If they are not, as Wiredu says, going to mistake thinking *about* phenomena in a colonial language with thinking *in* that language (1996, 137), African philosophers must be attentive to differences in conceptual frameworks. That is, they must be alert to differences between the conceptual framework that operates in their indigenous languages and the one that shapes thinking in the language of the erstwhile colonizers.

What Wiredu has in mind in distinguishing between thinking *about* a phenomenon in a language and thinking *in* a language seems to be the awareness one must have about the way languages predispose us regarding formulating philosophical problems. To decolonize conceptually, African philosophers must think through philosophical concepts in indigenous languages to find out if the inferences made in foreign languages, from which those concepts originated, also apply meaningfully in their own conceptual framework.

According to Wiredu (1996, 138), should an African philosopher carry out this task of "conceptual translation" and find that a given concept or proposition does not make sense in her or his language, then the way out is to "reason out the matter on independent grounds." This means to consider the meaning of the concept in a way that takes into consideration the dialogue between indigenous African conceptualization and that of the foreign language.

For instance, should an African philosopher find that the term *to be* (existence) does not make the sort of sense in Twi that it makes in French, what is required in this situation by conceptual decolonization is to step back and consider the meaning of *to be* (existence) from an angle that takes the dialogue of French and Twi as its starting point. Doing this will enable the African philosopher in such a situation to find out whether the meaning she or he attributes to the concept is dependent on the linguistic habits of either French or Twi.

Without wishing to go into a detailed evaluation of Wiredu's arguments, one thing that is useful for the goal of this chapter should be noted. Wiredu's (1996, 141) attempt to show how conceptual decolonization works led him to make recourse to the retrieval of concepts and ideas from his Akan tradition. In attempting to show that it is imperative to subject Descartes's "cogito, ergo sum" to conceptual decolonization, for instance, Wiredu reached back to Akan tradition to retrieve the concept *wo ho*, which is the equivalent of existence. Through analysis of the Akan equivalent of *cogito*, Wiredu established that existence of the form conveyed by Descartes's formula does not apply in the Akan conceptual framework. The reason is that to exist, in the sense of wo ho, is spatial. On this ground, one cannot say, like Descartes did with the cogito, that one exists because one thinks. And the reason is that, in the Akan conceptual framework, *to be* implies to be something or to be somewhere.

The implication of Wiredu's argument, then, is that he does not just retrieve concepts from his Akan tradition. In addition to retrieving concepts and ideas, he recovers the meaning of these concepts to demonstrate the plausibility of philosophical propositions handed down to him and other African philosophers through education and inculcation of the conceptual framework of colonialists. Although there are other important questions in African philosophy, those considered so far are sufficient to make the point of this chapter. The point of this chapter is, first, that major discourses in African political philosophy emerge from consideration of meta-philosophical issues and, second, that conceptual retrieval is vital in the debates in this tradition of political philosophy.

DIAGNOSING NORMATIVE DEFICIT

These two points show that African political philosophy embodies a normative deficit that must be remedied. To discover a path that will allow adequate reflection on the challenge of political failure, which is the center of contemporary African experience, African political philosophy must evaluate its reliance on conceptual retrieval. The question to address, then, is whether major ideas in African political philosophy provide a formidable means to deal with the challenge of political failure. In other words, does conceptual retrieval suffice as a means to address the challenge of political failure?

I do not think this is the case. The normative deficit implicated in the approach of conceptual retrieval necessitates a revision of approach that makes possible a different kind of response to political failure. We need to develop an approach that makes possible an answer that is grounded on where Africa finds itself today. To explain what I mean by normative failure, I would like to summarize, first, what the different concerns of African philosophers considered in this chapter amount to. Based on this summary, I then spell out the unifying point of the discourses on African experience in the works of African philosophers. Carrying out these two tasks clarifies the nature of the normative deficit I have in mind.

We can summarize the discussion so far by pointing out the implication of the issues considered for political philosophy. In this regard, the debate about the relationship of persons and community can be seen as a meta-philosophical concern about the constitution and goal of political community. In other words, how should the political community be constituted, and what is the goal of already existing institutions? If in African thought the community has priority over individuals, would this not mean that political institutions in postcolonial Africa ought to mirror communitarian principles? What ought to be the relationship of the state to persons or, as Menkiti put it, conceptions of personhood and citizenship?

From the discussion of the opposition between tradition and modernity, we can infer two implications for political philosophy. Firstly, the debate can be understood as a search for a source of the ideas needed to construct a new political community. It could be interpreted as a reflection on questions about how to make valuable ideas of traditional African society fit for application in the modern, postindependence era. This amounts to saying that it is an attempt to conceive of a way to apply concepts and insights embodied by the institutions and practices of traditional African society in light of the deep changes brought by colonialization, an experience whose effects currently persist in many ways. Secondly, discussion of tradition and modernity could be taken to imply a fundamental concern about the desirable society in all its ramifications—a society that will enable the realization of the good life in Africa. This sense of the debate amounts to saying that it is an attempt to envision the ideal society.

We can understand the debate about consensual democracy as an attempt to conceive a model of governance or political order that is authentic and free from undesirable, imported deficiencies. While authenticity consists in the fact that such a model of governance builds on indigeneity, undesirable deficiencies refer to things like the corrupting impact of money in democratic processes or the tyranny of the majority. Finally, conceptual decolonization is relevant for African political philosophy because it concerns authentic freedom. It is a quest for solutions to conceptual disorientation, which has distorted self-understanding and the conception of reality among Africans.

Putting together the implications of the concerns of African philosophers, we can say that African philosophers have conceived African experience in four ways—namely, as a challenge that demands the conception of (1) the nature of political community, (2) the sources of the concepts and ideas for normative political theorizing, (3) the nature and path to realizing the ideal of a good society and the political order it entails, and (4) a path to construct authentic freedom.

From these points, we can infer a general claim: that African philosophers take the condition of life in the continent as the starting point of theorizing. Given this, any deficiency one may notice in the theories they propose can be anything but inattentiveness to context. It is essential to note this point because the normative deficiency I find in the work of African philosophers does not aim to suggest that their theories are of no consequence for the African experience.

Rather than derive this normative deficit from what African philosophers failed to do, I contend that the deficiency relates to the weakness of conceptual retrieval as a method for addressing the problem of political failure. The discussion of normative deficiency is therefore a form of immanent critique that seeks to advance the horizon of the discourse on African political philosophy. It is an attempt to move the field beyond a fundamental limitation regarding method.

African philosophers rely on conceptual retrieval in tackling postcolonial experiences. The convention is to look back to traditional Africa to retrieve ideas or concepts that are useful for conceiving remedies to current challenges. This approach harbors a normative deficiency that makes it an unsuitable foundation for conceiving justifications of political theories. This is a significant shortcoming because of the link between the justificatory power of an approach to political philosophy and the viability of the theory proposed. The focus on retrieval in contemporary African political philosophy is normatively weak because it is out of sync with contemporary sources of meaning.

Political imagination in the African continent can move beyond the current experience of political failure if we develop an account of a political culture that is contemporaneously justified. By this I mean that conceiving and justifying a political culture for the African context in a way that speaks to people today is a causa sine qua non for solving the challenge of political failure. To address adequately the challenge of political failure, it is not sufficient to simply draw insights from the resources of the African past as the method of conceptual retrieval proposes. One must pay attention to the resources of the present and the sense that the conceptual resources of the past are no longer coherent. Having lost the essential legitimating conceptual connections in the sense of being embedded in widely shared conventions, conceptual resources of traditional African societies must be creatively refashioned with a view to enabling Africans to reorient themselves to reality, especially political reality.

Focusing squarely on the resources of the past may be taken to mean that Africans in the present century are incapable of independent, critical reflection on realities that shapes their lives and aspirations. The normative deficiency inherent in the approach of conceptual retrieval is the limited justification it can offer. Rather than ask how we can derive concepts from traditional African experience to make sense of current African reality, we need to move further to inquire about the way Africans think about their situation today.

In other words, given the concern with the past and current reality of political failure, how can Africans conceive a vision of the future using the resources available to them? And how can the envisioned future be justified here and now, through the mobilization of resources capable of speaking to everyone—not just some people who have access to the idioms and metaphors of traditional Africa? Conceptual retrieval can offer only a limited justification of a political ideal worth striving for by people existing in the here and now. Notwithstanding, an outline of a robust justification that avoids the current normative deficiency of African political philosophy can be developed by recourse to the approach of conceptual creativity I develop in chapter 6.

FOUR

—⚊—

PALAVER AND CONSENSUS— PROVENANCE OF A CONCEPTUAL APPARATUS

A PUBLIC MEETING BETWEEN THE people of two towns, Osu and Labadi, and the Danish stranger community in Christiansborg (present-day Accra in Ghana) took place on February 9, 1767. During the meeting, different individuals and groups presented for consideration forty-two cases against Carl Gottlob Resch, a Danish governor who had lost his post. The cases presented for adjudication varied, just like the forms of demands for recompense made by the complainants. One of the cases, for instance, was a complaint that former governor Resch had failed to pay for the service of a certain Caboceer Orsa, who provided security for Resch's "private trading expedition" (Hernaes 1988, 22). Resch was also accused of seizing Caboceer Orsa's animals without cause. Besides Caboceer Orsa's complaints, grievances against Resch and demands for compensation were made.

Some of the cases had to do with Resch's failure to pay for goods and services, such as a fee agreed on for the delivery of his gold to a goldsmith in another town, costs for the capture of his runaway slave, payment due for a slave he had purchased, fee for delivery of his letter to someone in a distant town, and the costs for teaching his attendants how to make candles. Beyond these, there were other complaints about Resch's refusal to pay his bills: his refusal to pay local laborers for working on a construction project, his refusal to pay the fee for the facilitation of the sale of a number of slaves, and his failure to pay for goods he purchased, such as a pig and timber. In short, because of the extensive list of the cases brought against him, there was little ground to doubt that Governor Resch was a notorious debtor and a breaker of contracts.

A man of high office in the Danish outpost in Fort Christiansborg, Resch had indeed a lot to answer for. He was not only in the habit of refusing to pay for goods and services; he was also involved in violent activities. One of the cases brought against him—a demand to compensate a young girl he had assaulted in Osu—provides evidence for this. Resch got drunk alongside his servants during a festivity called African New Year and led a gang to attack Osu. The man whose daughter sustained severe injury to her teeth because Resch had hit her with a stone during the attack demanded compensation for the assault (Hernaes 1988, 24–25). To resolve the problems, participants at the public meeting deliberated. Their goal was to resolve the problems presented in a manner that was acceptable to all involved—that is, to resolve the problems in a manner that would restore goodwill among the people.

PALAVER AT FORT CHRISTIANSBORG

Although one might be quick to consider this public meeting an event solely aimed at providing a means to deal with private quarrels, the experience of the Danish community in Fort Christiansborg in the 1700s tells a us a different story. In encounters between the indigenous African people and the Danes at Fort Christiansborg Castle, public meetings "played an important role as an instrument in solving the more principal problems regarding the relations between the Danish establishment as such and the local community" (Hernaes 1988, 25). Per Hernaes (1988) recounts how public meetings provided a framework for the interaction between the Danes and local Africans in the eighteenth century in his discussion of a remarkable public deliberation that took place at Fort Christiansborg.

Between 1768 and 1769, two Danish governors, F. J. Kuhberg and G. F. Wrisberg, expressed unwillingness to pay for firewood and timber delivered on a regular basis to Fort Christainsborg. This had serious implications because the provision of these services was an important source of income for the young people of Osu and Labadi. As a result, the youth vehemently resisted, through protest actions, the refusal of the Danish governors to pay for their services. In response to the resistance, the Danish officers promptly took leaders of the protest into custody, claiming that they would only be released upon the payment of a ransom. Rather than intimidating the youths, the outcome of the imprisonment of leaders of the protest and the demand that a ransom be paid to secure their release was even greater violent protests that disrupted the trading activities of the Danes.

The Danish governor convened a public meeting, giving people an impression of being sincerely committed to the resolution of the conflict. Unbeknownst to the people of Osu and Labadi, the governor's call for a public meeting harbored a hidden agenda. He had planned to "teach" the people a lesson in obedience. Thus, when the representatives of Osu and Labadi arrived for the public deliberation, they were arrested and thrown into detention. This action forced representatives of the two communities to agree to the terms presented by the governor and his associates. Not long afterward, however, the controversy resurfaced. Four young men came to the Fort Christiansborg on October 4, 1769, to demand payment for firewood delivered to the fort. When the Danish governor refused to pay, riots broke out.

The local people were so determined in their defiance that the riots brought every kind of trading to a complete halt. Sensing the danger this portended, the Danish governor offered to negotiate, but the people refused. His attempt to convene a public meeting after his offer was rejected also failed because the people refused to pay any heed to his words, because of his antecedent behavior of detaining the people who had come for a similar public meeting. In the end, the governor was compelled to ask mediators from Accra to help deal with the impasse. Notwithstanding the acceptance to participate in a public meeting following the intervention of mediators, the representatives of Osu and Labadi were not convinced that they could trust the Danes. They therefore stipulated a condition for their participation in the public meeting. They demanded that the Danes should send "two white officers to be held as hostages in Osu during the palaver" (Hernaes 1988, 27). The public meeting finally took place when this condition was met, and the matter was resolved.

The practice that defined the interactions, whether violent or peaceful, between the Danes that established themselves at the Gold Coast in the eighteenth century and indigenous African people reflects an important dimension of African political heritage. This is the case because of the manifestation in these interactions of the form of public deliberation that is a central feature of social and political life in African societies. The prevalence of the disposition to resort to deliberation in dealing with social and political issues in African societies, past and present, has been noted in many studies. Given its ubiquity, there are varied descriptions and interpretations of public deliberation in this context.

It is against this background that I pursue a twofold aim in this chapter. The first is to account for the changes that have occurred in the conceptual designations of the practice in extant literature. The second is to show, through cases, the core presuppositions decipherable from practices of the palaver. The overall goal of the analysis in this chapter is to conceive typologies that can explain the nature of public deliberation in relation to political and social experiences in Africa. I will clarify in this chapter the meaning of palaver as a conceptual reference for public deliberation. This is necessary because public deliberation possesses a meaning that has evolved over time due to the interaction of such factors as precolonial commercial encounters, colonialization, resistance to domination, military dictatorships, and the contestation for power under democratic arrangements.

A good starting point in the pursuit of the first objective of this chapter is perhaps a cursory look at one of the seminal works on African political thought. In 1940, M. Fortes and E. E. Evans-Pritchard published their book *African Political Systems*, which set the tone for subsequent works in the field. The authors noted that they did not find issues pertaining to political philosophy useful in their investigation of indigenous African political systems. This is an instructive point. They argued that "theories of political philosophers" are "of little scientific value" in the study of the societies investigated because "their conclusions are seldom formulated in terms of observed behaviour or capable of being tested by this criterion" (Fortes and Evans-Pritchard 1940, 4). They further contended that "political philosophers in modem times have often sought to substantiate their theories by appeal to the facts of primitive societies" (Fortes and Evans-Pritchard 1940, 4). However, since Fortes and Pritchard "do not consider that the origins of primitive institutions can be discovered" (Fortes and Evans-Pritchard 1940, 5), they thought it needless to follow the example of political philosophers who attempt to derive political thought, in the sense of reflection on an ideal political order, from analysis of practices in a primitive society or state of nature.

The mistrust of political philosophy by Fortes and Evans-Pritchard, especially regarding the study of Africa, is instructive because it implies that the work they produced on African political systems eschews attempts to offer justification of the concepts, norms, and principles of political practice in African societies. In this book, I pursue the exact opposite of the goal Fortes and Evans-Pritchard set for themselves. I attempt to theorize the political habits and institutions prevalent in Africa. The consideration of the practice of deliberation in this book differs from the positivistic political anthropology offered by Fortes and Evans-Pritchard because I attempt to formulate an understanding of African political philosophy that does not merely describe how Africans view politics. Unlike the descriptive analysis we find in the works of political anthropologists, my goal is to develop a conception of African political philosophy based on the theorising of a central category of African political heritage—namely, the phenomenon of public meetings.

Although *African Political Systems* was a collection of essays by established experts on Africa, one of the lasting legacies of the book is the introduction of a conceptual distinction that became influential in the study of African political thought. This distinction is the idea that we can view indigenous African politics through the lenses of two categories: "stateless societies" and "primitive states" (Fortes and Evans-Pritchard 1940, 5). In the latter type of societies, there is "centralized authority, administrative machinery and judicial institutions—in short, a government." In addition, these societies have "cleavages of wealth, privilege and status correspond[ing] to the distribution of power and authority" (Fortes and Evans-Pritchard 1940, 5). It is regarding these features that "primitive states" are unlike "stateless societies," where the opposite social and political pattern obtains.

Stateless societies "lack centralized authority, administrative machinery and judicial institutions." Such societies lack a government, and "there [is] no sharp division of rank, status or wealth" (Hernaes 1988, 5). The common feature straddling the dividing lines of the two categories, which, according to Fortes and Evans-Pritchard, can help us to distinguish between African political systems, is the practice of public deliberation. In stateless societies and centralized states in Africa, public deliberation constitutes a basic political principle, which serves as a center of social and political life.

Writing about the phenomenon decades ago, Robert Armstrong (1979, 15) argued that "African societies are intensely active systems, and public and private meetings of various kinds are principal channels for the expression of the interaction of the groups, subgroups and personalities that make them up." Although his study of the practice focused on West Africa, Armstrong was not in doubt that he was dealing with a phenomenon of wider significance for social and political thought. His conviction was based on the fact that palaver deliberation was commonplace among Africans in other regions of the continent as well. Armstrong noted that "the literature suggests that East, Central, and South Africa are no different in principle from West Africa in this respect" (15).

ON THE PHENOMENON OF PUBLIC DELIBERATION

The question to ask concerns the nature of the phenomenon of public deliberation. How should we understand the meaning and function of public deliberation? It is vital to raise this question because public deliberation bridges the conceptual divide between so-called stateless societies and primitive states, the controversies surrounding the distinction between the two forms of societal organization notwithstanding. To be sure, scholars of Africa have employed different conceptual categories in attempts to make sense of the practice of public deliberation one encounters in African societies. Those writing in English variously refer to it as "forum," "communal assembly," "people's assembly," "direct democracy," "public meeting," and "palaver" (Bidima 2014; Okeja 2020; Clark 2010).

When we turn to works published in German, concepts like "Volksversammlung" and "Gemeinderat" stand out as categories used to describe and analyze the phenomenon (Bujo 1993; Helfrich 2005). Publications in French generally have the convention of using the concept of "la palabre" to describe this sort of public deliberation (Atangana 1966; Bidima 1997). There are instances where scholars use the Portuguese concept "palabra" in discussion of the phenomenon (Armstrong 1979). More generally, the description of the practice of deliberation as palaver permeates the study of the phenomenon in English and French. To carry out the first task of this chapter, therefore, I begin with an analysis of the use of palaver as a conceptual reference for public deliberation. My goal in doing this is to determine the changes that have occurred over time in the usage of the concept. This will enable me to specify how conceptual change and the evolution of new meanings ascribed to the practice are intertwined.

Recognizing that, as a distinct feature of African cultures, palaver provides the space and means for social and political participation in African societies, the United Nations Education Social and Cultural Organization (UNESCO) commissioned a study on the social and political aspects of the palaver in 1979. Armstrong (1979) discussed in his contribution to this study the variety of names by which the practice goes. Although focused on the Idoma people in Nigeria, it is instructive that Armstrong's study emphasized aspects of the palaver that resonate with another study focused on the interaction between the Danes and Africans in eighteenth-century Gold Coast (Hernaes 1988). According to Armstrong, it is questionable in what sense it is useful to conceptually describe the African practice of deliberation as palaver.

He suggested that instead of using the palaver concept, a more appropriate concept would be *public meeting*. Unlike palaver, public meeting enables us to take "advantage of the wide range of possible meetings which [the phenomenon] can refer to and the fact that it always implies a certain formality of procedures" (Armstrong 1979, 11). On this view, even the constructive understanding of palaver, which proposes that it is "an open debate during which each participant, regardless of age or rank, expresses his or her opinion on the problem being discussed until the entire family or community reaches a general consensus," is wanting (11). This is because the view cannot account for the variety of deliberations that happen in public meetings in African societies.

Armstrong considered further the meaning of palaver in the context of its history to show why it inadequately accounts for the practice of deliberation.

He turns in this regard to an exploration of palaver's etymology. He found that "all authorities agree that the English word 'palaver' is from the Portuguese 'palavra' and French 'palabre' is from Spanish 'palabra'. The Spanish and Portuguese words are cognates. Both conceive the phenomenon as 'word' or 'act of speaking'" (Armstrong 1979, 11). What is relevant for the understanding of palaver as public deliberation relates to the differences between the Portuguese and Spanish concepts, on the one hand, and the English and French concepts, on the other hand (12). Notwithstanding that the root of the French and English variants of the concept are traceable to Portuguese and Spanish roots, Armstrong observes that the English and French concepts "are not borrowed directly from the standard forms of these languages" (12). The explanation for this is that there was a change of meaning in the English and French appropriations of the concept. Whereas palaver refers to "debate" or "conference" in Portuguese, in English and French, it is rendered as, among other unfavorable terms, "idle chatter" (12).

As mentioned earlier, Armstrong's study raises issues that were of paramount concern in another study of the phenomenon of deliberation in African societies. This other work focused on the interactions between the Danes and indigenous African people in the former Gold Coast. Drawing on what he calls "palaver books," Hernaes (1988) provides insights into the history of palaver as conceptual designation of public deliberation. Like Armstrong, Hernaes found that, although the conception of deliberation as palaver is "interesting," the concept itself has to be clarified because it is "too vaguely defined" (2). For this reason, Hernaes investigated the shifting meanings attributed to palaver as conceptual designation of deliberation. He did this by analyzing the encounters between the Danes and Africans in the Gold Coast in the period between 1658 and 1850. This was the epoch of Danish dominion over the region regarded then as the Gold Coast.

In the interaction between the African populations and the Danes, palaver was "used by Europeans in order to describe any kind of problem or conflict" and to refer to "an institutionalized framework within which inter-African as well as Afro-European matters" were handled (Hernaes 1988, 2). Hernaes avers that no single meaning is attributable to the concept because it "sometimes referred to conflicts, quarrels, even wars" (3). But, he underscores, one should not construe this very fact to mean the concept was used to refer to just anything. The concept denoted either problem, conflict, or negotiation (4). The specific meaning the concept came to embody in its invocation among the Danes in the former Gold Coast was that it referred to "the very proceeding or meetings where negotiations of different kinds were conducted" (4–5). Hence, the Danes did not only hold palavers but also had what they called palaver notebooks, which is a concept they used to refer to the record of the proceedings of the different palaver deliberations they held with indigenous Africans.

Unfavorable characterizations that accompanied the translation of the concept into English became an essential aspect of its meaning when it migrated into the parlance of urban consciousness in colonial Africa. In the urban imaginary in colonial and postcolonial West Africa, the concept came to denote trouble of the sort that is colloquially regarded as *wahala* in Nigeria, for instance.[1] In the parts of Africa colonized by the French and the areas colonized by the British, palaver came to refer to trouble or idle chatter due to its migration into urban parlance. This is not to say, however, that there weren't other sources of mischaracterization of the concept. But, as Hernaes (1988, 14) has argued, the unfavourable characterization of the concept has always been a pointer to "the speaker's racist contempt or ethnocentric or class prejudice against the people spoken to or referred to." This proclivity certainly comes about due to attitudinal dispositions fostered by colonialization.

The foregoing was not lost on Ernest Wamba dia Wamba (1996, 13), who observed that the reluctance of scholars to compare the democracy of the Agora with palaver is traceable to "the fact that you cannot deny civilization to people in whose modes of life you can discover civilisation elements." Besides changes in meaning arising from the mischaracterization of the concept of palaver in political anthropology and the reductive colloquial denotation it later acquired through colonial encounters, palaver took on a set of new meanings in the era of postcolonial democratic rule. The reconstitution of the meaning of the concept during this period occurred mainly in three phases, which I describe below.

The first phase was the period of anticolonial struggle. At the outset of anticolonial discourse, the concept was rehabilitated to signify the cognitive equality, if not superiority, of the dispossessed and oppressed African peoples regarding political organization. Later, in the second phase, it became an ideology of legitimation invoked by authoritarian regimes in the continent to justify their grip on power. The purchase of the meaning with which it was imbued in this period consisted in the opportunity the concept provided for the mobilization of the cultural sentiment already set in motion during anticolonial struggle. Finally, the third phase came alive in the era of national conferences and the accompanying apologies aimed at reconciliation.

---

1. Depending on the context, *wahala* in pidgin means "trouble," "stress," or "general state of discomfort."

The shifting meanings ascribed to the concept of palaver during the different twists and turns of the third wave of democracy inspired African philosophers to reflect more carefully on the concept. It was in the fertile soil of different conceptual studies carried out by African philosophers that the seeds of the discourse on palaver as instantiation of African democracy were planted. The seeds later germinated and bore fruits in the works of African philosophers whose work focused on consensual democracy. In this regard, one can point to the works of Kwasi Wiredu, Edaward Wamala, Kwame Gyekye, Jean-Godefroy Bidima, Ernest Wamba dia Wamba, Emmanuel Eze, Magobe Ramose, Marie Eboh, Michael Onyebuchi Eze, and Bernard Matolino. Consensus democracy continues to reverberate as a major concern in the works of African philosophers interested in political thought.

In the period of anticolonial contestation, intellectual and political elites held up the notion of palaver as a shining example of the cognitive equality of Africans and their colonial oppressors from Europe. Convinced by the insight of Cabral (1974, 14) that "the time when it was necessary to marshal arguments to prove the cultural maturity of African peoples has passed," anticolonial struggle leaders tried to revamp the damaged political heritage embodied by the concept of palaver. Their efforts in this regard were in line with the general anticolonial supposition that a revival of African culture ought to constitute the center of the struggle for freedom, the reason being that the denigration of African culture was at the center of colonial oppression. Against this backdrop, the rehabilitation of the concept of palaver, as a signifier of cognitive equality of Africans vis-à-vis European colonialists, came in handy. Anticolonial struggle leaders saw in palaver a demonstration to one and all that Africans had developed a sophisticated and desirable form of democracy long before colonial misadventurists and their counterpart secular missionaries "discovered" the continent.

Julius Nyerere (1968, 12), a leading light of the anticolonial struggle, has argued eloquently thus: "We, in Africa, have no more need of being 'converted' to socialism than we have of being 'taught' democracy. Both are rooted in our own past—in the traditional society which produced us." In his view, instead of taking lessons in democracy, what Africans needed to establish an authentic political system was to regain their "former attitude of mind" (8). One can thus say that leaders of anticolonial struggle imagined palaver as a reflection of a dignified African cultural achievement—that is, as a pointer to the reality that Africans are just as good as Europeans.

This point was aptly captured by Peter Ekeh (1975, 101) in his observation that Western-educated African elites "bent over backwards to show that their standards of education and administration are as good as those of their former colonizers. The point of reference in such demonstrations is to prove that they are the 'equals', but never the betters, of their former rulers." Given the intention to wrest power from officers of the colonial government, it is reasonable to argue that power struggle inflected the reimagination of the palaver during the period of anticolonial struggle.

In the writings of anticolonialists, the main transmutation of the meaning ascribed to palaver is that the concept came to serve as a marker of the cognitive equality of Africans and their colonial oppressors from Europe. This change in meaning served, on the one hand, the aim of galvanizing belief in their culture among the emerging African political elites. It was meant to inspire in them the conviction that their culture had all the requisite resources for the construction of a core of modern politics that was decidedly African in provenance. On the other hand, the change in meaning underscored that, as heirs to African heritage, where the palaver mode of politics played a central role, African elites were no less capable of piloting the affairs of their homelands. The point therefore is that the practice of palaver demonstrated and deconstructed at the same time. It demonstrated that African culture possessed resources that enabled one to see that African elites were as well equipped for governance as colonial rulers. At the same time, the concept deconstructed the myth of African cultural inferiority.

Wamba dia Wamba provides insights that are valuable for understanding the second phase of the reconstitution of the meaning of the concept of palaver in the era of postcolonial democratic experiments. According to him, "the palaver is often not very well understood" because of its obfuscation and mischaracterization by "colonialist anthropologists (organic intellectuals of colonialism) and leaders of neo-colonial Africa and their organic intellectuals" (Wamba dia Wamba 1985, 7). The most explicit instance of the mischaracterization is the claim by postcolonial African politicians that palaver, as an embodiment of African indigenous democracy, is opposed to multiparty democracy. Capitalizing on this mischaracterization, postcolonial political elites legitimized their ideology and interest in holding on to power.

One only needs to consider the misappropriation of palaver as legitimation for a single-party state in the modern history of African politics to see how palaver became an ideological tool. Proposing that palaver is not amenable to multiparty democratic politics, some African presidents proscribed a multiparty system of democracy. They justified the abolition of multiparty democracy on the ground that authentic African democracy revolved around a different and nobler ideal—namely, a one-party system in which consensus is a cardinal political virtue. Wamba dia Wamba correctly argued in this regard that this is a farcical justification for a one-party state by postcolonial African political elites. Appealing to palaver in this way served only an ideological end. It was a way for politicians to manipulate democratic processes and ensure that they held on to power.

Closely related to the above is the reconstitution of the meaning of palaver during national reconciliations in the African continent. At the end of the 1980s and during most of the 1990s, many countries held national conferences aimed at fostering reconciliation. The conferences were responses to the terrible human rights abuses by military dictatorships and authoritarian one-party regimes. In this period, the concept of palaver acquired a new meaning: the understanding that it is an African paradigm of justice outside the formal structures of the state. It is against this background that the national conferences held across the continent were understood as reenactments of the deliberative approach to pursuing justice in precolonial Africa.

As such, palaver came to refer to the pursuit of justice beyond the narrow margins of seeking to simply punish offenders. The reconstitution of the meaning of palaver as an African paradigm of justice in the era of national conferences emphasized that, of necessity, justice requires the reconciliation of parties involved in a dispute. Thus, the meaning of palaver came to embody two interrelated ideas in the period of national conferences and reconciliation. First, it came to imply that justice is, in important respects, an affair tied to a people's cultural self-understanding. Second, the concept of palaver took on the sense that justice requires a space for the participation of both those directly affected by an action and other relevant stakeholders.

With the buzz created by national conferences in many African countries also came concerted efforts on the part of philosophers and political scientists to understand what indeed the palaver phenomenon meant at a conceptual level. Of course, scholars were not ignorant of the shifting and contested meaning of palaver in the periods prior to the national conferences. The point is that scholars, especially African philosophers and political theorists, started to engage in a more sustained fashion with the project of the conceptual exploration of palaver due to the impetus of national conferences held across the continent.

Hence, we find in this regard the exploration of this theme in the writings of such philosophers as Ernest Wamba dia Wamba, Kwasi Wiredu, Emmanuel Wamala, Marie Eboh, Magobe Ramose, Jean-Godefroy Bidima, and Emmanuel Eze. These scholars attempted to spell out the implications of the retrieved conceptions of the palaver that can be useful in constructing a new understanding of politics in the continent. Thus, the scholars that explored the meaning of the concept in this period were primarily interested in articulating how the phenomenon of public deliberation that palaver designates can be expressed as consensus democracy, the pursuit of consensus, or democracy by consensus. They aimed at conceptual retrieval to recapture the principles embedded in the practice of public deliberation in traditional African societies that would enable the theorizing of modern African democratic experience.

The theory of consensus democracy ought to be seen as one of Wiredu's lasting legacies (Wiredu 1996, 182–190). I would argue that, generally, African philosophers regard the understanding of public deliberation they retrieve from so-called traditional Africa as an instantiation of consensus democracy. For a number of these philosophers, consensus democracy is a category of analysis that provides a unique African context for the analysis of problems of ethics and social and political philosophy. Thus, discussions about consensus proved fascinating in postcolonial African philosophy due to assumptions about how to deal with problems associated with the practice of liberal democracy. One of the prominent assumptions in this regard is the thought that consensus democracy, of the sort derived from palaver, opens the much-needed avenue for the imagining of a democracy devoid of the shortcomings of majoritarian democracy.

Thus, the main political question for African philosophers whose works were informed by this assumption became how to ensure that the practice of deliberation inherent in palaver is refashioned as a form of politics that enables inclusiveness. As Wiredu (1996) has put it, the goal was to ensure that deliberation was used to articulate a means of representation of everyone both in council and counsel. There are three strands of thought on this reconstituted meaning of deliberation. The first strand interprets the consensus ideal of palaver as a project of retrieval that reveals a mode of politics best suited to African reality. The second strand looks on the consensus ideal as the summation of the impossible task ethnophilosophy pursues, which is to produce an African philosophy devoid of all foreign inflections. The third strand looks at the consensus ideal of palaver as an embodiment of a strategy of justification in moral and political philosophy, specifically as an ideal to leverage in justifying moral and political theories.

Each of these three strands of thought underscores a fundamental point— namely, that the essence of palaver, as a specific form of deliberation, is to achieve the ideal of consensus. The deliberation invoked is not just an open-ended process but, in principle, a process open to everyone. Whereas philosophers like Wiredu considered consensus the foundation for a nonparty democracy, others such as Emmanuel Eze interpreted the claims of consensus democracy as a distortion of the fundamental sense of democracy. I return to the discussion of the implications of the plurality of meanings attributed to palaver deliberation in the history of African political thought toward the end of this chapter. In the meantime, I focus on summarizing the discussion so far to make clear the dimensions of the meaning of the concept of palaver.

As we have seen, the convention of designating public deliberation in African societies as palaver is traceable to events in modern African history. This way of thinking about the concept developed at a time of rapid expansion of trade and exchanges with non-Africans. It is instructive to note this point because it means that there are diverse paths to reconstructing the meaning we can ascribe to the concept. Depending on the context of usage, the meaning attributed could be public meeting, verbose and idle talk, discomforting everyday frustrations, ideology of legitimation in politics, a form of political institutional arrangement, a marker of cognitive equality of oppressors and the oppressed, an African-specific democratic practice, or a symbol of collective action aimed at doing justice outside the formal structures of the postcolonial state.

Given that some of these meanings of the concept are incompatible, a problem that arises is the possibility of articulating a coherent sense of the concept. Is it possible to arrive at a coherent description of the concept that will reflect generalizable meaning? The best way to proceed in answering this question is to conceive typologies of the meanings the concept acquired over time.

TYPOLOGIES OF PUBLIC DELIBERATION

To conceptualize a meaning or definition of palaver applicable to the different epochs of African history, let us begin with a discussion of instances where the practice played a central role. We consider in this regard five cases that show how contextual roles of the concept give an inkling of its normative implications and meaning. Before recounting these cases, it is important to underscore that the cases invoked are not meant to suggest that it is impossible to understand the notion of palaver through analysis of its abstract properties. The point I want to underscore is rather that the meaning of palaver, as a concept, emerges more clearly through a specific form of inquiry—namely, a practice-dependent inquiry.

By engaging in a practice-dependent inquiry, we are able to understand more clearly the presuppositions of the concept. The first case below shows how the concept of palaver is an idea of legitimation and a normative framework that structures contestations for power. In the second case, palaver manifests as a reference point of social interaction. In the third case, the concept transmutes into a principle that structures the process of culture modification and social change. The fourth case reveals an imagination of the concept of palaver as an ideal of economic interaction and resolution of conflicts. Finally, palaver functions in the fifth case as an orientation that enables the community to comprehend what it means to be a human being.

Let us consider the first case. This story unfolded in the modern political history of the different indigenous groups in Sierra Leone. Recounted by Bruce L. Mouser as the Forekariah Palaver or Grand Conference, this public deliberation served as the means for the pursuit of political legitimation. Mouser (1998, 219) points out that this deliberation, held between March 24 and April 6, 1805, was "one of the earliest large conferences described in detail" in the records of British officials in Sierra Leone.

As the records show, the participants comprised indigenous groups in the country as well as settlers engaging in different kinds of trade in the region. The deliberation took place at Forekariah, which was at the time the capital of Moria. It aimed to secure recognition—that is, political legitimation—for Alimami Amara Morani as the ruler of the people. Mouser (1998, 220) points out that "acceptance or acquiescence was required for there to be political and economic stability in the region."

The context of the quest for the political legitimation of the new ruler should put things in perspective. The death of Sitafa, the ruler preceding Alimami Amara Morani, initiated a period of disagreements and confusion among the people. Because of the divisions that arose from these contestations, trade was disrupted, and political stability was threatened. Thus, when it happened in October 1804 that Amara was elected as leader of the Forekariah people by means of consensus, the urgent need to sort out the disputes in the region could no longer be ignored.

The need to address the disputes necessitated a grand deliberation among the people in March 1805. The public deliberation was also an occasion for the new leader to legitimize his authority. The legitimation became essential because the election that brought Morani to power lacked the requisite recognition from the lineages (Mouser 1998, 229). The grand palaver aimed to resolve five major disputes that were relevant for the cohesion and peaceful coexistence of the groups in the region. As such, the stakes were high, meaning that consensual decisions at the grand deliberation were complex and delicate tasks. By deploying tact, persuasion, mediation, open and structured debate, and other tools that conveyed attentiveness to fairness, the grand deliberation proved successful in realizing consensual decisions on the matters discussed.

Although expectations and demands differed greatly at the outset of the Forekariah conference, at the end, surviving reservations were negligent, meaning that peace was allowed to reign and trade could continue unhindered. This goal was possible because everyone was invited to participate in the public deliberation. Evidence and testimonies were admitted and carefully considered before a consensual verdict was handed down. In addition, resolutions that were rejected were not seen as an affront on the authority of the groups concerned but rather as an exercise of autonomy that had to be respected.

The Forekariah Palaver is not an isolated case where deliberation functioned as a means for political legitimation. Historians, anthropologists, and other social scientists with interest in Africa have noted similar occurrences in many parts of Africa. Among the Setswana of southern Africa, for example, there are records that show that palaver is the default mode of finding solutions to political problems relating to disputes about succession and legitimation. This much can be gleaned from the records of British officers in the nineteenth and twentieth century regarding the practice of kgotla.

Notwithstanding the intricate and often acrimonious nature of contestations for power among lineage groups, especially when the order of succession is unclear, the Setswana had faith in kgotla as a space enabling the resolution of conflicts. Although the order of succession is tied to birth in most cases, succession crises, for whatever reason, often brought to the fore the vital role of public deliberation as a means to establish the correct order of succession, hence the legitimation of political power (Parson 1990). In this regard, the experience of a community in postindependence Botswana is an apt illustration. Drawing from fieldwork conducted in Letlhakeng, Jo Helle-Valle (2002) has reconstructed how rural communities give meaning to politics and the state in their changing context.

The story Helle-Valle (2002) tells is that of a contestation for power and the legitimation of claimants to a headman position in the community he studied. As the story goes, a headman in a rural town in Botswana transferred his duties to a custodian due to protracted illness. The plan was that the custodian, who was a younger brother of the headman, would pass on the position to the headman's son when he became old enough to take over. Unfortunately, the son of the headman was still too young when the custodian died. The custodian's son then took over the position pending when the son of the original headman would return from South Africa, where he had gone to work in the mines. This new custodian too passed away, and his younger brother took over the duties of headman. It was at this point that the son originally meant to be headman (after his father) returned and requested recognition as headman.

Oteng, the custodian at that time, and his uncle thought otherwise. Their interest was to retain the position. When the rightful successor to the position, who had just returned from South Africa, and the custodian failed to reach an agreement, they brought the case to the public forum. During the deliberations that ensued, the community resolved that the son of the original headman was indeed the correct successor to the position and should be given his rightful status. Oteng and his uncle raised an objection, which prompted further discussions. The deliberation became prolonged, prompting people to leave to attend to other tasks. The deliberation reconvened on another date, and discussions continued until the people arrived at a consensual resolution.

The community resolved that the custodian headman, Oteng, and his uncle must accompany the rightful heir to appropriate government offices to register him as the new headman of the community. The reason the three parties were instructed to embark on the journey together was to demonstrate that the appointment and thus legitimation of the new headman's power resulted from a consensual agreement of the community. Unfortunately, the custodian headman, Oteng, found ways to avoid making the trip. The result was a failure to resolve the conflict, at least not until the researcher left the community (Helle-Valle 2002, 185–187). We discuss the implications of this story toward the end of this chapter.

Let us in the meantime consider another case that demonstrates a different typology of palaver. As noted above, palaver is also a reference point for social interaction. In his novel *Things Fall Apart*, Chinua Achebe described a feast the protagonist of the novel, Okonkwo, gave to thank his kinsmen for the hospitality they showed him while he lived with them as an exile. The palaver dimension in the story can be seen when we consider the order of events in the story. First, all of Okonkwo's kinsmen were invited to the feast. Second, there was a clear order in which the event proceeded, especially as signaled by the care taken to ensure regard for age was observed. Third, everyone recognized the sense in which the food presented did not constitute the core of the meeting. It was clearly indicated that the focus of the meeting was social interaction.

Finally, the event was an occasion for older members of the clan to reiterate to the youth the value of sociality. As one of the elders noted, young members of the group ought to learn the value of "speaking with one voice." By this he meant the value and necessity of unity. The point of the feast was clearly conveyed in Okonkwo's observation that "a man who calls his kinsmen to a feast does not do so to save them from starving. They all have food in their own homes. When we gather together in the moonlit village ground it is not because of the moon. Every man can see it in his compound. We come together because it is good for kinsmen to do so" (Achebe 1958, 118).

In *Arrow of God*, Achebe (1964) provides a case where the third typology of palaver manifests. In this context, palaver takes on the role of a principle that structures cultural modification and social change. The background of the story is the experience of Ezeulu, the chief priest of the deity in Umuaro. Ezeulu was imprisoned by the colonial government because he rejected the government's offer to become a "warrant chief" of his community. While he was in prison, Ezeulu was hindered from performing an important duty related to his function as chief priest of the community. As was the custom of the people, Ezeulu was required to declare the date for the New Yam Feast, which officially opens the harvest season. He could make this declaration only when he had eaten a specified number of yams offered to the god, Ulu, from the previous year's harvest.

While in prison, the chief priest could not attend to his duty of eating the yam, which meant he could not declare the date for the New Yam Feast. Now, without Ezeulu's declaration of a date for the feast and subsequent observance of the event, the year's harvest could not begin. The implication then was that people in the community were at risk of losing their livelihood. On this account, there was an impossible dilemma to resolve. It was a tricky issue because, as one of the elders of the village quipped, the matter before the community was like asking one to find a way to carry a man with a broken waist. In attempting to resolve this contradiction that threatened the basis of coexistence in the community, the people of Umuaro resorted quite naturally to a deliberative process. The men of high title in Umuaro came together in Ezeulu's home to deliberate on the possible way forward to save their crops while respecting the wishes of the gods.

Because resorting to deliberation as a means of structuring conflict was an entrenched way of life of the community, the procedure of the discussion in Ezeulu's house could not but be carried out in an orderly, decorous fashion. Thus, the deliberation has a phase in which the conventional ritual to initiate the deliberation was observed. Afterward came interludes meant to establish the conditions necessary for a productive dialogue. Central among these conditions was the sharing of kola nuts to affirm trust and unity. The issue to be deliberated upon was presented, leading to arguments, counterarguments, and resolution on the way forward.

One of the ten elders presented the matter to consider. Ezekwesili presented the reason for the convocation of the deliberation as a concern that Ezeulu had not pronounced the date of the New Yam Feast. In response to Ezeulu's explanation that he can only do so when he had one yam left from what was offered to the gods from the previous year's harvest, Onenyi Nnanyelugo offered a rebuttal. He argued that what Ezeulu said was true, but then notice must be taken of the changes that had occurred in their epoch. The white man who imprisoned Ezeulu, he said, might have fouled the air, but he did not live with the people of Umuaro to breathe the bad air. He pointed out that the gods must have the survival of the community at heart, in which case they cannot allow the community to perish.

It was argued that Ezeulu should just go ahead and eat the remaining yam, so he could set a date for the festival. Assurances were given that the elders, whose unity represented the will of the community, would bear the consequences of Ezeulu's deviation from established custom. Disagreeing with the proposal, Ezeulu argued that it was not a prerogative of the elders to determine procedures about sacred affairs. Since his own interest was also at stake, like that of everyone in the community, Ezeulu argued that the objectivity of his stance is not in question.

In the end, a tentative resolution mandating Ezeulu to go back and consult further with the gods was agreed upon. Although the consultation did not yield a result that is different from Ezeulu's position in previous deliberation, the essential point was made—namely, that the community satisfied the requirements of culture to resort to deliberation as a means of resolving conflicts, even in intricate cases that threatened the very basis of the community's self-understanding.

The experience of Umuaro is instructive for several reasons, but one major reason is that the experience reflects a basic attitude of the community to a fundamental culture change. Although the people considered free discussion their default approach to resolving crisis, the encounter with the colonial state and the social confusions it precipitated led to a fundamental disruption of a cultural pattern, which could not easily be resolved through deliberation. The imminent culture shift for Umuaro seemed to entail irreconcilable perspectives, hence the limitation of palaver as the reference point for the community. Nonetheless, the point to note is that the palaver framework was a principle that structured culture change for the people of Umuaro.

Notwithstanding the dire choices before them, nothing was imposed by fiat. Following an established procedure, the community deliberated on how to proceed in dealing with the changes to their culture that have become imperative. It is of course open to argument what should be inferred from the outcome of Umuaro's deliberation. However, the recourse to deliberation demonstrated the wisdom of the ancestors of Umuaro. Passed down from one generation to another, this wisdom was a recommendation "that no man however great was greater than his people; that no man ever won judgement against his clan" (Achebe 1964, 287). Leaving further comments on this aspect of the palaver concept aside for a while, let us discuss the other two roles it plays.

In 1776, the Danish community in Christiansborg (present-day Ghana) was compelled by circumstances to form an alliance with the Akuapem people to secure their economic interests. At that time, the Danes were vulnerable due to a dispute with the people of Accra and the Dutch community. This necessitated that the Danes had to rally support of communities that were not their main partners at the time, that is the people of Osu and Labadi. The first step the Danes took to achieve their aim was to send emissaries to the head of Akuapem, called Atiemo. According to Hernaes (1988, 30), who examined the historical records that documented the event, the build-up to the formation of the envisaged alliance began with a "series of preparatory palavers." In these preparatory deliberations, the Danish and the representatives from the Akuapem presented demands and traded offers.

The Danes made three demands. First, they requested military assistance from Atiemo and his people to support them in warding off an imminent attack on an ally, Osu. Second, they wanted a permanent "friendship" from Akuapem. This was another way of saying that the Akuapem should not sign an accord with other European traders in the region. Third, they offered Atiemo and his people material goods and the promise of assistance in the likely event they were threatened in the future by other Europeans or any of their partners in the region. In response, Atiemo's representatives made their own demands. They requested a considerable monthly payment due to Atiemo and other material benefits. Atiemo's requests presented by his representatives fell through, however, when the Danes threatened to join forces with the Akuapem's enemies. Atiemo and his people accepted the offer made to ensure the threat did not materialize.

At the conclusion of the deliberations, a date was fixed for an oath-taking ritual that would conclude the palaver. On June 9, 1776, Atiemo and his party of six hundred people came to Osu for a closing palaver. The palaver was concluded on June 14, 1776. Afterward, Osu and Christiansborg were attacked in 1777, and Atiemo's assistance was critical because it was the ultimate saving grace for the Danes in the situation.

Leaving aside the skewed conditions under which the deliberations were conducted, we should notice that economic interaction happens in African communities during palaver. Sale, for instance, of land and significant commodities usually requires sanction through a deliberative process. This is symbolic because it signifies that economic interaction in relation to some goods is not just an exchange but a transfer of layers of values to a new agent. Thus, there is a convention among Africans of ensuring that everyone concerned is heard before an offer is accepted or an agreement is reached.

Goods of unquantifiable value—like community and family land, the exchange of culture-specific knowledge (such as unique skills in pottery, artistic style, and craftsmanship), and secrets of medicinal plants—are seen as more than something one can buy in the free market. For the exchange of such goods, it is necessary to engage first in a deliberation. This means there is a precondition attached to the acquisition of such commodities. The palaver serves as a regulative ideal in economic interaction, especially in relation to the exchange of some kinds of goods. The important point to note is that the transfer of value that occurs in the exchange of important goods follows a deliberative process, the reason being to emphasize the nonsubjugation of a people's self-understanding as ultimately free beings to the whims of economic calculations. In other words, one is not merely buying what one desires. Instead, one is entering into a vital relationship with equal and free agents.

Finally, palaver occurs in some instances as an orientation that enables one to find an answer to the meaning and implication of being human. We see this in cases considered in various national conferences on reconciliation in Africa, especially Gacaca in Rwanda and the Truth and Reconciliation Commission in South Africa. An example from Gacaca illustrates aptly how palaver serves as an orientation to tackling the meaning of human life. Recounted by Phil Clark (2010, 2), the story below is about an event that occurred in a session of the Gacaca trial:

> A murmur goes through the gathering as the prisoner walks to the front, standing between the crowd and the line of judges. He mumbles and the president tells him to speak up. The man, with his head bowed, explains that he has come to confess that he killed the wife of his neighbour in the first week of May 1994. He found the woman hiding in the bushes as a gang of killers walked the paths of the village searching for Tutsi. When he found her, she was crying, screaming at him to let her go. He pulled her out of the bushes and threw her to the ground, then slashed his machete once across her neck, then again, and left her to die. The prisoner, head still bowed, says that he has come today to apologise for what he did. When he was in jail, he had many years to think about his actions, and his conscience was so heavy that he confessed his crimes to the authorities.

How does a community make sense of this sort of tragedy? Obviously, the question about the humanity of the perpetrator of the crime recounted arises, not the least because of the nature of the ties to the victim—they were neighbors.

Is the perpetrator of this crime still human? What is the perpetrator's understanding of human nature? Did he withhold its attribution to the victim? If so, why? If human beings can find a space in their minds to contemplate such cruelty, what does it mean to be human, and what do the answers we propose imply? These are certainly not easy questions to answer. In African political experience, palaver provides an orientation that makes it possible for us to contemplate possible ways to respond to the situation.

I have argued elsewhere that it is by means of public deliberation "about the monstrous infractions of the guilt-plagued member of the community" that the community "attempts to re-capture the language it had lost in order to deal with a monstrosity it cannot name or resolve" (Okeja 2019, 14). This is because there is no clear sense in which we can deal with a conflict that has claimed lives, let alone find adequate means of atonement for the dead, whose fate is now an ultimate, eternal silence.

Serving as the means through which a community can find its bearing again when its reference point is disturbed, palaver provides the conceptual tool that ties together important dimensions of human understanding of reality. In this regard, palaver weaves together, at a conceptual level, multifaceted layers of perception of reality. These layers of perception may be legal, social, economic, religious, political, or cultural. Sometimes, it may be a combination of two or more of the different layers. The vital point is that palaver in all these instances deals with speechlessness by reenacting the power of speech. Through deliberation, it proposes that the sense of what it means to be human can emerge only by using the most potent resource available to humans—namely, communication, which may be verbal, nonverbal gestures, or silence.

To recapitulate, there are five typologies of palaver that can be inferred: the political, social, cultural, economic, and constructive typologies. In each of these typologies, deliberation serves as a normative framework for the pursuit and determination of the ideal of consensus. According to Bidima (2014), two basic categories map the nature of all the varieties of palaver. He suggests, following Frances Jacques, that the categories of the irenic and agonistic palaver account for all the forms of the phenomenon. The former type of palaver "occur in the absence of conflict (on the occasion of a marriage, a sale etc.)," while the latter "result from a differend" (Bidima 2014, 16). Although I accept that conflict—or, to use Wamba dia Wamba's (1985) terminology, "contradiction"—constitutes an important aspect of palaver, I think there are important dimensions of the phenomenon we will not be able to account for if we rely on this twofold categorization.

In the first instance, the absence of conflict does not presuppose that there is identity of viewpoints. There may still be competing views in those forms of palaver that occur in the absence of conflicts. For instance, on the occasion of a sale, although there may not be conflict to resolve, there will certainly be different viewpoints among the participants in the sale palaver. This may, for instance, have to do with differences in opinion regarding the value of the property involved in the transaction. Thus, the absence of conflict does not imply that there is absence of competing interests.

My point is not that Bidima's distinction is vague or unhelpful. My argument is that the phenomenon of palaver is multifaceted in each of the instances it obtains. Thus, it will be problematic to subsume all possible forms of palaver under two broad categories of irenic and agonistic palaver. This point should become evident when we consider that, in one instance of the palaver, deliberation might transmute from embodying a layer of an event to becoming a totally different kind of phenomenon. To give an example, an irenic deliberation about the sale of prized cultural artifacts could transition from a nonconflictual process to heated debate generating a differend. The change in the nature of the deliberation might even happen in a way that will necessitate complete suspension of the quest for consensus.

Having made this point, I now turn to an evaluation of the different manifestations of palaver to make clear what they entail theoretically. Regarding the political form of palaver, there are at least five principles that are taken for granted in the way deliberation unfolds in the context. Looked at closely, there is value placed on procedural faithfulness in this form of palaver. There is also a fundamental insistence on substantive and equal representation. In political palaver, debate is valued as the main vehicle for advancing political interests. In addition, it is accepted that differences in political opinion do not amount to a negation of the equality or weight of individual opinion. Finally, in this form of palaver, politics is seen as essentially a public act where customary norms provide the basis of political culture.

Procedural faithfulness matters in political palaver because it confers on the holder of political office the symbolic sanction attached to the exercise of power. The value of substantive and equal representation consists in recognition that an improperly constituted people cannot make a claim to legitimacy. For every voice to be heard, everyone must be represented both substantively and equally. Because of the recognition that the human faculty of reason is constrained and prone to mistakes, the emphasis on debate is not merely aimed at enabling political horse trading. The goal is to ensure that political communities do not fail themselves by accepting any perspective as undisputable. In addition, acknowledging the centrality of debate to politics makes possible the realization of aesthetic access to meaning in politics.

By aesthetic access to meaning, I refer to the power of a beautiful speech to shape our views and understanding of intricate political challenges. What I am describing is of course different from propaganda because the beauty of a speech here must pass the test of truth. It must, in other words, withstand the inquisitive examination of dissidents and other merchants of contrary evidence participating in the deliberative process.

In the political form of the palaver, politics is essentially a public act because it is only through insistence on this point that the community is able to guarantee that different opinions count equally. Furthermore, the publicness of politics advances the social coherence or symmetry that forms the basis of legitimate governance. In becoming political, custom establishes the norms that guide orientation in politics. It does this by making clear the type of politics possible or desirable, based on the people's understanding of themselves as members of a particular society.

Turning to the social form of palaver, a practice-dependent reading shows there are at least four basic presuppositions implied: procedural faithfulness, substantive and equal representation, the action-guiding role of customary practices, and the elasticity of ties of kinship. Just like in the political palaver, procedural faithfulness in the context of the social palaver underscores the place of protocol in the normative orders of the community. By doing A before B, it is emphasized that the social arena for deliberation is also subject to the governance of reasonability. Substantive and formal representation in politics demonstrates how the practice of communalism does not abrogate the separateness of persons. This amounts to infusing the principle "I am before we are" into the categorical injunction "I am because we are."

The communing person, in other words, retains the original individuality that makes sociality meaningful. The action-guiding role of custom becomes vital in this form of palaver because of the indispensable need for an orientation. Finally, kinship ties bind, presenting thereby the context for the social life of a people. But then, the ties of kinship are elastic because it is unlike the sort of ties that obtain in an elective community. The elder who addressed the younger people at the end of the feast Okonkwo gave for his kinsmen meant precisely this point when he bemoaned the fact that the younger generations did not know what it meant to speak with one voice. The point of this statement is that the inability to come to a consensus in a closely bound community is a fundamental defeat that leaves all the members of the group vulnerable.

The cultural modification palaver presents us with yet another set of pre-suppositions. Here it is taken for granted that it is essential to be attentive to procedures and remain open to reason and critique. Because of its nature, this form of palaver shows the sense in which whatever is customary is ambivalent. In the cultural modification form of palaver, the challenge is to decipher the way forward in the seemingly opposed constructions of custom—either as a static practice we may not change to suit our purposes or as a set of conventions we can opt to consensually modify. In the case considered earlier, while Ezeulu chose the former path, most of the elders present at the deliberation about the future of Umuaro chose the latter. Ultimately, the viability of this form of palaver presupposes a fundamental conviction that human beings have freedom of self-expression. And this self-expression encompasses both the use of words in speech and other forms of communication, such as sighs, silences, grumbles, and so on.

The constructive palaver has its basic presuppositions. From this form of palaver, we can infer the recognition of the sense that inhuman acts constitute a collective tragedy that demands an answer beyond retribution. By grappling as a community with the attempt to understand infractions that contradict very basic assumptions about what it means to be human, this form of palaver makes clear that the only way we can deal with new reality is through the constructive use of words. In doing this, we give new meaning to our experience of reality by moving in a new direction. Having considered the different shifts and changes that have affected the way deliberation manifests in the African context, I focus in the next chapter on the implications of the dynamic meaning of the practice for the construction of modern African political philosophy. Close attention is paid to a discussion of the ways in which the shifting meaning of the concept of deliberation constitutes a crisis of normativity.

FIVE

—∭—

INDIGENOUS POLITICAL CONCEPTS, CONCEPTUAL LOSS, AND POLITICAL FAILURE

MUSING ABOUT AN AFRICAN ELDER, Ifeanyi Menkiti (2005, 22) said: "An old man from Africa praying, may speech not choke us, but be our companion, now and in the future." Indeed, unspoken words pose the danger of choking the bearer of speech. For one who must bear witness about the past in interest of the future, this is true metaphorically and, of course, literally. In the quotation from Menkiti's poem *Mutatis Mutandis*, the "old man from Africa" has reasons to pray that words should not choke "us" but be "our companion," "now and in the future." It is through speech that the old man has come to know the past and is able to conceive an action-guiding ideal for the present and future. As an African, the oral character of his knowledge tradition gives him reason to be gravely worried about the destiny of speech because he relies on the spoken word for his comprehension of reality.

When speech therefore becomes impossible or when what is experienced can no longer be captured in coherent speech, speech itself ceases to be a companion. Instead, it becomes a choking danger. In such situations, the demise of *Homo dicere* (humans as speech-making beings) becomes a demise of *Homo propositum quod* (humans as beings of purposeful existence). The reason is that, bereft of concepts, no one can comprehend reality. Although simple, the point I wish to make with this observation is fundamental: when a people's conceptual resources become an inadequate reference for interpreting the perception of reality, the result is that perception of reality becomes a meaningless succession of disparate events. In such a situation, comprehension itself becomes impossible. To this end, concepts are central to our comprehension of reality. Thus, they are fundamentally significant as attempts to construct an ideal of a life worth living.

Looking back at the concern of the old man from Africa in Menkiti's poem, how can we comprehend his prayer? Is it expressing bewilderment at the fact that the concepts available to him have become inadequate for interpreting reality? Could his be a prayer muttered in anxious realization that he is unable to articulate what he experiences, what he sees, feels, or imagines? Does the situation of the old man reflect a crisis of meaning in Africa, whence he comes? Put differently, is an inability to articulate reality through a mode of speech accessible to the African mind at the root of the social and political crisis in the continent? In this chapter, I want to consider to what extent it may be reasonable to make this claim. The goal I pursue is to examine whether there is a connection between the experience of political failure and the collapse of African conceptual resources.

The question then concerns whether colonization distorted, erased, or displaced indigenous African concepts and the normative predispositions attached to them. To consider this question is to contemplate the connection between the problematic nature of African conceptual resources and difficulties involved in harnessing African conceptions of the ideal of coexistence to shape concrete politics. If colonization displaced, distorted, or erased African concepts and their normative predispositions, what is the best response to such an experience, especially in light of current political reality?

Is remaking the African conceptual world a viable response to political failure, or should an answer be sought in another realm? In tackling these questions, I begin by showing how a reimagination of African political concepts can provide a robust understanding of human agency in the sphere of politics. I proceed in this way because the challenge of political failure essentially relates to factors that occlude the agency of Africans in politics. Thus, the answer I offer is to conceive an approach to rethinking African political concepts to decipher their import for the task of reconstructing political agency. This is a necessary antidote to the experience of political failure.

EXOGENEITY, INDIGENEITY, AND THE DISCOURSE ON PUBLIC DELIBERATION

It is interesting that palaver remains the de facto concept for articulating perspectives on public deliberation in African societies. Despite the revitalization of indigenous concepts like *mbongi, kgotla, izu, imbizo,* and *gacaca* in African political discourse, little has changed in relation to the dominance of non-indigenous concepts in the study of African politics. This situation raises an important question about the relationship between what is described and the concepts used in the description. It is therefore pertinent to ask: What role do concepts have in the development of theories in African political philosophy? In raising this question, I wish to underscore the need to consider the problematic consequences that accompany the deployment of such concepts as palaver, palabra, and consensus, in the study of the public deliberation practiced in African societies.

The question therefore arises whether a reliance on exogenous concepts in the study of African political thought indicates that a debilitating instance of conceptual loss prevents the emergence of a nuanced comprehension of the phenomenon of deliberation. To consider this question, I think it is reasonable to begin with the remark that the history of nonindigenous concepts in the study of African social and cultural phenomena is complex. Also, it must surely be acknowledged that a reliance on equivalents of African concepts as a means of analysis has led to incredible cognitive inaccuracies. This point was not lost on African scholars as it played a vital role in their works, especially during the two decades preceding the 1960s when many African countries achieved political independence.

In their works, Chinua Achebe (1988), Okot p'Bitek (1970), and Kwasi Wiredu (1996) referred variously to the problem of language and meaning. The connection between language and meaning was a common central problem for the three thinkers, even though they worked in different disciplines. Whereas Achebe was a novelist, p'Bitek and Wiredu were, respectively, scholars of anthropology and philosophy. Notwithstanding disciplinary differences, the three scholars shared deep concerns about the place of language in the scholarship on Africa. In highlighting the problematic connection of concepts and meaning, p'Bitek was adamant that translation compacted the misreading of African practices and their normative foundation. Although he made his point through a comical rendition of encounters between the Acholi and European missionaries, his argument was clear.

P'Bitek recounted one of the encounters as follows: "In 1911, Italian Catholic priests put before a group of Acholi elders the question 'who created you?'; and because the Luo language does not have an independent concept for create or creation, the question was rendered to mean 'who moulded you?'" (p'Bitek 1970, 62). Notwithstanding the efforts by the interpreter to make the question intelligible, it remained meaningless to Acholi elders because in their conceptual world, human beings are born of their mothers. Not making sense of the question, the Acholi elders told the visitors they did not know the answer. Since the missionaries would not accept this as satisfactory answer, the elders had to improvise, perhaps to get rid of the deluded visitors.

One of the elders recalled that the "spirit" Rubanga "re-moulded" people who became deformed as a result of an illness (p'Bitek 1970, 62). Relying on this answer, the missionaries began to preach that the supreme being who created the Acholi people was the spirit they called Rubanga. Wiredu (1996) points to this case and the comic translation of St. John's gospel into Luo language to underscore the necessity of examining the role concepts play in articulating modern African thought. According to p'Bitek, the story of the logos poetically told in the Christian Bible in the statement "in the beginning was the Word and the Word was with God and the Word was God" took a comical turn once it was translated into the Luo language. This happened because the translation of the text back into English amounted to the following: "From long long time ago there was News, News was with Hunchback spirit, News was the Hunchback spirit" (Wiredu 1996, 82).

Wiredu made a case for conceptual decolonization due to his concern about the distortion of meaning that arises when there is a mismatch between concepts and the objects or phenomena they describe. His proposal that conceptual decolonization is an imperative for African philosophy can be appreciated better when we consider his insightful observation that "concepts of philosophy are the most fundamental categories of human thought" (Wiredu 1996, 136). But concepts do not fall from the sky; they are the outcome of cultural evolution. Where one culture develops a set of conceptual tools to articulate specific experiences, another may have no need for such concepts, given the absence of experiences that necessitate their development.

Even in situations where experiences are similar, there are diverse ways that meaning is shaped by culture. Thus, Wiredu (1996, 136) proposes that "particular modes of thought that yield these concepts may reflect the specifics of the culture, environment, and even the accidental idiosyncrasies of the people concerned." Communication is of course possible across cultural boundaries; however, there remains a sense in which the conceptual resources of cultures are context specific. Stated in another way, there is always a sense in which conceptual resources are rooted and relevant in articulating only a specific notion of reality arising from a group's historical experience.

Due to their training predominantly in the Western tradition of philosophy, African philosophers employ conceptual categories that are sometimes problematic. Wiredu (1996, 137) makes this point to argue that African philosophers should be wary of carrying on in their reflection "philosophical deadwood" arising from the "historically enforced acquisition of philosophical training in the medium of foreign languages." Although problematic conceptual categories can constitute a challenge in other traditions of philosophy, for Wiredu, the African case is different and dire. The reason he thinks so is because of the "situation of cultural otherness" with which Africans must contend (137). Wiredu, I think, wishes to draw attention with this claim to the widespread convention of looking upon everything African as exotic and strange. It is often the case that African conceptions of reality are seen through the prism of classical anthropological myths that Africa is one dark continent where mysterious beings and practices originate.

The aim of Wiredu's conceptual decolonization is to accentuate major philosophical concepts rooted in African cultures. His idea is that decolonization allows us to create a space that will allow African philosophical concepts to thrive. He believes that this is the only way to articulate philosophical problems that have an African pedigree. This amounts to claiming that conceptual decolonization manifests when we assess exogenous philosophical concepts and cast aside the particularistic "philosophical deadwood" they embody. Thus, against attempts to interpret the notion of conceptual decolonization as Wiredu's effort to refine intercultural communication, a more plausible view is to see it as a move to create a space for the emergence of unique philosophical problems arising from an analysis of African concepts.

To apply conceptual decolonization, Wiredu suggests that African philosophers need to think through basic concepts and problems of philosophy in indigenous languages. He says: "In regard to all these concepts, the simple recipe for decolonization for the African is: try to think them through in your own African language and, on the basis of the results, review the intelligibility of the associated problems or the plausibility of the apparent solutions that have been attempted when you have pondered them in some metropolitan language" (Wiredu 1996, 137).

It is easy to misconstrue the argument as a claim that we should dismiss anything that sounds unintelligible when translated into an African language. It is tempting to see Wiredu's views as a claim that questions in Western philosophy become pseudoquestions in situations where there are no conceptual equivalents in African languages to translate Western concepts. This would be a misunderstanding of what Wiredu is saying. His goal is to make a specific point. He wants to note that thinking *about* a concept in a foreign language is not same as thinking *in* a foreign language about a concept. Whereas in the former case we use language as a tool of thought, in the latter case, we reduce thought to the idiosyncrasies of a particular language. Wiredu's point is that we ought to avoid the latter approach because it is a source of the pseudophilosophical problems that he calls the philosophical deadwood of other cultures.

To cease needlessly carrying other people's philosophical deadwood, it is important to engage in conceptual decolonization. Should one employ Wiredu's (1996, 138) formula of conceptual decolonization and find out that a philosophical concept loses its meaning, the next step "is to try to reason out the matter on independent grounds." What this means is that, in such situations, one ought to "argue in a manner fathomable in both the African language and the foreign language concerned" (138). Wiredu himself adopted this approach to dispose of some philosophical problems in Western philosophy.

Take as an example his comment on Rene Descartes's "cogito, ergo sum." When this idea is viewed from the perspective of an Akan conceptual framework, it becomes problematic. For Wiredu, it is problematic to draw the conclusion Descartes proposed on the basis of the *cogito*. The reason is that existence in the Akan conceptual world is spatial. Thus, when one says that one thinks and, therefore, that one exists, the Akan person will be confounded. It will not be clear to the Akan what is meant by "existence" here. And the reason is that *to be* is to be *something*, to be *somewhere*, or to be *an entity* (Wiredu 1996, 141).

Besides Wiredu, another major African thinker that paid a great deal of attention to the place of indigenous African concepts in academic discourse is the novelist Achebe. Writing about literary criticism, especially in relation to his first novel, *Things Fall Apart*, he notes the need to "deal with some basic issues raised by a certain specious criticism which flourishes in African literature" (Achebe 1988, 46). Achebe's concern is the emergence of a crop of critics who carry on with the colonial attitude toward Africa in assuming that the African can be explained or understood entirely through simplistic Western assumptions and imaginings about Africa. In a bid to buttress his point, Achebe refers to the comments of some critics of his novel. He suggests that "the European critic of African literature must cultivate the habit of humility appropriate to his limited experience of the African world and be purged of the superiority and arrogance which history so insidiously makes him heir to." This position was, however, offensive to some Western literary critics. One of them felt particularly offended and "launched numerous unprovoked attacks against [Achebe]." The poetic justice, alas, was that the critic wrote "a long abstruse treatise based on an analysis of a number of Igbo proverbs most of which, it turned out he had so completely misunderstood as to translate 'fruit' in one of them as 'penis'" (49).

Achebe used this case to illustrate the importance of understanding the African conceptual world for scholars of African experience. For him, people who can only view Africa from the outside as cultural outsiders ought to proceed with caution in their claims to expertise on the African. Achebe should not be understood to be arguing for full-scale Westernization. His point is that there are ways to transform the tool of the language available to us. In other words, his view is that the important thing to focus on is the thought created, not the medium. We should thus pay attention to the creative way African scholars reshape the language they inherited while also creating new ways of understanding their reality as Africans using the medium of this language.

But what is it about concepts and meaning that makes having access to an African conceptual world so important? We shall return to this question in due course. The point about conceptual resources and meaning making is important in the African context due to the devastating experience of colonization. In effect, this experience is a major source of anxieties about the correct order of things and the light in which Africans can and should interpret social, political, and other phenomena. Before delving into the details of this issue, it is important to consider for a moment a number of preliminary concerns that provide a background for the view I propose regarding the relationship between political failure and conceptual loss.

The claims of the scholars considered above accentuate the importance of concepts for intercultural encounters and for the possibility of constructing propositions that can claim validity across contexts. If concepts matter because they are the compass that enables us to navigate and comprehend reality, we can assert that concepts also matter because they are the means through which people make sense of their culture. This is to say that concepts are essential because they enable us to understand ourselves as beings embedded in specific social and political milieus. Against this background, it is reasonable to infer that the distortion of a people's conceptual reference point leads to unpalatable consequences. This is the case especially concerning the imagination of possibilities beyond the status quo in social, political, economic, and cultural spheres.

CONCEPTS AND MEANING MAKING

Regarding the phenomenon of political failure in Africa, the link between concepts and meaning making demands that we take seriously the task of proffering answers to current problems through an examination of African conceptual resources. What I mean is that it is important to consider how the experience of colonization and the imposition of Islamic and Judeo-Christian conceptual frameworks on Africans complicated the African conceptual world, making an intractable task out of attempts to give meaning to political experiences afterward.

We ought to consider the best response to the devastation of African conceptual resources because concepts play a vital role in understanding political experience. This is an important prelude to conceiving an ideal of politics after colonization and other destructive experiences in Africa. I argue in the next chapter that developing a new conception of African political philosophy is possible only on the basis of a viable method for reimagining indigenous political concepts. I show there that the practice of deliberation presents a possibility to realize this aim because it embodies an African public culture.

In the meantime, I focus on analyzing the connection between meaning making in politics and the conceptual metaphors deployed to explain African practices of deliberation. What is the implication of referring to deliberation in the African context as palaver, palabra, or consensus? Is this a manifestation of conceptual loss, one that occludes the conception of a modern African political philosophy? To understand what is at stake, it is crucial to analyze the normative power of concepts in the study of indigenous social and political experiences.

Doing this enables us to come to grips with the nature of issues that arise for reflection on political reality when we graft supposedly universal concepts onto otherwise particularistic experiences. If exogenous concepts deployed to make sense of the political experience of Africans do not cohere with the way Africans conceive reality through indigenous concepts, a reasonable inference to draw is that there is a fundamental problem of comprehension. For this reason, I think it is essential to consider whether exogenous concepts are appropriate tools of analysis of African political experience.

There are two major responses to the career of non-African concepts in the analysis of African experience. But these two perspectives, I argue, are deficient and therefore must be discarded. The first response generally amounts to a claim that exogenous concepts are indispensable for any attempt to theorize African experience because there is a hermeneutic handicap that is specific to the African cultural context. The claim here amounts to saying that recourse to nonindigenous concepts is the most viable path in developing theories to explain African experience. The reason, it is often claimed, is that after the experience of colonization, Africans generally lack the conceptual resources needed to undertake this task.

The second approach is the claim that foreign conceptual tools must be rejected in the analysis of African ideas or experience because of their exogeneity.[1] Although this argument is stated in different ways, the common

---

1. Mazrui summarizes these two positions quite succinctly in his discussion of the attempts by the World Bank to influence language policy and education in Africa. See Mazrui 1997.

denominator is the idea that a reliance on exogenous concepts simply amounts to the perpetuation of the external domination of African culture. Scholars who rely on exogenous conceptual resources in their study of African political experience, according to this view, perpetuate the cultural domination of Africa because they disregard Africa as a context for production of *valid* knowledge, based on distinct African methodologies.

I have already indicated that the two perspectives are inadequate responses to the use of non-African concepts in the study of African experience. By making clear the shortcomings of the two perspectives, I point out a solution I consider more plausible. My view, which I expatiate on in due course, is that we ought to turn to conceptual creativity in attempting to formulate modern ideas in African political philosophy. Conceptual creativity is not new to the African context because it has, in some sense, been the hallmark of the social, economic, and cultural life in the continent. Although it is not something new or unique to Africa, when put into a more formalized schema, however, the method of conceptual creativity can help us uncover the path to a revaluation of indigenous African concepts.

This is a task that has become necessary due to the cultural flux in which Africans exist currently. Conceptual creativity helps us to reimagine African political philosophy so that we can take adequate notice of the promise of African political heritage, which includes nonindigenous elements and the current experience of political failure. In the next chapter, I discuss in detail the idea of conceptual creativity and how it could function as a method for developing contemporary African political philosophy. In the meantime, I discuss claims about the use of exogenous conceptual resources in the analysis of African experience.

Ideas articulated through such concepts as decolonization, epistemic injustice, African personality, authenticity, negritude, Afrocentrism, and Afropolitanism now fashionable in discussions in the social sciences and humanities point to problems associated with a reliance on exogenous concepts in the analysis of African experience in the postcolonial era. The problem these tropes of analysis seek to capture is perennial. For instance, it is interesting to note that one of the earliest calls for the decolonization of education was made in an immanent critique of the idea of an African university in the early nineteenth century.

Indeed, "as early as 1881 the elite in Lagos had asked that Fourah Bay College, which had always been the property of the CMS, be taken over by the Government and developed into 'the University of West Africa'" (Ayandele 1974, 16). This was in effect a call for the decolonization of the university. Decolonization, in their view, meant to put African culture and Christianity at the center of instruction. This is certainly a perspective that will sound ridiculous to many who advance the cause of decolonization today because of the emphasis on African Christianity as the center of education. That this view sounds ridiculous today points to the fact that decolonization is not a static idea. Just like the African societies it is supposed to improve in many ways, the notion of decolonization continues to take on new meanings, depending on trends in different parts of the continent. But, usually, the concept of decolonization refers either to concerns about space or knowledge practices.

Regarding space, for instance, decolonization at one point in time meant the quest for an end to foreign rule on African soil. Later it came to denote the struggle to bring an end to different forms of minority rule, especially those that were based on racial hierarchies. In recent history in Cameroon, decolonization has been mobilized as a conceptual resource that allows for the capturing of a just quest for emancipation from the domination of a linguistically defined group—namely, Francophone Cameroon. In terms of knowledge practices, decolonization evolves in various ways. At one point, it expressed a demand that Africans should take charge of the administration machinery of institutions of higher learning in the continent.

This meaning was later displaced by the framing of the concept as a demand to replace knowledge from colonial metropolises with indigenous ideas and homegrown methods of inquiry. Because of a convergence of disparate events, the meaning of the concept changed yet again to denote the domestication of foreign knowledge from the global north. This particular understanding owed its currency to attempts to realize the goals of knowledge transfer. These shifts imply that we cannot get to the core of the issue at stake in the invocation of the concept by merely looking at the surface of populist discourses.

Focusing on populist discourses would mislead one to reduce the concept of decolonization to populist attempts by educated African elites to wrest social control and political power from colonial misadventurists or their local competitors, like traditional chiefs. It is when we dig deeper into the underlying assumptions of decolonization and related concepts in the social sciences and humanities that we will get to the core of the problems they raise. Getting to the core of the concept is essential because that is the way to grasp the fundamental questions raised about power, mechanisms through which dominant knowledge systems currently operate, and the methods of knowledge creation worth pursuing.

To get to the fundamental issues, therefore, we need to ask if there is a basic problem that the tropes of African humanities and social science discourses aim to address. Is there such a common denominator of concerns, or are the discourses on decolonization, negritude, African personality, Africanization, authenticity, Afropolitanism, epistemicide, and epistemic justice unrelated and random quests? The connecting thread that unites these discourses, I want to propose, is that they are attempts to remake the African conceptual world. They are attempts to find an answer to challenges in the continent after the devastating colonial experience and forced amalgamation of disparate African peoples into political units held together by violent institutions.

Seen in this way, it becomes easy to imagine decolonization as a grand strategy aiming to remake the African conceptual world. Just like other similar concepts, the notion of decolonization is an attempt to respond adequately to the challenge of creating social and political ideals that will guide a brave new Africa that is emerging from colonization and its effects. The extent this assertion is true should emerge when we consider the arguments proponents of different theories of decolonization advance to support their claims. Scholars of African literature and African philosophy present materials to conceptualize this point, given that scholars in both fields share a deep concern about the authenticity of their disciplines. It is in the interminable debates about authenticity in the two disciplines that we see the full extent of the struggle to remake the African conceptual world.

In literature, hardly any case suggests itself for consideration more than a well-known debate between Ngugi wa Thiong'o and Chinua Achebe on the language and identity of African literature. Although an old debate, the issues raised by the exchanges between these two giants of African literature are emblematic of the anxieties engendered by decolonization discourse in the present decade. Whereas Achebe proposed that authenticity should not be interpreted to mean that African writers should discard English, French, and other European languages for the mere reason of their exogeneity, Ngugi argued the contrary position.

In his view, authenticity for African writers is a matter of understanding the cultural significance of language. Let us call this disagreement the *authenticity-language problematic* in African literature. The disagreement between proponents of the two contrary positions took a definitive turn when the definition of what African literature is became a prominent concern at a conference on African literature in English at Makerere University in 1962. Since then, positions in the debate have been refined, premises modified, and conclusions revaluated. Still, the issue that separates both sides of the debate remains unresolved. The question, simply put, is how Africans should tend to "the health of African culture" (Chinweizu 1983, xiii).

The arguments for the two positions can be stated in the following propositions. If, as Ngugi noted, "a people's roots were in their traditions going back to the past, the very beginning" (wa Thiong'o 1986, 1), tradition is what enables them to make sense of reality. Subduing a people's rootedness in culture amounts, therefore, to subduing their basic sense of reality. Since language was the means to this form of subjugation during the colonialization of Africa, the plausible conclusion to infer is that Africans ought to decolonize themselves by reconnecting to the conceptual resources of their indigenous languages, which essentially are the fountains of African culture. This explains why language was central in Ngugi's conception of ways to overcome imperialism. It explains his assertion that "the biggest weapon wielded and actually daily unleashed by imperialism against . . . collective defiance is the cultural bomb. The effect of a cultural bomb is to annihilate a people's belief in their names, in their languages, in their environment, in their heritage of struggle, in their unity, in their capacities and ultimately in themselves" (Ngugi 1986, 3).

The foregoing is perhaps the reason Ngugi considers the point of the 1962 debate with Achebe at Makerere University a straightforward matter of fact. For him, the issue is not a concern with a hypothetical possibility—namely, *if* it is only literature in English or *if* it is only literature in indigenous African languages we can regard as African literature; or *if* other criteria would do the magic of definition. The relevant issue for him is "the domination of our African languages and cultures by those of imperialist Europe" (Ngugi 1986, 6). What is the result of this domination? How does it distort reality for Africans and how can liberation come about? These questions define the project of decolonizing for Ngugi. Decolonization, according to this view, is urgent because language is culture. Thus, given that "culture embodies [our] moral, ethical and aesthetic values" and is "the set of spiritual eyeglasses, through which [people] come to view themselves and their place in the universe" (Ngugi 1986, 14), the idea of language as culture is the core of decolonization.

Language is culture because it "is the collective memory bank of a people's experience in history" (Ngugi 1986, 15). Because the domination of African languages implies the domination of the African mind and its conception of the world, the main challenge for postcolonial Africa inheres in freeing itself from the spiritual subjugation that accompanied imperialism, most especially the imposition of imperialist languages on Africans. Although I do not wish to claim that I have presented by these observations all the nuances of Ngugi's view on decolonization, I want to underscore the reason language is central to his ideas about decolonization.

Language is essential to the projects on decolonization because it is the means through which we can revive conceptual resources that will enable African people to regain their sense of self, which was lost because of imperialism. The destruction wrought by imperialism has to do with conditioning of the mind of Africans to conceive and contemplate reality through the lenses of exogenous languages and concepts. The implication of this thought, therefore, is that confusions in the social, political and other spheres of life in Africa is traceable to the suppression of indigenous African conceptual resources.

One of the tasks that accompanied independence in many African countries was to conceive ways of remaking the African world. In the pursuit of this aim, African scholars and statesmen conceived myriad social, political, cultural, and economic theories. As we saw in chapter 2, postcolonial scholar-statesmen proposed ideas that could bridge the gap between the ideals that obtained in traditional African societies and the ideal of the future Africa they aspired to bring about. Whereas Nkrumah proposed his idea of consciencism as the road map for the future, desirable African society, Nyerere articulated a conception of Ujamaa as an African political perspective that will guarantee Africans a bright future. Besides these two perspectives, there were other political ideologies proposed by disparate figures like Amilcar Cabral, Nnamdi Azikiwe, Obafemi Awolowo, Ahmed Sekou Toure, Leopold Sedar Senghor, and Kenneth Kaunda. The point for them was simple. It was how to give meaning to the state in Africa—that is, how to make the state less alien to the people.

Scholars too joined the chorus at different stanzas. In the process, interminable debates about authenticity, indigenous African governance, African personality, African literature, African philosophy, and a number of other Africanisms ensued. In all the prominent attempts to deal with the legacies of colonization and conceive new African ideals of social and political life, little attention was paid to the important role of concepts. This is true especially for works dealing with political philosophy. In this area, the literature developed to tackle the impact of colonial legacies excelled mostly in retrieving concepts. African political thinkers assumed that the essential thing to do in response to the legacy of colonial devastation of the African mind was to return to the traditional African past to retrieve principles and ideas that could be applied to modern African societies. This point was argued brilliantly by Bernard Matolino (2019).

Conversely, those who thought the experience of colonization was too devastating to allow for this kind of project turned to crippling cynicism and a blind pursuit of Europeanism. Thus, although it was clear for African scholars that African conceptual resources provided a promising path to conceptualize

responses to the challenges of life under postcolonial conditions, it was generally assumed that the answer possible was a matter of an "either/or." That is,
it is either you return to an unmitigated re-creation of the past, or you pursue
aggressively a blind imitation of notions of modernity dominant in former colonial metropolises. This matter has been debated exhaustively in the scholarship
on Africa. Thus, it is unwarranted to spend time rehashing the arguments conceived to justify the different positions advanced. The important point I want to
address is how misconceptions of the experience of colonization misled many
political theorists in the search for a new mode of politics for the continent.

The experience of colonization was misconceived due to the excessive focus
on two issues. On the one hand, there was exaggerated emphasis placed on
analysis of culture. On the other hand, there was a great deal of energy dis-
sipated on articulating how the state constitutes the primary site of politics. It
is surely reasonable to think that understanding the ends of the postcolonial
state is the starting point of attempts to address the legacy of colonization.
But, since thinking about the state often becomes thinking about the state as
an institution, one is quickly led astray to believe all that matters in African
politics, especially in the postcolonial era, is the state. However, the viability
of this kind of approach to political thought depends on two essential factors.

First, for such an approach to make sense, we must be able to ascertain that
questions about the "enpeoplement" (Menkiti 2002, 37) of the state is settled.
Secondly, the approach is viable only where there exists a consensus, however
minimal, about the ideal ends of politics. The idea of "we the people" becomes
meaningful only when these two factors obtain. But where both conditions
are not guaranteed, and hence, where we cannot talk about we the people, it
remains unclear why an ideal of politics is justified. In many African countries,
these are problematic issues. The reason is that colonization did not allow for
the realization of the two conditions that would have made a focus on the
analysis of culture and the role of state institutions viable paths to formulating
political theories. Thus, studying state institutions in a bid to decipher ways to
deal with the legacies of colonization is insufficient. This is because institutions
of the state themselves depend on foundational normative presuppositions that
cannot be guaranteed by the African state.

The opposite side of the focus on the state is consideration of culture as
a means to dealing with legacies of colonization. The idea, in this regard, is
to explore the cultural basis of politics in a bid to determine how to create a
new ideal of politics. The main shortcoming of this approach, which makes
it an unviable starting point, is that it reduces the political to a mere performance without substance. It is inadequate to consider culture a basic ideal of

the political. Doing so constitutes an error because, under postcolonial conditions, culture itself exists within the disciplining boundaries of politics. Said differently, the postcolonial state operates in a way that makes culture itself an inevitable target of daily enactments of politics. As can be observed in many places in Africa, whatever is considered cultural is shaped by political praxis. To this end, culture has to find creative ways to remain culture and not be reduced to a tool in the political contestation for power.

THE DILEMMA OF AFRICAN POLITICAL THOUGHT

Thus, given postcolonial conditions, African political thinkers face a dilemma concerning how to go about conceiving an ideal of politics in a way that transcends the limitations of the two obvious starting points—namely, exclusive focus on analysis of culture and exclusive focus on analysis of states. Bereft of these two starting points, the question to ask is what constitutes a promising path to conceiving a contemporary African political theory? A viable approach, I argue in chapter 7, is to reimagine public deliberation, which is the core manifestation of African political culture, in terms of an agency-based political ideal.

This, to me, is what is needed in the quest for a new, viable African political philosophy. Paying closer attention to the core manifestation of African public culture will enable us to go beyond enactment of culture as a political performance, like we find in Mobutu Sese Seko's Congo, where simplistic sophistry meant that African dress and other superficialities became branded as authenticity and the defining fundamentals of political praxis. Theorizing African political culture through the method of conceptual creativity is the means to transcend the despondency induced by a sterile analysis of state institutions in such theories as prebendalism, failed states, predatory states, and so on.

The point I have been trying to make is that concepts matter for the imagination of the ideal of political life. As we have seen, this is the reason consistent efforts have been invested in attempts to recreate the African conceptual world, especially in discourses in literature and philosophy. When we look beyond decolonization discourses, however, we gain further insights into the significance of concepts for political imagination. This point is evident in the study of conceptual loss by philosophers. To this end, I consider ideas about conceptual loss articulated by two philosophers: Jonathan Lear and Katrin Flikschuh.

In his book *Radical Hope*, Lear (2006) recounted the experience of the Crow, a Native American tribe, toward the end of the nineteenth century. Lear's focus is how to understand the community's experience of a devastating implosion of their conceptual reference point. He explores this issue in light of a general experience of cultural devastation among the Crow. *Radical Hope* is, for this reason, a great example of the way to understand significant historical events that have collective ramifications.

By analyzing Crow experience through the prism of Plenty Coups's struggle to come to terms with reality, Lear (2006) shows how best we can deal with cultural devastation. Plenty Coups was a Crow chief who, before his death, narrated his story to Frank B. Linderman, a white man who had become his friend. The point Lear places at the center of his reflection on the experience of the Crow is the possible meaning of Plenty Coups's statement that, at a certain time in the life of his people, things ceased to happen.

By making Plenty Coups's statement the center of his exploration in *Radical Hope*, Lear is not simply indicating an interest in unearthing historical or anthropological truth. His goal instead is to explore the realm of possible meaning regarding the experience of the Crow. Thus, the main question of *Radical Hope* can be stated as follows: How can we understand the claim that there exists a time when comprehension is impossible? To grasp the implication of this question, we would have to consider what could possibly bring about a situation where a people are unable to make sense of experience. To answer this question, Lear makes two vital claims.

First, he says we can make sense of the question by reflecting on what it means for "history to exhaust itself" (Lear 2006, 3). Exploring the sense in which history exhausted itself for the Crow provides clarity about the meaning of the statement that "at a certain point in time, things ceased to happen for a people" (Lear 2006, 3). Second, Lear argues that what it means to say things ceased to happen is tied to a disorientation arising from the collapse of the concepts through which the Crow understood reality. These two moves enable Lear to pose a question about an adequate response to the death of a culture. For Plenty Coups, the reasonable response is to choose *radical hope*. What is meant by radical hope is a choice to live and not to sink into cynicism or despair. Lear (2006, 103) argues that this response is reasonable because it genuinely engages with possible human events no one can anticipate or contemplate before they happen.

Although Lear focuses on the experience of the Crow, he raises fundamental questions about the ethically possible action to take in situations where one's conceptual resources become inadequate. In addition, Lear shows in *Radical Hope* the ontological implications of a particular human vulnerability—the experience of culture collapse. These points reflect clearly in his observation that "it is one thing to give an account of the circumstances in which a way of life actually collapses; it is another to give an account of *what it would be* for it to collapse (emphasis in original). And yet another to ask: How ought we live with the possibility of collapse?" (Lear 2006, 9).

Constantly threatened by possible or actual war, Crow culture revolved around the pursuit of excellencies expressed in war-inspired virtues. They planted coup sticks and counted coups. Bravery, courage, tenacity, and other virtues of a warrior were therefore central to the way the Crow perceived reality. On battlefields, in public life, and through private dealings, the Crow viewed reality through the eyes of their specific conceptual framework. According to Lear (2006, 34), the Crow operated in line with a law of the excluded middle, which in effect said, "*Either our warriors will be able to plant their coup-sticks or they will fail*" (emphasis in original). In this context, the Crow could grasp an experience of failure in the battlefield, "in the sense of being overrun by the enemy" (34).

But when it happens that this framework for perceiving reality collapses, when the framework itself ceases to give meaning or intelligibility to actions, then "the field in which occurrences occur" breaks down (Lear 2006, 34). This was the experience of the Crow tribe. Theirs was a situation that could not be anticipated by any human culture, for no human culture prepares its people for the task of meaning making in the event of its total collapse. Usually, culture provides the context to interpret reality, based on the supposition that it will continue to exist. As Lear (2006, 83) notes, "this inability to conceive of its own devastation will tend to be the blind spot of any culture." Thus, with the collapse of their culture, the ethical horizon for the Crow people was blurred because actions became unintelligible. They lost their "conception of what life was worth living *for*" because "their conception of *what happiness is* could no longer be lived. The characteristic activities that used to constitute the good life ceased to be intelligible acts" (55) (emphasis in original).

How did the Crow respond? And how should any individual or culture respond to the possibility of this experience? In answering this question, Lear explored Plenty Coups's courageous act of living and his even more exemplary act of leading his people in line with his commitment to radical hope. Before they were confined to life on the reservation, the Crow had a glimpse of what would befall them. This came about through means of a dream—a medium of imagination to which they attributed great significance.

Plenty Coups had a dream in which the forest suffered devastation because of a war of the Four Winds. In the dream, all the trees in the forest were knocked down except one tree. On this tree that was standing lived the Chickadee, who was "the least in strength but strongest of mind among its kind" (Lear 2006, 70). Plenty Coups was admonished that he should follow the example of the Chickadee if he wished to survive.

This dream was interpreted by Crow elders as a foray into what was to come. They saw it as a warning that the Crow would survive the impending danger to come and hold on to their land if they cultivated the qualities of the Chickadee, who listens and learns from the mistakes of others. As Lear (2006, 79) notes, notwithstanding this interpretation of the dream, it was unclear at the time of the dream "what holding onto their lands would come to mean," just as it remained unclear "exactly what [Plenty Coup] needed to learn" (75).

Conceiving an adequate response to the experience of cultural devastation is thus a matter of ethics. Although Plenty Coups was given a glimpse of an impending tremendous storm, there was no clue as to the substantive way to respond to the experience. Still, Plenty Coups, through personal courage, was able to "bear witness to the end of a traditional way of life." He attained this feat by committing "himself to a good that transcends these finite ethical forms" (Lear 2006, 95). He embraced "a peculiar form of hopefulness . . . the hope for *revival*: for coming back to life in a form that is not yet intelligible" (95) (emphasis in original).

But how was he able to do this? And what justifies his chosen path in comparison to other available options? Lear makes the case that Plenty Coups was able to do this because of his dream, which enabled him to commit to a form of goodness he could not conceive. It was an embrace of "imaginative excellence" (Lear 2006, 117), in the form of radical hope. Lear argues that the commitment to imaginative excellence on the path of Plenty Coups was justified because it is a choice to live rather than resign and sink into any of the extremes possible. To succeed, however, the embrace of imaginative excellence requires a reimagination of the basic concepts of Crow life. The implication is that dealing with the experience of cultural devastation demands the creation of new concepts (Lear 2006, 118). That was the case for Plenty Coups and his Crow tribe, and that might be the case for others struggling with similar challenges.

The concept of courage that was central to Crow life had to be reimagined to enable the Crow community recapture the ideal that could give meaning to their experience of the world. In other words, basic Crow conceptual categories, such as courage, had to undergo "internal transformation" (Lear 2006, 119). Courageous response to the experience of culture collapse requires therefore that people become alive to the demands of their situation. And, most often, this is a call to go beyond the bounds of established patterns of conceiving and interpreting reality.

To be sure, this demand is nothing short of a major psychological adjustment. In the case of Plenty Coups, Lear (2006, 135) notes that his dream "provides the psychological resources by which one might avoid despair."

Plenty Coups was able to choose an ethically plausible path in the face of the cultural devastation his people suffered because he realized the relevance of his dream to the situation. His choice, for instance, was unlike that of the Sioux chief Sitting Bull, who chose the exact opposite of Plenty Coups's radical hope. When he visited the Crow during the time both the Crow and the Sioux were confined to reservation life, Sitting Bull pointed out to Plenty Coups that it was unreasonable to cooperate with the white man. He was convinced that doing so would amount to capitulating and becoming the white man's slave (106).

Unlike Plenty Coups, who committed to radical hope by choosing to live, Sitting Bull chose to keep fighting even when the very possibility of giving meaning to such action had imploded. Besides the contrast to Sitting Bull, Plenty Coups's choice of radical hope stood apart from other attempts among the Sioux to find solace in false promises grounded on religion. The allure of the preaching that a messiah would come who would save the Native Americans from all their misery only deferred the inevitable—namely, a confrontation with reality.

Thus, the "teaching that the current task of the Indian was to perform a Ghost Dance, which will help usher in the apocalypse," was flight from reality. It was merely an attempt to capitalize on "a dream-vision to short-circuit reality rather than deal with it" (Lear 2006, 150). Such flight from reality, as we can tell from individual experiences, leads nowhere. In the end, one must confront reality, and that was what Plenty Coups was able to do through his commitment to radical hope.

Flikschuh (2017) extends the notion of conceptual loss to global normative thinking. She does so by interrogating assumptions by global theorists that political liberalism offers a secure basis for consideration of adequate response to global challenges, such as those that constitute the core of the discourse on global justice. Whereas Lear asks what it could possibly mean for a culture to experience devastation, leading to conceptual collapse, Flikschuh is interested in inquiring into what conceptual incapacitation would mean for global normative thinking.

Does liberal global theorizing suffer from conceptual loss? If yes, what implications can we infer? Like Lear, Flikschuh adopts a first-person perspective in her inquiry. She does not aim to consider the question of conceptual loss in global normative thinking from an impersonal, abstract point of view. She aims instead at getting global theorists to interrogate the grounds of confidence in sufficiency of their "grasp of emergent global normative realities" (Flikschuh 2017, 101). Given her commitment to articulating a perspective on how we can orient ourselves to think globally, Flikschuh ponders the implication of different ways we can respond to conceptual collapse.

What would be the implication for global normative thinking if, like Plenty Coups, liberal theorists were to bury their "coup stick"? Burying their stick in this context means to give up the historical assumption that liberal morality is superior to other ways of contemplating social and political reality (Flikschuh 2017, 114). What would liberal theorists lose if, in searching for an orientation in normative theorizing, they buried their "framework" of assumed superiority and accepted that liberal morality is just one among possible alternatives? Flikschuh argues that the implication of doing this for the liberal theorist is positive in the sense that it will lead to the sharpening of her or his cognitive capacities. Liberal theorists will learn greater self-awareness in doing this because it is a way to acknowledge that there are different sources of theorizing to draw from when we wish to consider normative global problems, such as the problem of global justice (Flikschuh 2017, 7).

Instead of merely assuming the universality of our own framework, the reasonable thing to do is to engage in "an act of reflexive moral modesty" (Flikschuh 2017, 130). This comes close to the experience of Plenty Coups considered by Lear. Realizing that his Crow way of life had come to an end, Plenty Coups laid down his coup stick, symbolically signaling that he was burying that way of life. Drawing from this insight, Flikschuh proposes that we can become better global thinkers when we consider seriously the possibility of conceptual loss in relation to our framework of thought.

This effectively demonstrates to us the contingency of our framework of thought or morality, making us aware that exogenous frameworks are possible ways of living and making meaning in existence (Flikschuh 2017, 130). The sense of this assertion is not to suggest that we should make these other frameworks our own. Rather, the idea is to note that we gain critical insight and acquire a desirable disposition for normative theorizing by imagining the contingency of our own framework—in the sense that it can also experience the faith of the Crow, whose conceptual world collapsed.

There are many interesting dimensions to Flikschuh's engagement with conceptual loss; here, I briefly consider one that bears on my goal in this chapter. In her analysis, Flikschuh distills (2017, 7) from the notion of conceptual loss an exposition of how we ought to reconfigure global normative theorizing. Her pursuit is crucial because of the global nature of major problems of humanity today. Understanding orientation in global normative theorizing entails accepting that all frameworks of thought can participate in normative global theorizing as equals. It means paying heed to Achebe's (1988, 89) admonition that universality means ensuring "every people bring their gifts to the great festival of the world's cultural harvest," so "mankind will be all the richer for the variety and distinctiveness of the offering." The question to ask is how to know whether these gifts of every people are gifts appropriate to the festival.

How is it possible to say that a framework is an appropriate way of knowing or living? Surely, we cannot, on the model of reflexive modesty, appeal to external, universal criteria to answer this question. Flikschuh addresses this issue in her discussion of relativism and value pluralism. She appeals to Kant and Velleman to construct a view that sees value pluralism as a coherent standpoint, while avoiding the dangers of relativism (Flikschuh 2017, 117). Even when accommodation has been made for the view that acknowledging the possibility of conceptual loss as a fate that could befall any culture leads to a better orientation in global normative theorizing, we would still not have answered a fundamental question. The question left unanswered is, how do we know that a framework of thought is indeed contributing something? This is no trivial question. If we are unable to answer this question, we cannot determine the quality of theorizing that emerges from the new orientation to global normative theorizing we acquire by adopting the proposal Flikschuh advances.

In raising this question, my aim is not to reject entirely the importance of Flikschuh's proposition about how we should reorient global normative thinking. What I want to point attention to is how thinking about new normative orientation involves, first of all, thinking about it for particular traditions of thought. What I mean is that thinking about global normative theorizing is not always *other* oriented. The need for a new normative orientation arises almost always as a result of internal critique within a thought tradition. The implication of this is that any attempt to conceive a new normative orientation must emerge from the self-reflexive questioning of a thought tradition. In the context of African philosophy, for instance, this means that a new normative orientation would only emerge when this thought tradition, on its own terms, self-reflexively considers how its concepts, theories, and way of knowing have become unformidable.

Discussions of conceptual loss by Flikschuh and Lear lead to the inference that there are two interpretations of conceptual loss. The first is to consider it as an experience whose consequence manifests principally in daily life. The second is to think of it as a problem of intellectual reflection in a specific context. Whereas Lear's discussion of the experience of the Crow can be taken as an articulation of a perspective on the former interpretation, Flikschuh's discussion of conceptual loss in normative thinking reflects the latter view. Notwithstanding the range of possible intersections between these two interpretations, the interesting thing to consider is whether our interpretation of the experience of conceptual loss determines the solution we can imagine.

It does not seem to me that the connection exists. Regardless of the way one conceives experiences of conceptual loss—be it as part of everyday, concrete experience or as a problem of reflection in a specific thought tradition—the central problem remains the same. The main issue remains how to overcome a severe limitation regarding understanding reality to deal adequately with cognitive disorientation. As such, it is immaterial whether the limitation brought about by conceptual loss manifests as an issue affecting everyday life or it is a problem about the construction of knowledge in a thought tradition. The question that matters remains a concern about what constitutes a plausible proposal on how to rectify the deficiencies imposed by limitations arising from the breakdown of conceptual resources.

In my view, conceiving an adequate response to conceptual loss requires us to be able to know that our self-perception has become inadequate—to know, for instance, that counting coups, as in the case of the Crow, is no longer a coherent way to perceive oneself as Crow. It is only when we know this that we are able to make inferences about adequate responses to the experience of conceptual loss. In the case of the Crow Lear considered, this knowledge was tied to the realization by Plenty Coups that after the buffalos went away, things stopped happening for the Crow. For many reasons, Plenty Coups could see at a particular moment that events ceased to make sense in accordance with Crow conceptual categories.

In the case of orientation in normative theorizing, which Flikschuh discussed, the awareness manifests in the recognition by liberal theorists that it is problematic to assume that liberal morality is not only universal but also superior. In making the diagnosis about the awareness of conceptual loss, we realize what is at stake in the possible responses to the experience. For Plenty Coups, his awareness of conceptual loss on the part of the Crow led him to realize that certain ways of responding to the experience, like Sitting Bull's idea that working with the white men was selling out, are unviable. In the case of global normative theorizing, Flikschuh's claim seems to be that the diagnosis of conceptual loss by liberal theorists would lead them to realize that an excessive focus on liberal resources for reflection on global normative problems is barren in the end, hence the need to pay attention to other ways of theorizing.

DIAGNOSING CONCEPTUAL DESTABILIZATION

Given my focus in this book, I want to consider the way we might think about these issues concerning African political experience in the postindependence era. Has there been conceptual loss in this case? If yes, is this solely due to colonization, or are there other relevant factors? But, as already noted, to know that conceptual loss has occurred depends on whether we are able to say that a certain sense of self-perception is not coherent anymore. To this end, the question in the African context is whether Africans today know that they are experiencing conceptual loss, that their assumed framework of knowing has become a disoriented approach to meaning making in politics and other spheres. And how do we conceive a solution to this challenge? These are questions that capture the steps required to develop a modern African political philosophy, which I explore in the remaining chapters of the book.

I considered earlier how ideas about decolonization point to a deeper concern among scholars of Africa. To reiterate, I argued that there are two perspectives on nonindigenous concepts, which are often presented as foreign ways of life, in the scholarship on Africa. The first view suggests that exogenous concepts are necessary because of the paucity of indigenous African conceptual resources that would enable us to comprehend the reality of life in Africa. The second view is that nonindigenous concepts must be rejected due merely to exogeneity. Being of foreign provenance, it is argued, employing nonindigenous concepts in studies of African phenomena or experience amounts to a perpetuation of external domination.

Earlier, I hinted that both approaches are ultimately flawed because they do not get to the heart of the matter at stake. Now, I show why this is the case by considering the relationship between conceptual loss and the deployment of nonindigenous concepts in the scholarship on Africa. In carrying out this task, I analyze African political experience to point out how we can reasonably talk about the manifestation of conceptual loss in contemporary Africa and conceive a viable solution to the problem. Let me turn to the first issue, which concerns the inadequacy of the two perspectives on the deployment of exogenous concepts in the scholarship on Africa.

Regarding the use of nonindigenous concepts in the scholarship on Africa, palaver is a case that aptly reveals many insights. As we saw in the preceding chapter, the notion of palaver has a provenance that is intricately connected to the history of Africa's relations to the world. The currents of this contact with foreign peoples stand firmly at the heart of the normative meanings associated with the concept of palaver. In the experience of the Danes in the former Gold Coast, palaver served a vital purpose in shaping their interaction with the indigenous African people. Palaver was the conceptual resource that enabled both parties to conceive a framework for the regulation of their interactions to enable them to realize their different ends, be it in politics, commerce, or social life.

Often, the Danes would call for a palaver when they perceived that there was a threat to their economic interests. Conversely, the indigenous African groups resorted to the palaver when they felt there was a credible threat to their interest in autonomous self-rule. Although their ends differed, palaver represented for both parties the means to frame and deal with the challenge of collective existence. While the practice of the palaver was productive in this context, it became a reductionist concept. The concept was whittled down to a mere strategy that catered to the economic interests and anxieties of the powerful stranger community of the Danes in Christiansborg Castle.

The point is that context matters because it determines what the concept can signify. Because the phenomenon designated as palaver largely revolved around contestations about economic interests, the sense of the concept as a fulcrum of the interaction between the Danes and the African groups reveals itself as a game governed by instrumental rationality. Although the concept was presented as a means through which norms of coexistence were generated supposedly to serve the economic interests of all, the main goal was to safeguard the interests of a powerful minority on both sides. This becomes apparent when we consider that the norms generated by the palaver between the Danes and Africans in the former Gold Coast were dutifully and successfully enforced, although they were generated on an ad hoc basis. That the procedural flaws that inflected the palaver did not occlude the binding force of norms generated shows that it was not the interests of all that were served.

When we juxtapose the phenomenon captured by the palaver in the interaction just described with other instances of the practice of public deliberation in Africa, what emerges is the sense in which the history of the use of nonindigenous concepts in the scholarship on Africa matters. Consider as a contrary example the nature of the palaver in the kgotla held by a community in postindependence Botswana, a story recounted in chapter 4. The kgotla, as a means of finding answers to the contestation for political power, did not yield an effective solution in this case. Oteng, one of the contenders for the headman position in the community, showed no care whatsoever about what the kgotla resolved to adopt as its consensual decision, effectively defeating the end of the kgotla. Although a consensual decision was finally attained by the community after many attempts, the consensual decision was innocuous as it lacked a binding force.

This makes it rather glaring that the capacity to sanction, be it socially or legally, has simply dissolved in the hands of the community. This is unlike the palavers held between the Danish stranger community and the indigenous people in the former Gold Coast. The kgotla held by the members of the community in postindependence Botswana could not make any claim to having a binding force of equal significance. The question to ask then is how it is possible to designate the same experience as the practice of the palaver in African society. Does it make sense to say that the public deliberation between the Danes and indigenous Africans in the former Gold Coast is the same as the public deliberation that was held in a postindependence Botswana community? Would applying this concept in this manner not amount to a category mistake? If one manifestation of the phenomenon is totally devoid of binding force whereas the other has all the force to bind, does this not mean we are dealing with a significantly different issue in each case? Herein lies the problem of the recourse to nonindigenous concepts in the scholarship on public deliberation in African societies.

As a concept, palaver fails to capture the turns and shifting constitution of meaning in relation to how public deliberation manifests in African experience. The reason is that palaver is an inelastic concept that is firmly rooted within particular histories. Tied as a concept to the experience of domination, palaver lacks the requisite dynamism to properly reflect practices it is supposed to describe. It captures the meaning of public deliberation in the African context but only to an extent. The concept captures the significance of the phenomenon it supposedly denotes only insofar its meaning coheres with historical currents that shape the manifestation of what is described. Thus, the concept of palaver could at one point in time mean empty, verbose talk but denote at another time the exact opposite of these ideas—namely, a fruitful conversation and framework for generating valid norms. It is for the same reason that the concept could at one moment refer to trouble in the postcolonial urban imaginary but change to connote the one-party framework for political organization in postcolonial Africa.

Nonindigenous concepts, like palaver, are problematic not only because they fail to provide accurate descriptions of experiences. They also lack the fluidity, in terms of meaning, that will enable them to reflect the dynamic nature of phenomena in the African context. Tied to a background of colonialization and oppression, exogenous concepts like palaver manifest as vehicles for contriving single, inflexible, and dubious stories about social, political, cultural, and even economic phenomena.

Although exogenous concepts describe aspects of African experiences, the ideas they reflect are mostly unviable across time. And because they lack a stable context for evolution, exogenous concepts fail to map the twists and spontaneous turns of experiences in this context. The reason is that deployment of exogenous conceptual categories aims primarily to help non-African audiences understand the goings-on in Africa, meaning that the subjects of experience are decoupled from the understandings proposed.

Does this mean we should discard nonindigenous concepts because of exogeneity? I think the best way to approach the issue is to resist the temptation to predetermine, in abstraction from context, what we should do with nonindigenous concepts. The challenge is rather to decipher how the reliance on exogenous concepts points to fundamental challenges we must address to better understand experiences. What I am pointing to here is the need to consider from a broader perspective the challenge of concept formation in the scholarship on Africa. Suggesting that nonindigenous concepts should be abolished from the vocabulary of scholarship on Africa does not amount to saying much that is useful.

Besides, the long career of nonindigenous concepts in the study of Africa is such that we will fail to account for a significant portion of African experience if we discard these concepts. Their inadequacies notwithstanding, exogenous concepts constitute a significant interlude in the history of reflection on reality in Africa. As such, they constitute an important dimension of theory formation and the conceptualization of guiding ideals for social and political praxis. That is to say, they are vital components of the conceptual economy that has shaped the history of the imagination of African reality.

What this implies is that we are faced with a complex challenge we cannot adequately address from the standpoint of the clean distinction between indigeneity and exogeneity of conceptual resources. By this I mean that exogenous categories are not problematic merely because of their provenance as conceptual apparatuses. The difficulty they raise relates to the sort of apprehension of reality they make possible. It is rather a challenge regarding the possibility they create for thought, for reflection on experiences. Exogenous concepts, it seems, raise a challenge regarding how we *should* think about African experiences in light of the past, present, and future: how, for instance, we should think about deliberation in light of the history of its manifestation as izu or kgotla, in indigenous Africa; later as palaver, in the era of colonial interaction; and, finally, as an ideal of governance today and tomorrow.

The very fact that the challenge regarding how to orient oneself to indigenous concepts exists indicates that the African conceptual world has become unsettled. In a settled conceptual world, there is usually an established reference point for interpreting experiences, whether economic, social, or political. This point leads us back to an issue noted earlier, which is whether Africans experience conceptual loss in their present situation. To address this question, it is necessary to ascertain first how Africans consciously grasp the manifestation of conceptual loss. In the case of Plenty Coups, for instance, his grasp of the experience of conceptual loss is seen in his awareness that at a certain point in the history of the Crow, things stopped to take place. Can we say the same of contemporary Africans?

It is pertinent to note that people in different cultures may not experience conceptual loss in the same way. Thus, although the cultural devastation the Crow people suffered led Plenty Coups to realize that certain ways of perceiving himself as a Crow had become incoherent, this cannot be said to apply to every other group that has a similar experience. Other cultural groups may perceive cultural devastation differently. Notwithstanding, I think there exists a point of intersection that alone can enable us to judge whether indeed conceptual loss has occurred in a given context.

A culture that suffers a devastation that unsettles its conceptual resources necessarily has to contend with the problem of cognitive disorientation. In the experience of the Crow, contention with cognitive disorientation came to light in their confusion about the nature of meaningful existence after the collapse of Crow virtue. For contemporary Africa, the problem of cognitive disorientation can be seen in the difficulties Africans face about naming the "trouble" with Africa in the different spheres of life.

A cursory look at different attempts to characterize what ails Africa today reveals a perplexing circularity. This circularity, I believe, is traceable to a difficulty in finding adequate concepts to express reality. An example should suffice to demonstrate this point. Many scholars, in attempting to stipulate the challenge confronting Africa, turn to the issue of good governance. They construe the problem of governance in Africa as resulting from a deficit in democratic institution building.

It is often suggested that the more democracy becomes entrenched in Africa, the more we will see good governance unfold. Doubt about the cogency of this view quickly emerges when the dialectical relationship between democracy and development is raised. The challenge posed by this dialectic is often stated in terms of whether Africa must choose between democracy and development. In response to the challenge, arguments are advanced to assert that democracy and development are complementary. Democracy, proponents of this view argue, does not preclude the pursuit of development. Rather, it is the foundation for building the institutions of a sustainable democracy.

The problem, however, is that this assertion leads back to the initial question—namely, in what sense can we say that governance is the trouble with Africa so that we can be certain that its realization through democratic means will resolve the current situation? This question usually leads to another circle of proposals, disagreements, and reconciliations of viewpoints. In the new circle of debates, new fundamental questions may be raised. For instance, concerns may be expressed about the meaning of concepts employed in the discourse, such as good governance. Arguments might arise as to whether certain ways of understanding central concepts conduce to the goal of conceiving a political ideal for Africa.

Proposals that show why reconstructing African notions of governance represent a viable path to an adequate answer to the questions might emerge. Conversely, perspectives may also be articulated to demonstrate that the viable option is for people in Africa to emulate the path that led to success in the West. In all this, we see that much is said about the situation in Africa but in circular fashion. This leaves many with the feeling that theorizing about African challenges is a waste of time, an academic entertainment of African intellectual elites and their Africanist friends. All it takes for the circularity of arguments to reboot itself and start all over is for someone to attack the basic assumption—for instance, the assumption that what troubles Africa today is lack of good governance, development, or the embodiment of right values and attitude of mind.

The foregoing speaks to an underlining insight concerning commonplace observations by many Africans that theory does not solve problems. A good number of African intellectuals will surely recall situations where people have cynically quipped that "grammar" cannot change the status quo of the continent. With this statement, it is underscored that what is at stake in Africa is more than merely giving tags or labels to experiences. I agree that doing so would amount to a gross misunderstanding of the situation. The political condition of the continent does not demand the development of a conceptual register to label specific experiences, the reason being that it will still be left an open question what the conceptual apparatuses proposed mean. If we say, for instance, that a political phenomenon is an issue of good governance, that is but only a starting point.

Further questions about meaning arise immediately. Questions about what it means to name a phenomenon in one way or another must be tackled. Thus, awareness of challenges about finding adequate concepts to name African experience does not imply that we instantly arrive at a comprehensive picture of the story of conceptual loss in the African context through the development of a conceptual register (e.g., through the creation of neologisms that could serve as labels for African experiences). There is a further question of meaning that cannot be solved by such a move. The conclusion to draw then is that a crisis of meaning is implicated in the notion of political failure. The challenge of political failure comprises, on the one hand, the way to name contemporary experience in the continent and, on the other hand, conceptualizing the meaning implicated in the way we name experiences in the continent by means of conceptual metaphors.

The crisis of meaning in the political sphere reduces at a fundamental level to political disorientation. Disorientation in African political praxis arises from cognitive disorientation. Africans struggle to name their experience because of cognitive disorientation, which arises from the experience of conceptual loss after colonization. And because they can neither name nor give accurate meaning to their experience, due to cognitive disorientation, a pernicious form of practical disorientation ensues. An example is the challenge of understanding what genuine political action entails. Given the confusion in this regard, contradictory actions are presented as conceptions of genuine political action.

The pursuit of development, radical environmentalism aiming to limit damage to the ecology wrought by projects of development, privatization of state-owned firms, socialism in the form of collective ownership, attempts to desacralize and detraditionalize politics, and the spiritualization of political authority all jostle for recognition as genuine political action. The claim advanced by proponents of each of these perspectives is that their project of action embodies that which is in the best interest of postcolonial Africa. This sort of confusion arises because of cognitive disorientation regarding the very idea of genuine political action.

This disorientation should not be misconstrued as an argument that one will inevitably act correctly if one has correct knowledge. This would be a normative prescription that does not follow from the premise—that is, it does not follow that possession of knowledge leads to acting correctly. The point I am making proceeds not from normative prescription but rather from historical reflexivity. Cognitive disorientation when imagined from the vantage point of historical reflexivity would reveal that the central challenge in the situation is certainty about the normative value of the past. Due to historical experiences, there exists a confusion in the African context about the normative predisposition that should shape practical life. Usually, people judge and decide what to do about X because they are historically reflexive—that is, because it is clear the course of action suggested by a historical lesson from the past.

Consider, for instance, the fact that liberty matters for most Americans because a great majority of Americans know the historical value of liberty. Populism constitutes a big threat for Europe because historical reflexivity makes them aware of the disaster the idea poses. In recognition of these facts, political theorists appeal to the conceptual repertoire of the history of political thought. In African political philosophy, this issue manifests in the recourse to conceptual retrieval.

To think about current challenges, a return to the past, presented often as reconnection to history and indigenous concepts, is generally seen as the way to proceed. However, this approach is problematic. I turn in the next chapter to discussion of the reasons I consider this approach inadequate. Most importantly, I go beyond merely offering a critique of conceptual retrieval to outline the more viable approach of conceptual creativity I deploy in chapter 7 to argue for an agency-based political philosophy. This is the approach I think is capable of resolving the problem of political failure.

SIX

—ᘚ—

CONCEPTUAL CREATIVITY

An Approach to Political Philosophy Here and Now

THE DISCUSSION IN THE PRECEDING chapter opens up the question regarding the way to proceed in theorizing African political experience—in other words, the approach that will yield a viable African political philosophy, if we discount conceptual retrieval, while still faced with the challenge of conceptual loss. In this chapter, I argue that conceptual creativity is a viable response to the challenge of method in African political philosophy. This method of analysis does not only correct the deficits of conceptual retrieval; it provides a basis for imagining a coherent political ideal capable of responding to the phenomenon of political failure, which is the main feature of contemporary African experience. To make this case, my starting point explores how conceptual creativity arises and what it means.

Analogies and thought experiments are vital tools philosophers employ in their work. Although this is true, it is hardly debated what makes these approaches to thought viable. In other words, what really happens when philosophers use thought experiments and analogies as tools for constructing arguments and philosophical theories? Why should we trust analogy and thought experiments as approaches capable of leading us to knowledge? In this chapter, a proposition I want to demonstrate is that part of what happens when these tools of reasoning are deployed is the manifestation of conceptual creativity. To explicate this view, I engage in three separate but related explorations.

First I recall the historical relevance of these tools of philosophical discourse. In this regard, I take notice of how they are deployed by African philosophers and philosophers working in other traditions. The second part of my exploration discusses how conceptual creativity unfolds in various domains of artistic creation. Engaging in this task is a way to conceptualize the background of the approach of conceptual creativity. To this end, I assess attempts to leverage epistemic resources to create new paradigms of interpretation of reality as the foundation of the method of conceptual creativity. Third, I show that conceptual creativity differs from conceptual retrieval. The aim is to note how the limitations of conceptual retrieval necessitate a turn to a new orientation in theorizing African political philosophy—that is, a turn to conceptual creativity as a more formidable way to take on the tasks of political philosophy in African philosophy.

Hardly anyone would disagree that *A Theory of Justice* by John Rawls (1971) is one of the best-known works in political philosophy in the Western tradition. Part of the appeal of this work is its creative reimagining of the foundational conceptual resources of his tradition of thought. Rawls was able to rekindle interest in political philosophy through his creative reimagination of two basic concepts: the social contract and justice. By constructing a narrative about an original position in which the veil of ignorance serves as a test of justice, Rawls breathed new life into Western political philosophy.

What was at stake for him was not just to deploy new narratives or thought experiments to conceive a theory. Implicated in this approach to political thought is an assessment of the validity of the proposition that says that a correct orientation to the use of conceptual resources available in any given tradition of thought is vital for an accurate formulation of practicable theory. If the approach or tool is broken, the theory proposed will also fail to fulfil the envisaged task.

ORIGINS OF CONCEPTUAL CREATIVITY

To explain how conceptual creativity is a viable approach to articulating an agency-based conception of politics, it is necessary to consider its context of emergence as an approach to theory formation. The inspiration for this approach to analysis and theory formation is my observation of the dynamics in different domains of life in postcolonial societies. Notable issues in this regard include contemporary African music and forms of artistic expressions, such as fashion, art production, and literature. In these domains, we find distinctive African creative agency in full display. Kwame Anthony Appiah (1992, 76) captured this point succinctly in his observation that "the relation of African writers to the African past is a web of delicate ambiguities. If they have learned neither to despise it nor to try to ignore it . . . they have still to learn how to assimilate and transcend it."

The impact of exertions in these areas of human endeavor is that there is increased visibility of African artists and literary icons on the global stage. In art, we find the late-lamented Okwui Enwezor and a host of other curators of African descent. In music, there is a catalog of Afrobeat musicians competing favorably with established counterparts from every corner of the world. In literature, we can surely point to dozens of African writers at home in the world.

In my view, the explanation of these success stories can only begin to emerge if we consider how the actors in question display uncommon capacity for conceptual creativity. To explicate this claim, let us consider how conceptual creativity is exhibited in music, literature, and art. I certainly do not claim that global attention to these areas of artistic self-expression is new, in the sense that people in different parts of the world are just beginning to appreciate, recognize, and respect the exertions of Africans in these fields. The point I am making is that the significance of works by Africans in these fields has to do with the innovations demonstrated through the deployment of forms of conceptual creativity.

African music currently travels around the world with unprecedented ease. The reason for this situation is certainly not because people are now less biased against foreign music or due to the disappearance of impediments to intercultural communication, such as racism, class bias, and other forms of prejudice. The reason is that producers and artists are expressing forms of creative imagination that are capable of commanding the attention of music lovers everywhere. They are not just digging up forms of music specific to African cultures and presenting them to the world as *authentic* African music. What is going on is that creative artists, both young and old, recognize the dormant potential in African musical heritage, which they are able to reimagine in ways that speak to the aesthetic desires of Africans and non-Africans alike.

Thus, rather than just retrieve supposedly authentic African musical expressions, they are busy recreating music itself by creatively drawing on the heritage of African music genres. Although the end product is still music, it is not music that is simply reducible to the mold and cast of the heritage from which the artists draw inspiration. This is why it is not a rarity to encounter African music today as sometimes a combination of highlife music and rap; *ogene* and highlife and pop; or a mixture of jazz and *makossa*. These mixtures create new forms of musical expression that are traditionally African, in terms of drawing inspiration from an African heritage of music production. Beyond this, the new forms of music are contemporaneous in that they are inflected and shaped by the musical and aesthetic desires of people living in present times.

The goal is not just to meet a need of people today. It is rather to create new forms of musical self-expression that enable a new conception of reality. Whereas a few decades ago there was the widespread perception that music for young Africans must come from the United States, this view is hardly tenable today. The change that occurred in this regard is not simply because current artists are able to satisfy the specific needs of young Africans, such as the desire for music that is rhythmical and hence danceable. The change seems to have come about because these new forms of musical expression are made in ways that enable Africans to be Africans in a manner that is in tune with a broader consciousness they embody. It is not the remaking of tradition, per se, that is key. Instead, what is key is the creative fashioning of new modes of self-understanding and engagement with the reality of what it means to be African in the here and now.

Some might dismiss new African music as superfluous. This attitude may be explained by reference to the claim that most of the songs lack meaning and are conceived to speak to a generation that is superficial. Barring problems related to the definition of *meaning* and concerns about whether conveying deep meaning is the main yardstick of creative self-expression, this argument does not take away the fact that artists in this context have engendered changes concerning African music.

Regardless of one's evaluative perspective, it remains true that fundamental changes in the imagination of music have occurred in the context of African music. It is this fact that is relevant for my attempt to explicate the context of the emergence of conceptual creativity as a method in African political philosophy. The point I want to make with the example of African music is simple. It is that aspects of life in Africa reflect experiences of conceptual creativity. Thus, the approach is not without a foundation in reality. Paying attention to the possibilities it opens up at the level of theory formation enables a different approach to theorizing political questions.

There is now a long debate about whether world literature denotes a distinct category of literature or whether the label is merely one among many attempts to perpetuate colonial practices of disciplinary hygiene and canon dictatorship. Related to this is the question whether it is in fact useful to speak about African literature, instead of just literature. I do not wish to go into the nuances of these debates to make the point I consider useful in understanding conceptual creativity. Without dismissing the importance of debates about authenticity, I would like to draw attention to the sense in which conceptual creativity manifests in the corpus of African literature as an important contributor to world literature.

The reading public almost everywhere cherishes the writings of African novelists. Some of the literature produced by African writers has inspired new forms of self-understanding and imagination for Africans. By this I do not mean to suggest that these works have inspired political revolutions but rather that people have come to see the world in new ways due to the insightful perspectives offered by these writers. In works regarded as African literature, there is largely the manifestation of the creative conceptualization of African experience.

Contemporary African literature does not just retrieve conceptions of X from the indigenous African past to hold them up as instances of the imagination of the human condition that is uniquely African. It seems to me that these works attempt to capture in some deep way what it means to be human, on the foundation of the heritage of specific experiences designated as African. They draw on variegated conceptual resources made available by their heritage and experiences to articulate new meanings of phenomena in the world. It is because of this that people have stopped looking to African literature for anything less than creative self-expression aiming to capture things in ways that yield new orientations to reality.

It is, of course, true that some literature by Africans does not aspire to these aims or, even if they do, that they fail to reflect what is noted as a marker of the manifestation of conceptual creativity in contemporary African literature. I would readily grant this point. But accepting that this is a possibility does not nullify that it is largely true that there are numerous instances where the opposite trend obtains. Most of the literature that is highly regarded by Africans does express approximations to conceptual creativity. And the reason is that the rootedness of African writers does not constitute the core of their artistic creation. They surely draw on the heritage of their place under the sun to imagine reality, but they do so in a manner capable of speaking to the human condition as such.

We also find the manifestation of conceptual creativity in art. African-born curators, such as Enwezor, have been able to reposition African art to be imagined in ways that go beyond the artisanal largely through a reliance on conceptual creativity. As a result of their success, people have come to develop a new orientation to African art. Instead of outsourcing the valuation of the forms of artistic expression produced by Africans to prices attributed to them by art markets, talented African curators and artists take a different route. They aim to refashion African art so that it can speak to human imagination on its own terms. The success recorded in this regard translates to further success on the global stage because this approach to African art enables artists to speak to reality in ways that produce new meanings capable of changing people's orientation or perception of reality.

Creativity at the level of conceptualization has enabled Africans in different spheres of creative endeavors to transcend the limitations of circular arguments about things African. This is an important feat because circular arguments point to gaps in theory that arise from reliance on inadequate conceptual metaphors. To use a recent example, consider what could have been the case if Britain and the European Union did not have the concept of Brexit. In the absence of such a concept, how could it have been possible to comprehend and address adequately the moral and material implications of the departure of Britain from the European Union? Although it is debated what would constitute a good action regarding Brexit—that is, what will give substance to "Brexiting"—there is nonetheless a shared meaning introduced by Brexit. This is the sort of thing we see manifesting in the fields considered above.

The reliance on conceptual creativity is useful in the African context due to specific reasons. Like we saw in chapter 5, a challenge that emerges in attempts by Africans to make sense of political reality, for instance, is complicated by the experience of a form of conceptual disorientation owing to the impact of colonization. This is the reason the challenge of developing a viable orientation to reality is such an important issue. Realizing that returning to indigenous African concepts alone cannot solve present problems in the continent, because the problem is more complex than what one is able to capture using these concepts, Africans in different fields turn to other ways of apprehending reality. The most successful of these new ways of giving meaning to reality is at the foundation of what I refer to as conceptual creativity.

Given the flux that is characteristic of contemporary Africa, indigenous concepts on their own are no longer formidable ways to know reality. However, postulating a position that is outside this context as a solution does not work because of the reasons considered in chapter 5. This means that we must decipher how people can know themselves through recourse to their conceptual resources that, although they still exist, have become seriously undermined by factors of history. This is like a situation where what is available does not work but we are unable to abandon it altogether to adopt an external standpoint. The theoretical potential of the method of conceptual creativity should become apparent when we come to full grips with its meaning as an approach to political philosophy.

As an approach to political philosophy, conceptual creativity insists that different sites of justification rely on different forms of normativity. The point of this is to underscore that contexts of justification demand an account of normativity that is contemporaneous, even though historically grounded. Thus, the reflection on African experience advanced by African political philosophers needs to do more than just draw from the past to explain the present and conceive a vision for the future.

Interpreting African experience in this manner is inadequate because the vision of the future conceived on the basis of this approach will face the issue of not speaking to contemporary Africans in concepts and idioms they understand and relate to in terms of political sentiments and aspirations. The experience of political failure cannot be plausibly addressed by reaching back to norms and ideals of African traditional institutions or practices to recover concepts that were put to successful use in conceptualizing political reality in times past.

The method of conceptual creativity takes a different approach. It merges attempts at conceptual retrieval with contemporary sources of meaning to conceive concepts and ideas that robustly explain the problem of political failure, while offering a vision of future politics. The explanation this approach offers concerning phenomena bridges both the justificatory grounds of concepts of traditional African experience and the conceptual apparatuses of modern Africa. The aim of conceptual creativity is to refashion, rethink, and merge the paradigms of Africa's traditional and modern conceptual resources. What emerges from this undertaking is thus a toolbox for political thinking grounded in the wisdom of history and the dissatisfactions with present reality.

As a method, conceptual creativity does not merely attempt to extract concepts that can be put to use to dispute whether propositions of other traditions of philosophy are relevant in the African context. For example, instead of retrieving a concept such as wo ho, which the Ghanaian philosopher Wiredu retrieved to challenge Descartes's idea of cogito, ergo sum, the method of conceptual creativity would aim to refashion the general sense of the notion of existence in Akan thought in light of what the concept must confront today, due to questions raised by new sources of meaning in modern African experience. Rather than ask on the basis of a retrieved concept whether Descartes's paradigm applies in the Akan context, the approach of conceptual creativity will seek to reimagine the very idea of existence in both traditional Akan society and the contemporary epoch of Akan experience. The aim will be to think about the notion of existence in both contexts to refashion the concept in a way that enables one to explain the totality of the African experience of being.

Relatedly, instead of extracting ideas from traditional political practices or institutions concepts that can be applied to modern realities, the approach of conceptual creativity aims to refashion the conceptual apparatuses of both the past and the present. This is necessary because both the retrieved concept and present sources of meaning harbor fundamental shortcomings, having proven themselves inadequate as means to solve contemporary African challenges. Although the approach of conceptual creativity is similar to conceptual retrieval, it differs in important areas. This is because conceptual creativity as an approach to political philosophy emphasizes the need to make retrieved concepts fit to do the work of reframing our reference point in the political sphere.

The goal of this approach is not to attempt to deliver outcomes by means of updating indigenous concepts in light of modern experiences—that is, by merging the positive aspects of indigenous concepts and modern realities. The approach instead moves beyond emphasis on the positive aspects of retrieved concepts and concerns about how to apply them to the present. It goes beyond both issues in the interest of engaging in the task of forging new idioms that enable us to conceive new ideals, using the resources of the past and the sources of meaning that shape the present. Conceptual creativity, thus, relinquishes attempts to "retraditionalize" as a means of inventing the future. The reason for this move is the conviction that the future is shaped by how we use the sum of our contextual experience of reality to imagine a different state of affairs.

What, however, does one need to do should one wish to deploy this approach to doing political philosophy? What, in other words, is the test of conceptual creativity as an approach to political philosophy? Although the description above does not suggest that there is a specific way the manifestations of this approach to meaning making proceed, I think having clarity about this point adds to the persuasiveness of this approach to meaning making. For this reason, it is useful to work out a broad outline of this approach. The preliminary thoughts about the notion of conceptual creativity I am putting forward come from the notion of the revaluation of African ideas that Richard Bell says is operative in the works of thinkers like Wole Soyinka.

Bell (2002) refers to Soyinka's proposal in *Myth, Literature and the African World* that Africans should "translate the inherent or stated viable values of a social situation into a contemporary or future outlook" (Soyinka 1976, 98) to develop a perspective on problems confronting African philosophers. In his view, the narrative dimension of African philosophy refers to the point that an effort must be made to "revaluate" African values in the sense proposed by Soyinka. Doing this requires a "lifting up of the deeper traditional values of a community and recasting them to meet today's realities" (Bell 2002, 116). The idea, therefore, is to do more than just retrieve traditional values or concepts. There is the further work of "recasting" concepts to meet the contemporary cognitive needs in the sphere of political imagination.

Although Bell and Soyinka pointed to the need for further reflection on retrieved ideas, the outstanding task they did not address is what is required to recast retrieved concepts. How should one conceive this task, and what does one need to do to realize this goal? Conceptual creativity is an attempt to provide an answer to these questions. As an approach to political philosophy, conceptual creativity serves the purpose of orientation by detailing the core of what needs to be done in response to the inadequacy of retrieved concepts and the problems associated with contemporary sources of meaning.

While we cannot lift ideas from the past and apply them wholesale to the present, we cannot also rely on contemporary sources of meaning because of their shortcomings. Thus, although prefigured by notions of retrieval and revaluation, the method of conceptual creativity differs both in terms of its constitution and aspiration. We consider how this is the case in the discussion of the relationship between conceptual creativity and conceptual retrieval. To provide a context for that discussion, the first step is to understand the sorts of things we need in order to be able deploy this approach to political philosophy.

STEPS AND PROCEDURE OF CONCEPTUAL CREATIVITY

As noted above, it is not clear what we need to do if we wish to deploy the method of conceptual creativity. It is vital to underscore that the nature of this approach is shaped by its emphasis on concepts. As such, the conditions useful for its deployment must be conceived in such a manner that allows for creativity at the level of concepts. This means that there are conditions that make conceptual creativity possible. They include the following:

1. Recognition of a dormant potential
2. Imaginative competence
3. Abstraction fluidity (malleability, ability to yield ideas rather than restricted to events)
4. Hypothesizing through analogy and logical inversion
5. Contextual independence (must neither be of the past or present or even future—aorist)

One cannot engage in conceptual creativity if there is not dormant potential embedded in a given practice or phenomenon. The question, however, is what is dormant potential, and how is it possible to recognize its existence in practices or phenomena? Dormant potential refers to a new possibility of imagination that is capable of taking the mind beyond the status quo. It means the existence of grounds upon which a leap in thinking, perception, and imagination can be premised. For instance, in relation to a practice X, a dormant potential obtains if X presents the possibility to think Y beyond its conventional understanding as X_1. This is similar to recognizing that a resource could be reshaped in a way that enables it to serve a function that was hitherto unimagined, although possible. For an example, we can think of spokes in a bicycle, which could be reshaped to become an improvised key that can open a lock whose original keys are lost.

How then can one recognize dormant potential? This would depend on one crucial factor: there has to be an acknowledgment of an acute need of a new orientation to concepts. Just as we are nudged to recognize the dormant potential in a bicycle spoke due to an acutely felt need for improvisation required to open a lock whose keys are lost, so too would we be in a position to recognize the dormant potential of any phenomenon if we feel an acute need for improvisation to do something different with the phenomenon. Viewed in the context of this book, an acute need for improvisation would be the realization that some form of what is called conceptual loss has occurred. It would mean coming to grips, like Plenty Coups, with the reality that something does not work in relation to the concepts we deploy to make meaning of political or other forms of experience. Given the framing of the manifestation of conceptual loss in the African context as cognitive disorientation, dormant potential refers to the need to realize that the normative order of the African conceptual world has become unsettled. With such a realization comes an acute need for improvisation at the conceptual level to enable the creation of new meaning rather than attempt to remake the old order.

The second condition that makes conceptual creativity possible is what I regard as an imaginative competence, which linguistic access or competence makes possible. Spokes of a bicycle can be attached to the wheel in different ways. However, the creative possibilities that exist in this regard arise from experiments in thought carried out by different individuals. The possibilities require that experimenting individuals have access to spokes on a bicycle wheel, in the sense of knowing that things of a certain nature are bicycle spokes. It is on the basis of this kind of knowledge that the experimenting individuals are able to think beyond the status quo. In the same vein, imaginative competence refers to linguistic access or competence that makes possible an engagement with the conceptual resources of a given context.

Imagination of this sort does not refer to the general human capacity to contemplate reality. It refers instead to a specific human capacity to contemplate reality in a particular context. Although one may be in a position to use one's imagination to apprehend reality as such, it is possible to fall short of this ability if one lacks the requisite access to the epistemic resources necessary for the contemplation of reality in a given context. This, however, should not be taken as a suggestion that a condition for conceptual creativity is that those interested in engaging in the task must be able to speak an African language.

Although the ability to speak a language may be a crucial asset for someone interested in engaging in conceptual creativity, lack of access to a language is not an insurmountable barrier. If one lacks the requisite language skills that guarantee access to the epistemic resources of a thought tradition, recourse can be made to other means of guaranteeing access, such as translation. The point in this regard is that access to a language by itself does not translate to sophistication of thought or capacity for deployment of conceptual creativity. The possession of the requisite language skill may get the task off the ground, but it is insufficient to ensure success in using the method of conceptual creativity to tackle the task of remaking the African conceptual world as it relates to the quest for existential repair in the sphere of politics. Translation thus plays a mediating role in the method of conceptual creativity.

For my concern in this book, imaginative competence refers to the possibility of accessing the epistemic resources of African cultures, regardless of the unabated cognitive disorientation characteristic of contemporary African existence. It is not a suggestion that one should be able to speak an African language or draw insights from an African culture to formulate political theories. What is crucial for this condition of the method of conceptual creativity is to ensure that there exists a possibility to apprehend reality in a way that captures various aspects of African experiences.

It means taking the relevant dimensions of African experience into proper account concerning a concept in order to have a proper horizon about the phenomenon addressed through deployment of the method of conceptual creativity. An example here would be the often-invoked distinction assumed to exist between colonial and postcolonial epochs. This distinction is usually invoked in attempts to address African challenges through conceptual retrieval. The complicating factor, however, is that we disregard the continuity of reality when we try to address contemporary African challenges in the way suggested by this distinction.

To be sure, the African is aware of herself or himself as a continuity. It is for this very reason that it occurs to her or him that there is a problem with available epistemic resources. For instance, when confronted by the impersonal nature of institutions of the state and the alienation arising from modern economic interaction, the African does not become perplexed because she or he has come into contact with alien reality. One is instead perplexed because one is living a reality one can no longer understand, a situation devoid of meaning.

Facets of precolonial, colonial, and postcolonial worlds become a lived experience of disoriented continuum.

The African is forced to deal with things that happened in the past and those that are happening now with conceptual resources ill-suited for the task of meaning making. Thus, imaginative competence is a condition for conceptual creativity. It underscores the necessity to think about the defining ideas or problems of the African world through a broader horizon. This means to think from a perspective aiming to account for all relevant experiences. Without imaginative competence, experience can neither be historicized nor understood as a totality.

Abstraction fluidity is the third condition of conceptual creativity. This condition refers to the malleability of concepts. The aim is to guarantee that conceptual creativity yields a form of imagination that is not restricted to a specific event, era, or place. This condition relates to the recognition of the violence of cognitive disorientation and its effect of truncating perception. It underscores the importance of being able to contemplate the sense in which the experience of cognitive disorientation, which is currently a basic feature of Africa, requires a disruptive form of violence to be resolved.

Abstraction fluidity points to the necessity of unearthing the complexity implicit in the coherence assumed to inhere in concepts supposedly embedded in the African world to produce a new orientation to reality. It points to the need to subject to critique assumed ways of apprehending reality that are said to be uniquely African to decipher whether what is assumed about these ways of apprehending reality is justified in light of current experience. Abstraction fluidity entails considering, for instance, how the assumption that the concept of witchcraft can explain certain experiences is justifiable in light of technological possibilities and scientific progress that shape current experience in Africa. How do the assumptions that make possible the explanation offered by this concept hold up in relation to discoveries about causality? That is the question to ask.

As a condition for conceptual creativity, abstraction fluidity underscores that we ought to stretch the conceptual resources available to us in a way that will make them yield insights capable of reorienting our apprehension of reality. The idea is that concepts are malleable in the sense that they are epistemic tools we can redesign to deal with the changing patterns of challenges we face in apprehending reality. By suggesting that it is necessary to subject to thorough critique the ways Africans are assumed to orient themselves to reality, this condition of conceptual creativity makes possible the introduction of the disruptive forces capable of relocating African epistemology, given the experience of cognitive disorientation arising from conceptual loss.

Once subjected to thorough critique, assumptions about African conceptions of reality should be reconfigured in a way that allows the fluidity of concepts to emerge. By subjecting the concept of witchcraft to thorough critique, for instance, insights about causality embedded in the concept will manifest in ways that reveal aspects of the concept that can be abstracted and merged with other sources of meaning currently salient in the African world. To this end, one can say that abstraction fluidity aims to produce "raw materials" for conceptual creativity through the process of immanent critique. Here, immanent critique is a form of discourse that points out the inconsistences of assumptions about conceptions of reality said to be uniquely African.

Next is the condition of hypothesizing through analogy and logical inversion. This step arises from abstraction fluidity. This condition addresses what should be done with the raw materials gained from abstraction fluidity. Hypothesizing through analogy and logical inversion means consciously attempting to create new parameters for thinking about concepts. This entails elucidating how previous imaginings that shaped thinking about experience should be reconfigured to yield a new mold of thinking. Once the task of critique of a concept is accomplished, remnant cognitive insights or raw materials cannot be recast in light of the mold of the old pattern that held sway prior to the critique. This implies that it is necessary to find new parameters of thought that enable us to recast fluid cognitive insights gained from immanent critique.

Since engaging in this task entails forging an idea or concept that can enable the creative conceptualization of reality, the new parameter for thinking must not merely reconstitute old ways of knowing. The criterion must be a form of logical inversion, in essence, a move outside the box. Instead of thinking, for instance, of the witchcraft concept by associating it with an old pattern of thought, which sees it as having to do with an explanation of mysterious events, logical inversion would suggest thinking about the remnant insight or raw material of this concept in light of other associations. And this may include associations opposed to causality or other possible associations hitherto unimagined in relation to the concept. This might, for instance, mean to think of the remnant insight gained from immanent critique of the concept of witchcraft within the parameters of the political oppressiveness of secret societies or the explanation of the logical foundations of modern science and technology.

With this, we come to discussion of the last condition of conceptual creativity: contextual independence. This condition underlines that it is important to recognize the sense in which theories created through deployment of conceptual creativity must aspire to be more than ideas of the past, present or future. For conceptual creativity to occur, a basic condition is recognition of the inadequacy of generating concepts that explain once and for all the totality of reality. The life and times of concepts are tied to their relation to reality. By this I mean to say that concepts and what they make possible are closely related to the location in time of agents attempting to apprehend reality. The notion of contextual independence is similar to the Greek sense of *aorist*. It construes concepts as a relation of the position of the agent to time. This means that, for conceptual creativity to be deployed, there has to be an acutely felt need to create concepts aiming to produce meaning transcending the past, present, and future. Such meaning is constituted entirely by the relation of the agent of knowledge to reality.

This location in time could be location in forms of temporality, such as political times or even cultural times. It could also mean location in the forms of spatiotemporal horizons, such as experiences specific to regions or epochs of history. The importance of this observation is that conceptual creativity does not yield conceptualizations of reality that are fixed. This approach to analysis leads us to ways of orienting ourselves to reality that will enable us to deal with phenomena in their specific contexts. It is only in this way that conceptual resources can be liberated from attachment to events and history. And, liberated from these trappings, it would be easy to put them to use where they are clearly relevant rather than where their application is conventional. This ensures progress in knowledge.

Given the discussion of the conditions for conceptual creativity, it is important to ask whether it is an approach to political theorizing that can be replicated by everyone. If this is not the case, should we conclude that it is a unique or special way to do political philosophy, which is too unique to be viable? To be able to address this question, we must consider a prior question—namely, what conceptual creativity entails. If all the conditions for using conceptual creativity obtain, what does one have to do to deploy this approach?

A formula for the method is the following: think about phenomena in a way that is not trapped in the past or confined to symptoms of the present and anxieties of the future. Stated different, the recommendation is to do the following: in contemplating the explanation and solution to problems in the African context, proceed by forging conceptual links between different facets of experiences. This is an injunction to look on facets of experience and the epistemic resources attached to them as grounds for fashioning viable metaphors and idioms capable of speaking to people in the here and now.

In attempting to fashion a theory about a phenomenon, consider whether the relevant problem arises from conceptual disorientation. If this is the case, attempt to find an answer through exploration of the most relevant concept available. If available conceptual resources exhibit all or most of the conditions for conceptual creativity, re-create the central concepts in that situation by means of immanent critique. From the raw materials gained from immanent critique, forge new conceptual idioms capable of offering a new orientation to reality so that the problem can be imagined differently and resolved. Doing all this entails engaging available conceptual resources in a manner transcending appropriations from the past. It requires an activity similar to the work of blacksmiths, who fashion new objects from scraps of old metal.

To fashion new objects, the blacksmith has to engage in specific tasks, such as putting the metal through fire, gradually chiseling off parts of the red-hot metal, pounding hard on what remains of the metal, creating a new mold for the new shape that will be created, and then meticulously smelting and pouring the ore into the new mold that forms the shape of the new object created. Anyone engaging in conceptual creativity is like the blacksmith in that she or he puts the conceptual resources of the past through processes that make possible the creation of new concepts that are capable of redirecting our orientation to reality. The concepts emerging from conceptual creativity enable us to deal with tasks that are too complex for our subsisting conceptual resources.

CONCEPTUAL CREATIVITY: MATTERS ARISING

With this understanding, we can now turn to the question regarding the possibility of replicating the process of conceptual creativity. Is this approach to theory formation accessible to everyone? Or is it rather something accessible only to a few individuals gifted with this sort of creativity? Since the notion of creativity is implicated, there is cogent ground to assume that approaching the task of political philosophy through the lens of conceptual creativity is something that is open to a select few who are lucky to possess the gift of such creativity. I think this would be a wrong assumption. There is nothing about conceptual creativity that says anyone wishing to deploy the method must be exceptionally talented.

However, just as we have to learn the processes necessary to carry out the tasks of a blacksmith, so too do we have to learn the processes necessary to engage in conceptual creativity. Thus, to deploy this method in contemplating political phenomena, what we need to do is to find out whether the conditions necessary for the deployment of the method obtain. Thereafter, we can apply the suggested formula and determine the viability of the results we arrive at. Before applying this method of political philosophy to address the phenomenon of political failure, it is pertinent to examine three issues: first, the difference between conceptual creativity and conceptual retrieval; second, whether neologisms are instances of the deployment of the method of conceptual creativity; and third, the difference between the method of conceptual creativity and the idea of hybridism, which is a salient approach in postcolonial theory. Earlier, I hinted that there is something unique about the method of conceptual creativity. This uniqueness manifest in at least three ways, regarding (1) the goals, (2) the procedure, and (3) the context of conceptual creativity.

In terms of its goals, conceptual creativity is unique because it does not aim to re-create something exclusively African that lies in the past. Its goal is to enable political philosophers to accomplish the task of forging new conceptual tools suited to the task of reorientating oneself to reality. Rather than rehabilitate concepts embedded in the past, it aims to enable a form of creativity necessary for the contemplation of reality in the present. The concepts generated through the deployment of conceptual creativity do not aspire to timelessness, in the sense of being relevant for an infinite period. This is unlike conceptual retrieval, whose goal is to remake the conceptual world of the African on the assumption that these resources are in some sense timeless. Overall, conceptual creativity is unique because it aims at furthering new forms of imagination.

Another difference between conceptual creativity and conceptual retrieval has to do with the procedure of both approaches. Whereas the project of retrieval consists in excavating from cultures the essences of categories of understanding, conceptual creativity proceeds on the assumption that such essences do not exist and, even if they ever existed, that they cannot be recovered once they have become unsettled. Unlike the approach of conceptual retrieval, conceptual creativity accepts where Africans find themselves today as a possible starting point of theorizing. This is the reason the method proceeds by an appraisal of conceptual resources as they manifest today, not how they manifested in the past. Conceptual creativity considers the past only in the way it has shaped the present. In doing this, it forges a conceptual link between different epochs of African experience.

Rather than proceed on an assumption of separateness of the traditional and the modern, this approach circumscribes the spuriousness involved in the postulation of such a dichotomy. The approach offers a litmus test for assessing the viability of possible solutions to challenges Africans confront in the present century in the sphere of politics, which I have noted earlier are challenges that arise from cognitive disorientation. In this way, conceptual creativity provides justifications that are accessible to modern Africans living in the here and now. Because of the aim it is designed to attain, conceptual creativity proceeds differently compared to the method of conceptual retrieval. The conditions and formula of this method imply that doing political philosophy in an African context ought to involve a process of making fit concepts embedded in an African tradition of knowledge. This is because one cannot conceive a viable political theory for the present by retrieving and applying concepts embedded in the African traditional context.

Given the disruptions, shifts, and distortions that severely destabilized systems of reality in the African context, conceptual creativity proceeds by making the concepts of these systems of reality fit again as guides for contemplating reality. The reason is that the dehumanization of African people also implied the devaluation of their conceptual tools for knowledge creation as cogent tools to guide one's orientation to reality. Consequently, conceptual creativity proceeds by fashioning ways to make concepts embedded in an African framework of knowledge fit for the task of addressing cognitive disorientation, which is the core of the phenomenon of political failure. This sets the method of conceptual creativity apart from conceptual retrieval, whose sole aim is to recover concepts and attempt to create so-called African stories about different phenomena or experiences.

At the outset of this chapter, I discussed the manifestation of conceptual creativity in different areas of human activity, such as music, literature, and art. The idea was to describe the background for this approach to doing political philosophy. This method is unique and different from the approach of conceptual retrieval because it constitutes a formalization of an already operative mode of knowing and dealing with reality in the African context. It does not seek to introduce into theory formation a perspective on reality that that has no basis in reality. The method systematizes and formalizes disparate attempts to creatively engage the human condition in the African context. This is unlike the approach of conceptual retrieval, which is focused on recreating a reality that is hardly correlated to the lived experience of modern Africans. The context of conceptual creativity is the here and now—that is, engagement with the concerns and situations of existing societies today.

This is, however, not a suggestion that we should not attempt to retrieve concepts from the African past. What is important for conceptual creativity is the goal envisaged and how to get to this goal. The aim of conceptual retrieval must be to do something theoretically promising with the concepts we retrieve. The goal is not just to retrieve concepts from the past. We retrieve concepts precisely because we see in them certain dormant potentials, which could be relevant in resolving problems we face. Accomplishing this task demands that we put retrieved ideas or concepts through a systematic process that will make them fit for this task. The uniqueness of conceptual creativity inheres thus in its provision of a means to make concepts fit again, a task necessitated by changes that have occurred in the African conceptual world.

Having made these points, I can now address the question about neologisms. Is there a sense in which it can be claimed that neologisms reflect the results envisaged by the method of conceptual creativity? This concern arises because neologisms construct words and phrases that are supposedly hybrid enough to invoke new meanings. In African philosophy, there have been many instances where neologisms are misconstrued as reflections of original insights.

More than anyone working in African philosophy, Pantaleon Iroegbu (1995) was adept in constructing and deploying neologisms. In his works, we find such neologisms as *kpim* of X, where X would refer to a phenomenon or aspect of life in Africa. In short, Iroegbu came close to recalibrating philosophy as an exercise in "kpimology." Another way neologism is deployed in African philosophy is by infusing words derived from some African languages into statements supposedly expressing a theory. Thus, we find Innocent Asouzu's (2007) postulation of "ibuanyidanda" as an original African thought. Some scholars now use terms like "Ubuntuism" to denote an African normative theory (Fourie 2008).

Do neologisms constitute instances of conceptual creativity? In my view, neologisms do not reflect in any way the idea of conceptual creativity. This is because they do not embody the goal, procedure, and context of the approach of conceptual creativity. Rather than engage relevant questions, the reliance on neologisms conveniently dodges the challenge. Although those engaged in this way of theorizing African reality express concerns about the problem of essentialism, they end up smuggling essentialism into their discourse through the back door. Generally, neologisms are constructed by plucking words out of their linguistic context to anglicize and make theories out of the decontextualized words. The problem with this is that words do not become concepts or theories merely because an -*ism*, -*ogy*, or -*ity* has been added as a suffix. There is more to theorizing and concept formation than adding suffixes to words.

If a word in an African language shows itself to be harboring a dormant potential that will enable us to conceptualize a phenomenon, instead of making a neologism out of the word, the best way to proceed would be to translate the word into the primary language of discourse in the text. Such translations would then serve as foundation for the more serious conceptual work necessary to make sense of the phenomenon. Given that many African philosophers conduct their work in English, French, and other European languages, smuggling words or concepts of African languages into any of these languages to express "an African perspective" convolutes the discussion in ways that are apt to mislead. This is the case because we come away with the impression that theorizing in African languages is impossible, hence the need to append concepts found therein unto the languages in which African philosophers conduct their work. It is surely not the case that theorizing in African languages is impossible. Rather than create a mismatch of concepts through the construction of neologisms, the reasonable way to proceed is to maintain the separateness of domains of discussion and rely on translation.

Lurking around the corner is a concern about the understanding implicated in the idea of conceptual creativity. How is conceptual creativity different from the notion of creativity? The difference between the two consists in the fact that, whereas conceptual creativity is a necessity born out of a complicated history and anxious present, creativity itself is a human capacity that manifests as unique value. We cherish creativity as such because it is *einmalig*—that is, unrepeatable by another. This thought does not apply to conceptual creativity, which is merely a method of thinking about political questions or phenomena to address issues related to the general cognitive disorientation characteristic of life in Africa today.

It is a way of recognizing that the breakdown of the African conceptual world is at once an opportunity to create new modes of thinking that will guarantee progress toward the realization of freedom, another space for freedom. This reorientation to freedom is pressing today because conceptual disorientation entails an emergence of a paradoxical situation where Africans have become prisoners of the freedom their forebears fought long and hard to achieve in the form of political freedom or independence.

How do concepts forged through the deployment of conceptual creativity gain their power of signification or meaning? In other words, how do concepts become potent tools that can enable one to reorient oneself to reality, given the experience of cognitive disorientation? There are different ways to make concepts operational in this way. However, the most viable means is to infuse new meaning to creatively fashioned concepts. The concept of nonviolence, for instance, became a tool of social transformation in the United States, even without the cultural presuppositions that accompanied its understanding in India. This was attained because civil rights activists infused into the concept new meaning that was powerful enough to command people to reorient themselves to reality. Not only did the concept shatter ossified racist belief systems; it produced moral empowerment that enabled oppressed African Americans to make progress in their struggle for equality and racial justice.

This proposition brings conceptual creativity close to the aspirations of the theory of hybridity. As such, it is worth explaining the distinction between these concepts. In the main, I regard hybridity as an approach aiming to explain who or what one is if defined as a postcolonial subject. Conceptual creativity, on the other hand, is an approach aiming to explain who one wants to become and how one ought to position oneself to reality to achieve this goal. Conceptual creativity goes further than hybridism in dealing with the challenge of knowledge creation because it does not focus attention on essentialism and its pitfalls. Instead, the approach casts light on the steps required to enable Africans to emerge from their long night of cognitive disorientation, which is at the center of the challenges confronting the continent.

The reason for this focus is that the challenge of the postcolonial subject is not so much an issue of self-knowledge as it is the ability to conceive an adequate orientation to reality. It is hardly useful to set about attempting to define who postcolonial people are because their humanity is not in doubt. What is unclear is how to orient oneself to reality as a postcolonial subject to have a proper apprehension of experience. Besides, even if we accept that it is necessary to define the problem of the postcolonial subject as having to do with knowledge of the self, as the idea of hybridity proposes, we still have to consider the further question regarding the nature of this subject as an agent of knowledge. Who is this postcolonial subject that defines her or his being in this particular way, with these sets of concepts? How does this agent of knowledge come to possess and deploy these concepts in the situation of disorientation in which she or he exists?

That is the second-order question to address. To answer the question, I argued that we need to conceive an approach to theorizing that is capable of dealing with the challenge at hand. I proposed conceptual creativity as an approach to political philosophy that entails a set of conditions. Applying the method requires ensuring that the five conditions described earlier are fulfilled. These conditions are prerequisites for the application of the formula. It should be noted, however, that conceptual creativity does not aim to propose how political philosophy must be done or the sort of political philosophy that will necessarily emerge from applying the procedure it suggests. The method is squarely an attempt to capture the refinement that can aid the rehabilitation of an unsettled conceptual scheme.

CONCEPTUALIZING POLITICAL PHILOSOPHY THROUGH CONCEPTUAL CREATIVITY

HOW THEN CAN WE ADDRESS the challenge of African experience discussed in chapter 1 as a phenomenon of political failure? Responding to this question demands that we first determine what it entails. To do so, it is vital to recall the diagnosis proposed about African political experience. I have shown how political failure expresses the core of the experience. African political experience, I have variously noted, is ultimately to be understood as a situation in which individuals experience powerlessness in relation to social and political factors shaping their lives. The problem with this state of affairs is the inertia it brings about. Specifically, it is the demobilization of Africans as citizens, a situation that cripples the agency of Africans in the political sphere.

With this in mind, we can address the goal in this chapter by restating African political experience in a way that clarifies the main issue just highlighted. The diagnosis of political failure is not just a point about the state of affairs in politics. It is not, for example, about a situation where citizens are failing to participate in politics. If the diagnosis represented no more than worrying about the involvement of citizens in politics, it would mean that the idea of political failure is not a useful category of explanation, given that Africans participate in periodic elections. In fact, there seems to be too much participation in politics in some African countries because politics is regarded as the only means of dealing with every conceivable issue.

POLITICAL EXPERIENCE AND COGNITIVE DISORIENTATION

The diagnosis of political failure as the main feature of political experience in Africa is a claim that politics in Africa has become a meaningless performance.

The reason, as I explained in chapter 5, is the cognitive disorientation afflicting Africans. The situation of cognitive disorientation results from experiences whose combined effects have unsettled the African conceptual world. Although the experience of colonization did not lead to a complete conceptual loss, it brought about anxieties that negatively affect the organization and performance of the state in Africa. The outcome is that citizens of African countries are put in situations that make difficult, if not impossible, the imagination of a coherent orientation to politics as a differentiated sphere of reality.

Against this backdrop, addressing political failure requires first that we conceive an answer to the experience of cognitive disorientation. The reason for this is that cognitive disorientation is the factor that complicates the exercise of political agency in this context. To tackle this challenge, I think it is best to begin with a reflection on what it entails—that is, to first understand cognitive disorientation. We can gain clarity about cognitive disorientation by exploring how Africans relate to politics currently. One thing that is certain in this regard is that the performances of states in Africa have failed to impress Africans and non-Africans alike.

This dissatisfaction manifests not only in different protests against the state but also in sustained attempts to overcome the state itself. The streets of African cities bear witness to reverberating voices of anger, just as the pages of books and other media of public discourse are filled with protests. Constantly, the mind is put to task to conceive possibilities to overcome the state in Africa. The result of all these events is the creation of covert and overt movements aiming to carve out spaces for people to cooperate and flourish unhindered by the apparatuses of the state. Dismas Masolo (2010, 132) argues in this regard that "circumstances have changed for many aspects of everyday life in African societies, and there are many indications of our awareness of these change in our daily utterances, which signal the spirit of disapproval. . . . Our disapproval signals dissatisfaction with society's failure to adjust to today's pressures."

It takes a little reflection to realize that the core of what is implicated in this situation is anxiety regarding how to protect the freedom won from colonial administration and ensure at the same time survival of the individual human person. This concern manifests in a widely held belief in the continent today that there exists a dialectical relationship between freedom and survival. To this end, the issue becomes how Africans can guarantee freedom and engage fruitfully at the same time in the struggle for survival, which is a defining feature of the human condition. This is an urgent question for politics in postcolonial Africa because the dialectic assumed to exist between freedom and survival, when framed as a dilemma of politics in postcolonial Africa, raises further concerns.

For instance, it raises concerns about what it really means to survive. Is survival the realization of social justice, equality, and freedom from racial and other forms of oppression, or is it just the satisfaction of basic needs? How should Africans organize their societies to ensure the realization of these ends? Given that the concepts deployed to articulate perspectives on these questions are rooted in specific political histories, namely in the history of Western political thought, what theoretical options will enable Africans to imagine a worthy political ideal they should strive to attain? Conceptualizing a position around the dialectic assumed to exist between freedom and survival is therefore only a prelude to conceiving a theoretical path that will lead to a new imagination of political philosophy suitable for modern Africa.

Reduced by a common denominator, the anxieties in Africa today reflect uncertainty regarding the purpose of politics. It is not certain whether the goal of politics is to gain power for the sake of asserting dominion over a territory. It is not clear whether the goal is instead to ensure the efficient distribution of goods and services. Should one listen to economists, one would think that the goal of politics in Africa is to advance economic development and guarantee, at minimum, the enforcement of contract and property laws. However, it does not take a serious exertion of the mind to see the limits of this view. Even development theorists who hitherto expressed faith in economics and development as the sole aim of politics have now recognized the limits of the economic conception of the ends of politics.

Indeed, there is no shortage of proposals about what is or should be the aim of politics and the state in postcolonial Africa. Powerful organizations like the International Monetary Fund, the World Bank, and many NGOs have not relented in producing white papers on the goals states in Africa should pursue. Sometimes, these white papers focus on getting the African state to commit solely to the advancement of economic development. Other times, the aim they envisage for the African state comes in the subtle form of collective goals of the comity of nations to protect human rights. An example here is the so-called sustainable development goals. Besides these externally generated ideas about what the aims of the African state should be, there is also the reality that African states are hard at work in producing with great care official pronouncements about their goals. As we saw in chapter 1 and again in chapter 4, there are many endogenous ideas about what the goals of the state should be. The pursuits of these proposals, sadly, quickly turn into nightmares, resulting in further ascription of urgency to the question regarding what ought to constitute a *worthy ideal* of politics.

The disorientation in the sphere of politics, in the sense of uncertainty in the African context regarding a *worthy ideal of politics*, accounts for the reason postcolonial African politics is structured by meaninglessness. Politics in the continent is a circle of the impossible, where what makes sense does not matter and the things that matter do not make sense. The question to ask, therefore, is why there is a contradictory relation of political praxis and meaning. As we saw in chapter 5, the answer has to do with the unsettling of the conceptual resources that served as a reference point for the interpretation of experience. This explains why there is a sharp distinction between the daily struggles by individuals to survive and the reality of politics as a collective act.

Faced with this sharp distinction, individuals in Africa have largely chosen to focus on survival, meaning that politics is left to a few powerful individuals and their coterie of expert advisers. The exclusive focus on survival manifests in situations like military coups and other forms of social vices that entrench a nonchalant attitude toward accountability. We see how this nonchalant attitude in the fact that, for instance, when the military takes over government by coup d'état, the default reaction of Africans is to develop strategies to survive under the military rule that succeeds in establishing itself. In the event that another authoritarian regime takes over governance from the military regime, the reaction of people remains the same. They simply adjust to any new regime in power, while focusing their energy on the struggle for survival.

This sort of disposition has led to a situation where individuals in postcolonial Africa have become like a large search party seeking a treasure called survival. But this treasure is, alas, one they are unable to recognize even when they find it. With this analogy, I want to note that, although the struggle for survival is taken to be the very meaning of existence, it is largely impossible to tell what constitutes survival for almost every contemporary African. This situation points to the fact that there is a mistaken assumption about the way the relationship between political agency and the struggle for survival ought to be construed.

The dire consequence of this mistaken assumption is the postulation of a dialectic between exercise of political agency and the struggle for survival. This dialectic leads to an entrenchment of the understanding that politics should be confined to the realm of probability, where something good may or may not happen, the reason being that nothing can be done to bring about real and desirable change. Because politics is now confined to the realm of probability, the only thing that makes sense is to focus on making ends meet.

Given this situation, addressing the challenge of political failure requires us to articulate a viewpoint capable of reorienting Africans toward political reality in a way that does not conjure a dialectic between political agency and survival. Doing this requires us to conceive a perspective that shows how to overcome the perceived dialectic between political agency and survival. This constitutes the first necessary task to address the phenomenon of political failure. Conceiving a perspective that enables the transcendence of the falsely assumed dialectic between political agency and survival would put us in a position to articulate the nature of a viable, modern African political philosophy.

My argument is that an agency-based account of politics, derived from a new interpretation of the practice of deliberation in Africa, enables us to tackle the phenomenon of political failure. The question that arises immediately is, why focus on deliberation in conceptualizing this agency-based account of politics? The reason is simple. It is due to the nature of public culture in Africa. There is high esteem for deliberation in the public culture of African societies, and this is not merely something true about the precolonial African past. Present realities in the continent reenact the high esteem of deliberation through its negation.

Thus, whereas traditional Africa prized deliberation as a core principle of coexistence, the organization of coexistence in modern African states inverts the logic of deliberation by prizing secrecy as the core of politics. As a result, the state and its enactment of authority and control thrive on secrecy. Not only are reasons for coexistence of disparate people within the structures of the states inherited from colonialists not obvious; secrecy plays the role of enabler of governance through state institutions. It is at the core of the daily performance of politics, as Bidima (2015) has shown.

Although the practice of deliberation no longer constitutes the regulating principle of coexistence, it is precisely its negation that structures the coexistence of Africans today in the confines of state institutions. As such, conceiving a response to the challenge of cognitive disorientation in politics requires taking deliberation seriously. And the reason, I show, is that deliberation embodies a dormant potential capable of revealing the way African societies ought to deal with the challenge of political failure.

Having made these clarifications, let me now return to the question noted above, which I indicated constitutes the first step in articulating a response to the phenomenon of political failure. This is the question about how to address the dialectic presumed to exist between political agency and survival. Earlier, I pointed out that the dialectic assumed to exist between the exercise of political agency and survival entails the postulation of a false assumption about the nature of these values. This is why I think the most for-midable way to transcend the logic of this dialectic is to explore the false con-sciousness it embodies. Proceeding in this way demonstrates that, instead of being antithetically opposed, the exercise of political agency and daily struggles for survival are intricately related because they are both necessary factors in the ever-evolving human aspiration toward the realization of a higher degree of freedom.

BETWEEN POLITICAL AGENCY AND SURVIVAL

Before delving into discussion of the details of this view on the relationship of political agency and survival, it is important to consider briefly the false consciousness implicated in the postulation of a dialectic between political agency and survival. I set about this task in three steps. First, I trace the genesis of the postulated dialectic to put into perspective why it exists. Second, I show the function served by the postulation of an opposition between the exercise of political agency and survival. Third, I examine how the postulated dialectic relates to the task of reimagining African political philosophy—that is, how the postulation of a dialectic between political agency and survival is connected to the task of conceiving an African political philosophy that is capable of tran-scending the current mode of politics.

An important consideration in tackling these tasks is to make clear the link between event and thought. This is to say that the analysis offered does not imply, in any way, a supposition that African political experience unfolds as a succession of events playing out in accordance with a predetermined plan. My aim instead is to show through a three-tiered analysis how certain patterns emerge from dominant social imaginaries that shaped different epochs of his-tory and, on this basis, demonstrate what we can infer as coherent theoretical explanations.

One of the earliest articulations of the idea that there exists a dialectic between political agency and the struggle by individuals for survival was offered by Cabral. Reflecting on the struggle for freedom in light of mistakes of the past and plans for a better future within the confines of the postcolonial African state, Cabral (1969, 86) notes that it should always be borne in mind that "people are not fighting for ideas, for the things in anyone's head. They are fighting to win material benefits, to live better and in peace, to see their lives go forward, to guarantee the future of their children." Read closely, Cabral can be taken to mean by this statement that the realities of everyday life should take precedence over theoretical exertions by African elites. His suggestion is that political reality should not be understood from the perspective of lofty ideals envisioned by political theories.

He could be read to be saying that attention should be paid instead to concrete struggles by individuals for survival. Viewed from the perspective of the widespread poverty of the majority at the time who were not integrated productively into the economy, Cabral's point would sound cogent. Surely, it would border on insanity for one threatened by hunger and malnutrition to be preoccupied by the study of which political theory is most fitting for Africa. Implied in this outlook is that political agency is an empty concept if its meaning is unconnected to the daily struggles by individuals for survival, in the sense of satisfaction of basic needs. This view establishes a connection between the scope of a desirable ideal of politics and satisfaction of the basic needs of people, albeit a connection that assumes priority of the latter over the former.

Important figures in African political thought shared this view about the scope of politics and its connection to the concrete reality of individual struggle for survival. Views elevating basic instinctual impulse on the part of human beings to survive as a *primum bonum* were not only expressed by important postcolonial African politicians; their actions in most cases demonstrated a firm conviction that politics was a means to enrich oneself. In 2002, Olusegun Obasanjo noted that "corrupt African leaders have stolen at least $140 billion" (Ayittey 2006, 490). Paul Biya of Cameroon, Henri Bedie of Côte d'Ivoire, Mobutu of Zaire, and many other postcolonial African leaders are accused of stealing several billions of dollars from their countries (Ayittey 2006, 490). These leaders strongly believed that their training and position were supposed to provide them the means to make their lives better through the acquisition of material comforts.

It is, of course, a legitimate aspiration for people to desire a better life seen in the terms of the improvement of their material condition. That is, it is perfectly good for people to be ambitious in pursuing the acquisition of material riches through the deployment of the talent nature has bestowed on them. A leader who believes that one of their goals in life is to acquire as much riches as possible through legal means is certainly not suffering an unheard-of disease of moral deficiency. My aim is not to condemn postcolonial African leaders for the beliefs they may hold about the acquisition of material comforts through legal means. This is not my goal. I bring up the issue of the framing of survival in terms of the acquisition of material comforts to underscore that there was a widespread perception at the onset of state building in postcolonial Africa that survival meant the acquisition of material comforts at the expense of political agency.

Two phenomena in modern African history entrenched the perception that survival means the pursuit and acquisition of material comforts. These are the experiences of civil wars after the attainment of political independence in many African countries and the implementation of structural adjustment programs advocated by the International Monetary Fund (IMF). These two experiences, which unraveled in quick succession, left the landscape of countries in Africa desolate spaces suffering from the effects of traumatized social psychology.

These experiences unfolded hand in hand with the recurrent use of excessive violence by postcolonial states to secure the consent or, put more appropriately, submission of the governed. The effect of these experiences is that individual human persons in Africa were set on a path of existence that prized the perpetual pursuit of ways to guarantee daily survival. The outcome is the entrenchment of an outlook that suggests that the pursuit of survival constitutes the ideal of all human striving. Consequently, attempts at affirming the value of political agency metamorphized into a marginal and unaffordable luxury.

To contextualize the phenomena that made the pursuit of individual survival the goal of life in postcolonial Africa, it is necessary to paint a picture that lends substance to the issue implicated—namely, the view that the bifurcation of survival and political agency is the most feasible response to the postcolonial situation. War, poverty, and disease are often said to underpin how the continent has been imagined when viewed through the lens of the so-called developed world. The crystallization of this perspective, however, comes about largely due to the ravaging effects of bitterly fought wars in the continent. Less than two decades ago, such concepts as guerilla warriors, rebels, warlords, and traitors punctuated descriptions of events in Africa.

The discourse analysis of newspaper reports on Africa in the global north in the period between 1965 to 1990 would lend support to this point. Unlike today, when terrorism, immigrants, insurgents, and militants have become the main iconic images of newspaper reports on Africa, the widespread perception of Africa a few decades ago was through the prism of war. This trend issued from the reality that large swaths the continent were soaked in the blood of both protagonists and antagonists murdered in all kinds of wars.

The ascendance of humanitarian intervention as a compelling narrative regarding how to bring an end to the woes of the African continent is traceable to the successful use of images of Africans damaged by wars to canvass for humanitarian aid. Images of the suffering victims of war provided a lot of support to aid advocacy. These images were mostly of dismally malnourished, hopeless, and poor African children, child soldiers, and destitute women and men.

But Africa did not go to war with itself for no reason. In most cases, wars were fought in the interest of peace, progress, development, recognition, and even democracy. Students of military history and conflict studies in Africa have educated us to a certain extent on the reasons for some of the devastating wars experienced in this part of the world. Regardless of the lofty ideals they sought to achieve, the wars fought in Africa left behind an indelible footprint of agony in people's minds. It changed the social psychology of African societies. These changes relate to the political imagination of citizens. When wars fought to entrench material progress, freedom, and related ideals established nothing but vicious exploitation after the skirmishes, the logical next step is to become skeptical about what is worth sacrificing in the pursuit of freedom.

Consider the example of Zimbabwe, where the ascendance of Robert Mugabe brought only "sorrow, tears and blood," to use the idiom of Fela Kuti. The civil war fought in Nigeria supposedly in the interest of freedom or the assertion of sovereign integrity, depending on one's preferred side in the war, ended in a bitter defeat for all—officially, there was no victor or vanquished. The ideals for which the war was fought as parroted by the military and the political elites on both sides did not translate into meaningful results. Even the short existence of Biafra did not give the people a feeling of being better off in "freedom." Evidence for this is the disaffections that unraveled rather quickly (Ojukwu 1969, 66). Making a claim that the nation of Biafra would have been a political space where individuals experienced true freedom is certainly an exercise in sophistry, for there is no evidence to suggest that Biafra would have been different from other countries in Africa battling with the problem of political failure in the present decade.

Seeing that their lives did not improve, even as they continued to endure the devastating effects of wars fought to achieve lofty ideals, individuals in Africa express a reasonable response when they separate political agency from the struggle to survive. As many African countries were already fragile prior to the wars they experienced, the suffering caused by wars was particularly excruciating. This is because, with the veneer of existing infrastructure destroyed, people had to watch as loved ones perished because of a lack of medicine that should have been readily available.

Of course, one of the certainties in war is the severe constraint of agriculture. Thus, lacking access in most cases to imported food, many who survived the wars that plagued their countries had to practically feed on garbage until it became possible to reestablish a functioning system of agriculture. Beyond food and medicine, cultural ways of coping with reality were either destroyed or devastated. Age-old alliances and other mechanisms of social solidarity and trust came under unbearable pressure, leading them to tear apart at the seams. This was disconcerting as these factors constituted the core of cultural mechanisms that helped people to cope with reality in African societies. One has to imagine in this regard the value of alliances built across ethnic divides prior to these wars. The cultural value of such alliances went up in smoke due to the mutual suspicion entrenched by war propaganda.

Structural adjustment programs were also devastating in no small measure. I still recall the perception I had about these programs as a child whose parents were severely affected by not only the inflation they brought about but also the danger the job retrenchment that accompanied them posed for the mental well-being of civil servants. As an employee in civil service, my father would tell my siblings and I countless stories about developments in the implementation of the IMF programs. Although it consisted of diverse policy instruments and social and economic measures, structural adjustment programs are difficult to explain in terms of theory. Their implementation, however, caused real havoc on families. Of particularly destructive potential were the measures of privatization and retrenchment of government employees.

These two measures worsened the prospects of advancement for middle-class Africans. In many countries, these measures made the middle class feel, for perhaps the first time, the violence of life under postcolonial conditions. I remember the moonlighting practices of professors at the University of Nigeria Nsukka, who would leave their jobs and turn to farming in a bid to augment the paltry salaries they were paid. Suddenly, people whose jobs were supposed to give an assurance of a secure livelihood and generous benefits at retirement found themselves struggling to feed their families. Formulas such as 0-1-1 (0 referring to meals to be skipped by necessity and 1 a meal one can hope to have) became popular.

Such an experience was a recipe for the entrenchment of social vices and disillusionment with politics. The effect of this experience was dire in that it broadened the scope of disaffected people. Whereas war was a calamity that can be understood if one shared the ideal propelling it, structural adjustment programs could not stake a similar claim. Because they mostly affected the middle class, the outcome was that they disillusioned the part of society that could have been a driving force for the exercise of political agency. They drove the citizens that mattered most in terms of genuine political action to vehemently disavow politics. Indeed, the pauperization of African economies by the implementation of structural adjustment programs increased rapidly the ranks of the poor.

Seeing the faith suffered by the middle class who vigorously challenged their sophistry, the political elites turned their rhetoric to the poor. Overnight, they became the champions of poor people fighting the self-seeking middle-class people, who were concerned only with their advantages. This was a smart strategy because, in pandering to the poor, the numbers of which had drastically increased as a result of the structural adjustment programs, the elites easily won elections. All that was needed in most cases was to deploy the correct anti-middle-class rhetoric and hand out a few food items or cash or both. So whatever was left of the will to exercise political agency after the experiences of wars was wiped out by the experience of structural adjustment programs and the exploitation of the conditions it created by political elites. The experience was humiliating for the educated middle class in Africa because of its neoliberal origin and mission.

Although I have not found till date conclusive data to confirm this suspicion, I think there is something to the belief that structural adjustment programs are the reason there are numerous African diaspora intellectuals in many countries in the global north. Engineers, professors, medical specialists—in short, a majority of the people who had critical skills—left en masse for so-called greener pastures overseas because of the effects of structural adjustment. This was, in no small measure, an essential aspect of the factors responsible for the creation of the myth that migrating to the global north from Africa was an aspiration worth even one's life. If the leading lights of the society have no faith in staying back in their countries, what could justify the commitment on the part of the less fortunate? This in effect entailed a near eclipse of belief in postcolonial African states. Someday when a social history of the structural adjustment programs in Africa is written, I believe their role in eroding the trust in African states will be a central point.

To realize that the losses brought about by wars and economic experiments did not yield a better state of affairs was even more devastating. Career politicians, proving at every opportunity that they could surpass colonial officials in the use of violence to secure forced consent, demonstrated to ordinary citizens the limited stakes they had in the struggles for the realization of lofty ideals in postcolonial Africa. It became clear to everyday citizens that what was in their true interest was to occupy themselves with what it was they must do to ensure they could survive—and this while avoiding hazardous, empty promises reeled out by the political elites during election campaigns.

The experience of wars, especially the realization that these wars could not bring about the envisaged future, entrenched in the social imaginary of citizens of African countries the idea that political agency must be separated from the struggle on the part of individuals to survive. Although this separation is a rational response to the situation, it becomes a false consciousness when it pretends to be an adequate response to the political failure that defines post-colonial experiences.

To this end, the question to ask is whether the bifurcation of political agency and survival is a sufficient response to the situation Africans found themselves in as a result of the experiences of war and structural adjustment programs. The answer must be in the negative because responding in this way entails mistaking a false consciousness for a solution. The response, while giving the inkling that it is the only feasible answer, serves in fact to prevent an imagining of responses that will encourage the sort of action necessary to change the status quo. Thus, although the experiences that lead to the separation of political agency and survival are diagnosed correctly as having to do with the damaging consequences of incessant disappointments, the response offered bypasses the core task of addressing the problem in order to ensure two things.

One of the things the pseudoresponse does is to ensure the sustenance of a mode of politics that operates to serve a few elites. The other thing it does is to offer individuals a chimera in place of the perception of their true interest. We see why this is the case in the discussion below. What is important presently is to note that disparate experiences combined to give rise to the assumption that survival ought to take priority over the exercise of political agency in the African context. In this assumption, however, is implicated a form of false consciousness that must be transcended if we wish to develop a political philosophy that is capable of changing the status quo of political failure and guiding the coexistence of disparate groups within the structure of the state in Africa.

So the task before us is to proffer a view of the relationship between the exercise of agency and the struggle for survival that transcends the dialectic assumed to exist between the two factors. In the preceding discussion, I pointed out that the first step in conceptualizing such a formidable perspective is to unearth the false consciousness implicated in current perceptions assumed to define the relationship between the exercise of agency and the struggle for survival. Three tasks are to lead us to the realization of the goal of this first step.

TRANSCENDING THE DIALECTIC BETWEEN POLITICAL AGENCY AND SURVIVAL

The first is to trace the genesis of the postulated dialectic. This was the task pursued in the preceding pages where we looked at the experiences that led everyday citizens in Africa to make sharp the separation of the exercise of agency and survival. Having done this, I can now move on to the second and third tasks. The second task is to show the function served by the postulation of a dialectic between agency and survival, while the third task is to point out how this dialectic relates to the task of conceptualizing an African political philosophy that responds adequately to the challenge of political failure.

Tackling the second task implies two things. One is to clarify the manifestation of the dialectic between political agency and survival in the social and political imaginary in Africa. The other is to show how the manifestation of this dialectic is instrumentalized to maintain the status quo, instead of transcending it. Taken together, these two considerations demonstrate why a different answer to the challenge of political failure must be sought. One obvious place to begin considering the manifestation of the dialectic between political agency and the pursuit of survival in contemporary social and political imaginary in Africa is to analyze how political and social institutions function.

The common experience is that institutions of the state thrive on vices, such as corruption, nepotism, violence, and lack of accountability. These vices are now hallmarks of public institutions in Africa because they constitute the conventional norms that define the reality of these institutions and their relationship to citizens. Reforms are often proposed when elections are around the corner because the government in power or opposition parties want access to foreign aid. As such, reforms are often proposed, but none of them amounts to anything desirable. Even local activist struggles do not succeed in bringing an end to the problems. Although context-specific reasons can be given to explain the persistence of deficiencies in public institutions in Africa, it cannot be denied that a notable dimension of the problem is opportunism.

The idea is that every means is acceptable in the struggle to survive, given that survival has been elevated to take priority over every other value. Like Peter Ekeh (1975, 108) has pointed out in his idea of the two publics, public goods and resources of public institutions are appropriated to guarantee survival, either for one's group or private individuals. No one seems immune from the affliction of this malaise because having access to public resources is an opportunity to make one's survival feasible. This disposition fuels and sustains extensive networks of patronage in public institutions. On the basis of this logic, anything done in the interest of survival is justified because it is unwise to hope for a way out of the current situation of political failure.

Should one choose a different path that yields nothing materially beneficial, one is looked on as a fool. Thus, every decision taken by individuals is directly or indirectly constrained by the outlook of survival. The prioritization of survival, defined as the acquisition of material benefits, encourages imagining that the ostentatious show of material possession is a standard of success—hence the convention in contemporary Africa to reduce all values to the value of material wealth. Conspicuous, vulgar consumption becomes, in such a situation, a vital aspect of life for the rich and poor. And the reason is that one is what one *shows* oneself to have, essentially.

Upon close examination, it should become clear why this outlook is problematic. Giving priority in this manner to the struggle for survival is an incapacitating reaction to the challenge of political failure because the separation, as a response, serves the function of ensuring that politics is perceived as a realm of life that is divorced from the realities of citizens. Although this is the function served by the separation of political agency and survival, in the sense of prioritizing survival, the true nature of the issue is masked in diverse performances.

Religion, ethnicity, Africanization programs, and superficial social convention constantly nudge people to think they are trapped in a battle with a phenomenon akin to the law of nature—that is, that they are up against a fixed reality. The experience of political failure is by this means taken to represent a law of nature to be dealt with through personalized mechanisms that guarantee individual advantage. The issue therefore becomes how to get ahead of others engaged in the same struggle for survival and not how to reflect differently on the reality that sets political agency against the struggle for survival. But by focusing solely on ensuring individual survival, the true nature of reality is masked. This function of masking the true nature of reality should become clear when we consider the consequence of prioritizing individual survival in situations such as the one that obtains in African societies in the present century.

If survival becomes the most important goal to pursue, no one really survives in the end. This is both a logical fact as well as a truth established by historical experience. It is a logical fact because no one can survive if everyone is battling to survive. The reason for this claim is that survival is only possible in a situation where life is not a brutish war of all against all, a situation we cannot hope for if survival is taken as the sole aim worth pursuing. From the angle of historical experience, it is evident that in all the years priority has been given to the pursuit of individual survival, the situation of lone individuals has not improved. The reason is that survival as a singular pursuit in certain social and political contexts is an impossible dream.

Certain changes must occur for that goal to be guaranteed. But those changes will not come about without the reactivation of the exercise of political agency by individuals that constitute the polis. Herein lies the cogency of the proposition I indicated earlier—namely, that responding to the challenge of political failure demands that we develop an outlook that is more positive in the sense of emphasizing the ways to recover and put to use a political agency suitable to postcolonial reality. This is what I aim to achieve through the articulation of an agency-based ideal of politics. Before delving into that, I would like to consider the implications of the dialectic assumed to exist between the exercise of political agency and the struggle for survival for the political philosophy I propose. This is the third task noted earlier.

Three implications should be pointed out. Firstly, the challenge posed by experience of political failure in Africa cannot be satisfactorily tackled by proposing a balance between the exercise of political agency and the struggle for survival. Although one may get this impression from the discussion of the dialectic between the two factors, it simply does not suffice to serve up a version of African communitarianism, or any other theory claiming to balance the relationship of the two factors, as a panacea to the challenge of political failure. The reason is that political philosophy ought to express and justify the ideal of politics worth pursuing.

This goal cannot come about merely by resolving a tension implicated in the analysis of the reason it has become imperative to conceptualize a new, modern political philosophy in the African context. The second is that the response proposed for the situation discussed must harbor no pretensions of separating ideal from nonideal theories. This means that it must be taken seriously in the context the proposed African political philosophy speaks to. Finally, discussion of the dialectic assumed to exist between the exercise of political agency and freedom implies that the challenge of political failure demands that we develop an action-guiding political philosophy. This means to engage in a form of normative theorizing that will in some form guarantee emancipation both in terms of thought and praxis.

This brings us to the task of stating the agency-based conception of political philosophy that is capable of adequately addressing the challenge of political failure, which we have seen constitutes the core of contemporary African political experience. I think we should begin by clarifying that an agency-based political philosophy refers to a theory that is more than an action-guiding ideal. It is an attempt to conceive a new imagination of African public culture—that is, the practice of public deliberation—to conceptualize an ideal that could become a source of meaning and an action-guiding principle. The ideal aims to respond to the challenge of political failure by addressing two essential parts of the problem. The first is the problem of cognitive disorientation that arises due to experiences that have unsettled the African conceptual world. The second is the problem posed by the experience of powerlessness of individuals in relation to the social and political events that shape their lives in the postcolonial era.

It must be noted that the diagnosis of current political experience in the continent as a manifestation of the phenomenon of political failure is a philosophical diagnosis. As such, it is set apart by its all-embracing nature. By this I mean that the diagnosis invites one to think the whole—that is, to think about what in present times ails Africa in an encompassing manner, not merely from the prism of putative concerns. As a philosophical diagnosis, the notion of political failure demands a response that embodies a specific kind of reflection—namely, a reflection on the human condition.

The reason is that an attempt to deal with the current political experience in Africa must go deeper than providing a surface accounting of cause and effect vis-à-vis the situation. As we saw in the first three chapters, attempts to deal with this experience through the purview of linear logic are insufficient. The problem of this approach, we noted, is that it does not offer adequate reflection on the human condition. This is why the agency-based political philosophy I propose engages the task differently. An agency-based African political philosophy begins with the following question: What is modern African political philosophy supposed to be philosophizing about?

To answer this question, we must begin with an analysis of contemporary African political experience. Contemporary African political philosophy ought to be philosophizing about meaning in politics, given the subsisting experience of political failure. This is because the current political praxis in the continent is structured by meaninglessness. Most importantly also, this is the case due to the reality that genuine political action appropriate to this experience demands that we conceive a justified sense of meaning in politics. To conceive such a sense of meaning, we can take as a starting point identifying the relevant resources embedded in the political heritage of African people.

These resources provide the building blocks needed to construct the envisaged sense of meaning in politics. In addition, the methodology that enables the construction of this meaning from identified resources must be spelled out. The reason for this requirement is the normative destabilization that was noted in chapter 5 as a feature of life in contemporary Africa. The relevant resources embedded in African thought that will help us conceptualize a sense of meaning in politics are those embedded in African public culture. Here, I have in mind resources embedded in the practice of deliberation as a manifestation of public culture in Africa.

As we have seen, public political culture in Africa manifests through public deliberation. As such, sifting through its various aspects will enable us to discover the relevant resources needed to construct a worthy ideal of politics. The question of appropriate methodology is addressed by the method of conceptual creativity developed in chapter 6. Thus, by applying the method of conceptual creativity, I show how the resources embedded in deliberation as a manifestation of public culture provide the sense of meaning in politics and constitute an adequate response to the challenge posed by the experience of political failure.

Before getting to this task, let me discuss a prominent political philosophy derived from practices of deliberation. This is Wiredu's (1996) proposal that a modern African political philosophy, derived from deliberation, entails that politics ought to be regulated by the ideal of consensus. Wiredu's proposition is that the pursuit of consensus through deliberation should constitute a worthy ideal of politics. His theory of consensus democracy relies on insights retrieved from Akan practices of public deliberation. The core assumption is that dilemmas and paradoxes are the mainstay of politics, and given this, the *worthy* political ideal entails understanding politics as conflict resolution that terminates in a specific form of agreement.

The agreement is a type of consensus that enables a political community to take collective action without alienating any individual or any one group. Said differently, the sense of this type of consensus focuses on ensuring agreed actions, not agreed notion. Because we must reckon with dilemmas as constituting *the* constant of political reality, it is proposed that the overarching ideal of politics ought to be the furtherance of the art of persuasion needed to effectively harmonize conflicting interests. The ideal of politics, in Wiredu's vision, prioritizes the *harmonization* of opposing views to secure agreed action without agreed notions. As I show shortly, the shortcomings of this proposal necessitate a different articulation of the sense of meaning in politics that should constitute the worthy ideal of politics in the African context.

Wiredu's account has been criticized for different reasons. Without wishing to engage exhaustively with rebuttals to his consensus democracy, it is pertinent to point out a shortcoming that informs most of the attempts at critiquing his proposal. This shortcoming is the assumption that Wiredu argued for the understanding that the reality that deliberation is practiced in African societies, like in his Akan society, is the reason we ought to interpret the practice as an African democracy. This is erroneous.

I understand Wiredu (1996) instead to be interested in showing how the experience of public deliberation in Akan society provides the foundation to imagine a new form of democratic ideal. Stated differently, Wiredu is not making a retrospective claim that there exists an African form of democracy. Instead, he is interested in showing the form of political philosophy we can imagine by exploring the basic manifestation of public culture in Africa. Thus, it is not a persuasive critique of Wiredu's idea of consensus democracy to argue, as some have done, that the proposal does not cohere with a widely shared sense of the meaning of democracy.

The problem with Wiredu's (1996, 183) proposal has more to do with his failure to consider whether the theoretical foundation he assumes lends credence to his postulation that consensus constitutes the worthy ideal of politics. The assertion Wiredu makes can only gain plausibility when we consider whether it can be derived from the theoretical foundation upon which it is premised. The point I am making is that it is not clear how the consideration of the practice of deliberation in Akan society yields the postulation that consensus ought to constitute *the* worthy ideal of politics. To be able to make this assertion, Wiredu must show the way the ideal of consensus, derived from the practice of public deliberation in traditional Akan society, is fit for the task at hand.

How does this ideal become fit again as a reference point for modern African political praxis, given the destabilization of its normative foundation through colonization and other factors that shape the postcolonial condition of existence? Wiredu, I think, assumes that the mere historical experience of public deliberation in traditional Akan society is a sufficient condition regarding the theoretical background needed to conceptualize consensus as a worthy ideal of politics in contemporary Africa. This assumption is problematic because the historical fact that an ideal regulated the political praxis in an epoch of a people's experience does not necessarily imply that that ideal can serve the same aim in another epoch. This is because no two epochs of history are the same so that we can transplant lessons and principles from one epoch to another without any further ado.

Against Wiredu's view, I argue that a contemporary African political philosophy will not emerge from an argument that assumes the historical manifestation of a principle provides enough of what is required for the development of such a philosophy. More is required. We must put whatever we identify as a worthy ideal of politics in traditional African society through a test that makes it fit again for a changed context. This in effect entails approaching the task from the perspective of a methodology of discourse that is fitting for the changed context. As I have argued, conceptual creativity enables us to attain this goal, given that it offers the possibility to assess the way resources of African political heritage can be harnessed to develop a modern political philosophy. This is a task that comes before the justification of the principle gleaned through the process of conceptual creativity. Thus, conceiving arguments to justify why an ideal of politics in traditional African society is cogent does not suffice. We need to first know how the ideal enables the new conception of the reality in question. Much of this has been discussed in chapter 6.

To enable creativity at the level of concepts, conceptual creativity entails the recognition of dormant potential, imaginative competence, abstraction fluidity, hypothesizing through analogy and logical inversion, and contextual independence. I indicated earlier that a relevant resource to consider in the attempt to articulate a modern African political philosophy capable of responding to the challenge of political failure is to look to deliberation as a manifestation of public culture. To see if this practice enables the conception of a worthy ideal of politics in light of the experience of political failure, let us apply these conditions of conceptual creativity to the resource—deliberation.

DEVELOPING THE IDEAL OF POLITICS
THROUGH CONCEPTUAL CREATIVITY

Thus, we ask, how does the recognition of dormant potential manifest concerning practices of public deliberation? Recall that this condition requires us to ask whether there exists a ground to recast an identified resource for it to yield new ways of thinking, imagining, and perceiving. As noted earlier, in relation to a practice X, for instance, a dormant potential obtains if X presents the possibility to think Y beyond its conventional understanding as X1. In light of the practice of public deliberation, this means to consider whether there is a ground to recast the practice for it to yield new ways of thinking about its meaning beyond its conventional understanding. To determine whether this is the case, let us begin by recalling the conventional understanding of public deliberation discussed in chapter 4.

The attempt in chapter 4 to determine the meaning of deliberation when expressed as palaver revolved around three considerations. First, I considered the way different phases of the evolution of the practice produced different meanings attributed to the phenomenon. I proposed that there are three phases decipherable from the modern incarnations of the palaver. In the first phase, the period of anticolonial struggle, palaver signified the primordial cognitive equality of disposed and oppressed African people and their colonizers in terms of the craft of political organization. The second phase was a time in which palaver came to represent a form of ideology of legitimation invoked by authoritarian regimes to justify their grip on power. In the third phase, the concept became an ideology of political renewal concretized through the acts of national apologies and reconciliation.

Given the differences in the meanings attributed to the concept, the discussion in chapter 4 sought further to unearth an interpretation of the concept that embodies a generalizable meaning—that is, conception of a meaning of palaver that speaks to different contexts and epochs of modern African history. The reason for pursuing this inquiry was due to the consideration that palaver can only serve as a category for normative political analysis if it can be shown that it embodies a functional ideal uninhibited by time and context.

Determining a generalizable meaning of palaver led to the exploration of five cases that were to reveal the typologies of the concept. By fusing together meanings gleaned from the typologies, it becomes possible to conceive a context-transcending connotation of the concept. The five typologies propose these ideas about the concept: (a) it is a process of legitimation and a means of structuring political contestation for power; (b) it is a reference point of the ideal of social life; (c) it is a principle that structures cultural modifications and social change; (d) it is a regulative ideal of economic exchange and resolution of conflicts; and (e) it provides the orientation that enables the community to determine and maintain a vision of what it means to be human.

These five typologies that can be used to understand deliberation in African societies yield its political, social, cultural, economic, and constructive meanings. Given the differences between the different domains of life where the concept has salience, there is a risk of categorial mistake if one attempts to generalize the political, social, cultural, and economic meaning of the concept. It is only the constructive typology that embodies the potential for such generalization. Because it embodies a vision of what it means to be human, the constructive typology is not hindered by specificities of the different domains of life that form the center of the other four typologies.

The question to ask is whether the constructive typology embodies a generalizable meaning of the concept. Recall the meaning this typology proposes. It is that public deliberation provides the orientation that enables a community to determine and maintain a vision of the meaning of being human. This typology, as it is, is not generalizable across contexts. I believe this is the case because it is vague concerning the principle it proposes. Herein lies a possibility to think about deliberation in the African context beyond its conventional manifestation in the typologies through which it is understood. The vagueness of the typology that has the potential to be generalized is the dormant potential that allows us to recast the concept of public deliberation to create new ways of thinking, imagining and perceiving in the domain of politics.

The dormant potential consists, thus, in conceiving a generalizable sense of the meaning of public deliberation. Doing this requires us to articulate a principle that is aligned to the five typologies discussed earlier and capable of transcending them to respond adequately to the experience of political failure. Such a principle can be conceived through the application of the steps of conceptual creativity that extend beyond the recognition of a dormant potential in a concept or phenomena. These other steps are imaginative competence, abstraction fluidity, hypothesizing through analogy and logical inversion, and contextual independence. I now apply these steps to the concept of public deliberation.

Imaginative competence is a condition of the method of conceptual creativity that puts emphasis on the possibility of accessing epistemic resources of African cultures, notwithstanding the unabated experience of cognitive disorientation. It requires that we take all relevant dimensions of African experience into account as a united whole. This implies that, concerning a concept, to ascertain whether there is the possibility for conceptual creativity, all the relevant dimensions of imagining the concept should be considered.

Imaginative competence entails establishing how a concept whose dormant potential we recognize can be accessed as an epistemic resource, regardless of the cognitive disorientation characteristic of contemporary reality in Africa. To apply this step of conceptual creativity, therefore, we must be guided by the following question: How do we determine that the concept of public deliberation, whose dormant potential we have identified, can be accessed even in the face of the unabated experience of cognitive disorientation? To find an answer to this question, it is useful to point out the importance of this step regarding the idea of deliberation.

To see how cognitive disorientation manifests in relation to deliberation, it is necessary to consider current practices, like the La Sape movement. The Societe des Ambianceurs et des Personnes Elegantes (Society of Ambiance Makers and Elegant People) is, in a sense, one of the modern incarnations of deliberation in aesthetic form. Recall that public deliberation is a practice where a community comes together for irenic and agonistic performances. Public deliberation is therefore an act of coming together that is not limited to staging the word through conversation. It could also be enacted in other forms of performative expressions that allow individuals to express themselves as free people. The reason is that public deliberation is a gathering of members of the community for the purpose of celebrating the enactments of individual expression.

Seen in this light, the La Sape movement is an aesthetic manifestation of public deliberation that makes possible the communal act of individual expression through aesthetic means. But, given its flamboyance and nihilistic social and cultural sensibility, how can access to the idea of public deliberation be guaranteed in such a situation? When we consider current framings of deliberation, in La Sape and also its framing in the institutionalized negation of deliberation as a norm of governance, how can one have access to the epistemic resources of public deliberation as a concept?

This question is important because it problematizes the imagining of the concept in a way that pushes us to sieve out its meaning that is useful in realizing the goal at hand. Put differently, it provides a framework for the cautious extrapolation of the meaning attached to the concept. This is the way to ensure that we do not injudiciously hold on to beliefs associated with the concept merely because such beliefs constitute how we think about the concept. Applying imaginative competence to the idea of deliberation implies we must show that, notwithstanding cognitive disorientation, access is guaranteed to the epistemic significance of the concept. In addition, we must point out the epistemic qualities that are relevant and show why that is the case.

Apart from a few exceptions, practices of public deliberation do not constitute the central fulcrum of political action in contemporary African societies. It is mostly confined to the margins, in the sense that neither the principles nor the procedures of the practice are mirrored in the formal institutions of the state. This gives the impression that public deliberation is no longer a part of the social and political imaginary of African societies and, by implication, that its epistemic resources are inaccessible. It would be wrong to think in this manner about the fate of the concept. Although it is true that the principles and procedures of public deliberation do not currently form the basis of contemporary politics in Africa, this does not mean that the epistemic qualities of the concept of public deliberation are inaccessible. The experience of cognitive disorientation may have had negative impact on the normative stability of the imagining of the concept. However, the concept and the ideal it entails persist in different forms.

In the present circumstances, philosophical fieldwork guarantees access to the epistemic resources embedded in the concept of public deliberation. As a means of conceptual discovery, philosophical fieldwork is a process that enables us to engage with the persisting practices of deliberation in a way that guarantees the specific kind of access envisaged by conceptual creativity and ensures the sort of extrapolation that does not amount to injudiciously carrying over beliefs. The meaning I ascribe to the idea of philosophical fieldwork comes from recent work by Flikschuh (2014), especially in her work aiming to reorient global normative theorizing (Flik-schuh 2017).

Flikschuh (2014, 15) argues that, by exploiting as much as is judicious the sort of access philosophical fieldwork provides for conceptual discovery, global normative theorists will develop the capacity to adequately deal with the cognitive inaccuracies they will otherwise fail to recognize. Although I fully agree with Flikschuh on the potential of philosophical fieldwork in the context she explores, I take philosophical fieldwork to represent a way of ensuring access to the epistemic resources embedded in specific practices with normative significance. It is a way of gaining access to the epistemic resources of public deliberation today because of the emphasis on theorizing with an eye to conceptual discovery. Philosophical fieldwork entails engagement with distant peers—people at the margins—for whom deliberation still forms part of their social and political imaginary.

This engagement must go beyond "mere reading, insofar as it proceeds on the basis of familiar background assumptions[, which] may reinforce rather than challenge settled philosophical intuitions" (Flikschuh 2014, 15). As philosophers primarily working through the medium of the written word, we are involved in philosophical fieldwork when we engage with thinkers whose medium of discourse is predominantly oral or nonphilosophical, in the sense of academic philosophy, to sharpen our reflection on practices with normative significance.

Unlike the sort of engagement privileged by ethnographers, engagement in the sense I mean here is not meant to record practices but to interrogate reality collectively. And the aim is to bring assumptions of written modern African philosophy about concepts and their normative content into dialogue with our distant peers. As already hinted, these peers are so described because of differences in terms of methods of reflection. Philosophical fieldwork guarantees access to the epistemic resources embedded in the concept of public deliberation because it enables engagement with distant peers embedded in three domains of the practice of deliberation: imagination of the concept in kgotla, imbizo, and izu.

From this engagement, important insights emerge regarding the meaning attributable to the current experience of public deliberation. These insights culminate in a revision of belief in public deliberation as a means for the negotiation of power in relation to the structures of the state. Rather than being looked on as a practice aimed at the realization of consensus as noted by modern African philosophers, public deliberation manifests for peers steeped in its imagination as kgotla, imbizo, and izu as a site for the enactment of agency aimed at combating the stifling ignorance and ahistorical stance of state institutions. Its aim is no longer essentially to attain consensus but to enable communities and individuals to defend themselves against unilateral impositions by the state.

The salient epistemic resource that emerges through philosophical field-work is the discovery that emphasis on agency now constitutes the main value of political life. Epistemic resources—like free speech, equal and substantive representation, participation, and discussion—aim to ensure that agency is enacted and realized as a core value of political life. The relevant meaning of deliberation emerging from imaginative competence is thus the idea that agency is the main value of political life. A contemporary African political philosophy derived from analysis of African public culture—deliberation—must take as its core the exploration of this current meaning of the concept of public deliberation. In other words, such a philosophy ought to be built on the idea of agency as the central value of political life. In chapter 8, I explore the implication of this view. In the meantime, I continue with explication of how the other steps of conceptual creativity apply to the concept of public deliberation.

Abstraction fluidity is the step that enables us to fashion a principle from the epistemic resource accessed through imaginative competence. The aim of this step of conceptual creativity is to forge the concept accessed into an imagination unrestricted to a specific event and time. To this end, the relevant question to ask is the following: In what does the normative content that allows the extrapolation of agency as the core value of political life consist? To answer this question, I focus on spelling out the disruptive effect of making agency the main value of political life. This disruptive effect will operate in two dimensions—firstly, the conventional construal of deliberation in modern African philosophy that renders its normative content innocuous and, secondly, the current mode of politics that breeds political failure.

The change of framework for imagining meaning in politics must be disruptive in the two senses because it is the way to strip the new concept proposed of any pretensions that it is a unique African concept. This is necessary to free up the normative force of the concept, making it thereby a potent category for contemplation of the challenge of political failure as a manifestation of the human condition. Without this move, the proposed concept will be unable to explain African political experience in its current form, given that the experience is a phenomenon encompassing an array of factors of every conceivable provenance.

Regarding modern African political philosophy, the proposed understanding that agency is the core of political life is disruptive in the sense that it displaces the centralization of consensus as the framework for imagining the meaning of political life in the African context. African philosophers, such as Wiredu, Wamba dia Wamba, Bidima, and a number of more recent commentators that follow Emmanuel Eze's lead in critiquing consensus democracy, take consensus as the framework for imagining political life. This means they are either invested in articulating ways to demonstrate that consensus is a justified ideal of politics, or they essay to disprove this conclusion. Given this, it is disruptive for the discourse to postulate that agency constitutes the core framework for imagining meaning in politics. As noted, this disruption is necessary to free the normative force of the concept proposed.

To see how this freeing up of normative force occurs here, we need to pay attention to the innocuousness of the discourse on consensus. Generally, the structural problems that arise for any attempt to institutionalize consensual democracy in Africa today renders the theory of consensus democracy innocuous. In other words, cogent concerns about practical relevance limits the currently available articulation of the sort of political philosophy conceivable on the foundation of African public culture—public deliberation. The second kind of disruption introduced by the imagination of public deliberation in terms of agency relates to the possibility of altering the current mode of politics in the continent through the proposal advanced.

How does the postulation of agency as the core framework for imagining meaning in political life constitute a disruptive force in the current mode of politics in Africa? The agency framework constitutes a disruptive force for reasons that can be brought together under the umbrella idea of collective ownership of politics. By this idea it is implied that there are ways meaning and the capacity to exercise agency reinscribe vigor into politics in contemporary Africa, transforming in the process currently prevalent feelings of powerlessness on the part of individuals about their social and political circumstances.

Hypothesizing through analogy is a way to determine new parameters that should shape theorizing in view of the changed imagination of deliberation. This step of conceptual creativity answers the following question: In what light or parameters should rethinking the concept of public deliberation in terms of agency proceed? What should be our guide in deriving a new normative content from the idea of deliberation in the context we are exploring? The goal of this step is to merge previous and current parameters that shape the imagining of the sense of public deliberation. Given that previous parameters emphasized consensus as the foundation for the conceptualization of deliberation but the current manifestation of African public culture emphasizes agency as the main value of political life, how should we merge the two parameters of meaning making? In my view, we can do this by framing experience as a continuum.

Political experience in Africa is a continuum in the sense that political events occur for specific human beings who persist through time. Differences between epochs of history and their frameworks for meaning making in politics notwithstanding, the subject implicated remains the same. As such, the parameters of the different epochs merge in the consciousness that the subject of political experience has about political reality. The experience of powerlessness constitutes the uniting point of previous and current parameters of imagination of the meaning of public deliberation because powerlessness constitutes the consciousness of Africans about their social and political reality. It is thus the experience of powerlessness that should be taken as the center of attempts to conceptualize a new form of political philosophy in this context.

Concerning contextual independence, the essential point to note is that deliberation in the form determined through the preceding steps of conceptual creativity covers the horizon of the past, present, and future. The imagination that agency is the core of public deliberation is context independent precisely because it enables us to reflect on the concept as a category of explanation that deals with the human condition as such. That is, it enables us to reflect on the experience of political failure as a manifestation of human experience devoid of any essentialist presuppositions about the people implicated or as restricted to a specific epoch of history and society.

Thus, although the point of departure is a reflection on a specific experience having to do with what I called the phenomenon of political failure, and although the possibility of finding an answer is through the normative resource found in the context it manifests, there is no assumption that the theory one arrives at cannot be a universal theory. The theory is context independent in the sense that it constitutes a reflection on the human condition as such—that is, as a fact of existence experienced everywhere in different shapes and forms.

Having determined that conceptual creativity yields the understanding that agency is the core framework for meaning making in politics, it is pertinent to ask why it matters that this should be the case. In other words, why should agency be a core value of the conception of political public culture today? Is it because of changes in social, economic, and cultural spheres or due to something that is totally different? The answer I offer is that, by putting agency at the center of normative political theorizing, the logic of conformity to the community, which is expected of individuals in a context where deliberation is public culture, is inverted.

This inversion is essential to revise assumptions about the concept of public deliberation that do not have purchase in the present circumstances in Africa. In a context defined by the experience of political failure, clinging to consensus as the framework to imagine the most relevant value of political life lacks normative potential. This is the reason for the turn to agency as the relevant value for the contemplation of meaning in politics. Against this backdrop, I turn in the next chapter to discussion of the core proposal of agency as the core value in the imagination of meaning in political life. This will enable us to see the concrete way a reimagined conception of public deliberation deals adequately with the challenge of political failure.

EIGHT

—ɯ—

DELIBERATIVE AGENCY AND MEANING IN POLITICS

KWASI WIREDU (1980, 30) WAS perceptive in his observation that "the African youth, more or less bereft of the securities of tradition orthodoxies, stands in need of a new philosophy. . . . But, what philosophy should the modern African live by?" In this chapter, I attempt to respond to this perplexing situation aptly articulated by Wiredu. My goal is to consider in detail the claim that agency should constitute the main value of political life. This will be done through a two-tiered analysis. The first is to conceptualize the basic principle that expresses the claim advanced—namely, that the main value of political life should be agency. The second is to demonstrate the concrete implication of the principle. This means to show how the principle advanced tackles the challenge of political failure. As we saw in chapter 7, deliberation currently manifests as the site for contestation and negotiation with the state.

This change in meaning implies that the concept of public deliberation is predominantly a practice that allows people to situate themselves in relation to one another and, collectively, in contestation with the postcolonial state. For this reason, agency constitutes the main value of political life because it offers a replacement for consensus, which previously constituted the ideal of deliberation. The aim of the two-tiered analysis I pursue is therefore to explain the notion of this agency that crystalizes into a modern African political philosophy capable of resolving the challenge of political failure.

To begin the first task of elucidating the idea that the main value of political life should be agency, it is necessary to take note of the context of this claim. As we saw in the previous chapters, the experience of political failure is related to cognitive disorientation and normative instability. Given this, the question to ask is whether imagination of the sort of ideal we seek in this chapter is possible—that is, whether it is possible to develop an ideal of political life that takes agency as the core in a context that has the credentials noted about political failure. Raising this question amounts to asking whether imagination of a political ideal worth pursuing is possible while living under the nonideal circumstances resulting from political failure.

EXPERIENCE OF COGNITIVE DISORIENTATION
AND CONSTRUCTION OF POLITICAL IDEAL

If we take this question as an indication that context matters in the theories we develop about political experience, the point of contention becomes whether a context steeped in cognitive disorientation and apathy can make room for the construction of a worthwhile political ideal. Like Lear noted about the Crow experience of conceptual loss, the relevant issue in such a context is the possibility of imagining a meaningful way to live and act genuinely. For the African context, the problem is not whether imagination of a political ideal is possible, per se. The issue is the possibility of conceptualizing such an ideal using the conceptual resources available in this context.

This concern, I have argued, arises because the experience of colonization and other factors that negatively affected African conceptual resources did not lead to complete conceptual loss but rather cognitive disorientation. This means that what is needed is to stipulate how to recover and recast residual conceptual resources to function as building blocks in the construction of a contemporary political ideal. The discussion of how to make conceptual resources fit again for theory formation carried out in chapter 7 attended to this problem. There, I showed how conceptual residues can be transformed into tools we can use to conceptualize a viable political ideal.

Regarding deliberation, the issue is not whether the concept can be transposed from the so-called traditional African context to the contemporary situation. It is rather the way to recover a sense of the concept that has normative potential under current circumstances. Through one of the steps of conceptual creativity—namely, imaginative competence—it was determined that the sense of deliberation that has normative potential in the present circumstances puts agency at the core of deliberation. To answer, therefore, the question posed above, the issue at stake is to consider the nature of the agency postulated as the core of political life. What does this sense of agency mean, and what form of political philosophy does it enable us to articulate? Asking this question is the prelude to finding a resolution to the first task of this chapter—namely, to conceptualize the basic principle that expresses the claim that the main value of political life should be agency.

Agency is taken as the core of deliberation because it presents the means to leverage the imperfect leftovers to remake the political selves of individuals and communities in a nonideal circumstance. Imperfect leftovers refer to discarded conceptual tools used to imagine and regulate coexistence. As imperfect leftovers, these tools of cognition and the normative potential they embody are ascribed marginal significance by official political institutions. The destabilization of the African conceptual world and entrenchment of a new form of political organization that emerged from colonization led to a situation where public deliberation and its ideal of the pursuit of consensus came to assume a marginal significance.

Thus, postulating agency as the core of political life implies mounting a vigorous challenge to the marginality hoisted on public deliberation as a concept of political imagination. It is an assertion that a specific imagination of human individuals, not the formal apparatchik of state administration, should be at the core of politics. This move indicates a revision of belief ascribed to the concept of public deliberation. It points to the fact that belief in public deliberation is revised from being understood as a means to attain consensus to being seen as a practice of contestation. So what is the nature of this agency I urge should be the core of political life?

This agency should be understood as a claim that, as political beings, individuals are cocreators of meaning and purpose. It is an assertion that politics is a sphere of human action where individuals primarily exist in the mode that entails cocreating meaning and purpose. Through deliberative practices, the postcolonial state and its institutions are challenged to see politics as a sphere of action where the relevant actors—namely, individuals—are cocreators of meaning and purpose. Leaving aside for now the consideration of whether this idea is justified, let me consider the political philosophy we can imagine on the basis of the understanding that the core of political life ought to be agency that asserts that individuals are cocreators of meaning and purpose.

I would like to call this form of political philosophy deliberative agency. The principle of this political philosophy is the postulation that the ideal form of politics is one that advances a specific expression of what it means to be a person. In the sphere of politics, the necessary mode of self-expression that is true to the nature of human beings is the enactment of the capacity to cocreate meaning and purpose. To understand what this view entails, two points must be noted. One is that deliberative agency is a form of individual self-understanding located in the sphere of politics. This means that it does not

describe the kind of agent human beings should ideally become or are. Deliberative agency is concerned with the description of a value that ought to form
the core of political life.

The second issue is that the postulation of deliberative agency as the core of
political life is not contingent on a prior articulation of a robust conception of
a theory of agency. Because it is not meant to describe the type of agent human
beings should strive after or already should embody, the idea of deliberative
agency is not constrained by the absence of a robust theory of human agency.
This means that developing a robust theory of agency is not a prerequisite
for the postulation and explication of the nature of deliberative agency as an
imagination of the ideal of political life.

To fully understand the vision of politics deliberative agency embodies,
what is needed is to lay out its principle and spell out the imperative derivable
from the principle. Once this is achieved, the stage will be set for the justification of deliberative agency as a vision of political ideal—that is, justification
of why it is cogent to consider deliberative agency a political ideal in a context
where cognitive disorientation and its attendant political failure define political
experience. Below, I discuss accounts of deliberative agency as a political ideal
through analysis of different meanings we can infer from the thought that, in
the political sphere, the self-understanding of human beings is of necessity that
they are cocreators of meaning and purpose.

Doing this will enable us to determine the best conception of the meaning
of deliberative agency. Once we are able to establish the plausible understanding of deliberative agency, we can move on to two further tasks. One is to
conceive a justification of deliberative agency as the conception of the ideal
of politics in the context of our discourse—the current political situation in
Africa. The other is to discuss the implications of the principle. These two
tasks are meant to answer the following question: If we accept that the claim
of deliberative agency is a plausible, justified ideal of politics, what follows from
that acceptance?

I turn now turn to the first task: determination of the meaning of deliberative agency. At least three possible meanings of deliberative agency can
be imagined. The first is to see it as a specific form of governance. The second
possibility is to see it as a political morality. Thirdly, it can be understood as
an articulation of the structure of the sphere of politics as a separate sphere
of human action and existence. Let us consider separately what is germane to
these three ways to understand deliberative agency.

The first conception of the meaning of deliberative agency amounts to saying that this notion of a political ideal constitutes a form of governance where

primacy is placed on the ability of people to deliberate. This view is similar to Wiredu's idea of consensus democracy where emphasis is placed on how to establish a form of governance that prizes engagement in deliberation as a means to consensus. Understood this way, the meaning of deliberative agency inheres in the sorts of institutions it necessitates. This simply means that it reduces, in the end, to a conception of institutional arrangement based on the ideal of advancing the deliberative capacity of the political community.

The second perspective is a claim that deliberative agency is a way to evaluate politics. This is to say that it is a code of conduct for holders of political offices and the yardstick for assessing public policies. In this sense, one could say that deliberative agency is a principle that allows us to determine whether a public policy is morally right or wrong and whether holders of public offices act ethically.

The third view is essentially a proposal that deliberative agency is primarily an imagining of what politics ought to be, especially in a context with a specific debilitating experience. The goal of deliberative agency, according to this view, is not to tell us how to act or how to structure the daily affairs of governance. Instead, the concept reflects a correct understanding of the nature of political life for a context with a specific political history or experience.

To this end, deliberative agency is a signpost that clarifies the right direction political life ought to take. The reason is that it articulates the correct way to frame the understanding of politics as a sphere of human action. To make this claim is to suggest that politics is the work of individuals acting as partners in the pursuit of meaning making. To be cocreators of meaning means to take collective responsibility for the generation of meaning in politics. It means to see the task of collectively giving meaning to politics as a duty to be fulfilled through constant negotiation and contestation with structures of the state and with each other. I argue that the third option captures best the essence of deliberative agency. I return anon to consideration of this view. In the meantime, let me spell out why the first and second senses of deliberative agency are insufficient proposals.

The first and second perspectives on the meaning of deliberative agency do not capture accurately the ideal that the concept evinces. The first view misses the point because it conflates the concept with concrete practice. The consequence of understanding deliberative agency in terms of the first view is that what is at stake is no longer a search for the proper definition of an overarching meaning of politics as a sphere of human action that is shaped by specific experiences. Instead, the focus shifts to a quest to determine the details of a specific capacity—namely, deliberation and the sort of political practice it necessitates.

This perspective does not suffice because by merely saying that deliberative agency is a form of governance, nothing normative in terms of principles can be inferred. This is the case because normativity has to do with an imagining of what ought to be the case, which is to say it is not a description of a practice. Since deliberative agency is essentially a normative claim regarding what should be the core of political life, a perspective that explains its meaning from a nonnormative standpoint is inadequate. It is important to note that the argument is not that a system of governance based on deliberation is wrong. My point is different. It is that a nonnormative conception of deliberative agency is incapable of explaining the point of political life in the context discussed in this book.

The second view is also an insufficient account of the meaning of deliberative agency. This is the case because it reduces the ideal of politics embodied by deliberative agency to a moral prescription. Although deliberative agency makes a normative claim, it is not a rule of morality. The normative claim it makes is about the nature of politics as a sphere of human action. It is not about specific ways activities within this sphere of human action should be evaluated. To say, as the second account does, that we should understand deliberative agency as a method of evaluation of actions of political officeholders and public policy means to suggest that deliberative agency articulates a form of political morality.

The shortcoming of this view is that it reduces the scope of deliberative agency as a political ideal from being understood as a conception of the nature of the political sphere to being seen as a mere perspective on activities that take place in the political sphere. Given that perspectives on political morality can be inferred from our conception of the nature of the political sphere, it would amount to a reduction of the scope of deliberative agency to limit its possible meaning to political morality. Once a sufficiently broad view of the meaning of deliberative agency is achieved, it becomes clear the form of political morality recommended. Besides this shortcoming, other reasons must lead us to reject the second account of the meaning of deliberative agency. There is at least one more reason to reject the second account of deliberative agency noted above.

This reason is the consideration that the second account is logically incoherent and tells an incomplete story. The logical incoherence objection relates to the fact that the postulation of an account of political morality requires the prior justified notion of a political ideal to make sense. This is at least the case in the context discussed here because, as we saw earlier, the feature of political experience in Africa is political failure arising from cognitive disorientation. In such a situation, it will be logically incoherent to propose that the meaning of a reconstructed political ideal is that it is an expression of political morality.

The imperative in the situation is first and foremost to conceive a vision of the overarching aim of politics as a sphere of human action. It is only against this background that it is possible to determine how any formula of political morality validly applies. The second view, therefore, tells an incomplete story because the ideal of politics encapsulated in deliberative agency ought to take on board the feature of political experience in the context it addresses. Having made these points, I now focus below on the consideration of why the third account captures accurately the salient meaning of deliberative agency.

The third account of the meaning of deliberative agency is the most plausible account. To see why this judgment is correct, it is important to draw attention to the reason political ideals are conceived. What is the essence of thinking about politics in the light of ideals? There is a need to underscore that the sense of political ideal invoked here has nothing to do with what might be called the idealization of politics. This is to say that the imagination of the nature of African political experience and how to tackle the challenge it raises, which is the main question of this book, does not entail sidestepping reality in the interest of formulating a utopia Africans ought to aspire to achieve.

Given that the concrete experience of politics is the very foundation of the reflection in this book, the notion of ideal borne in mind is not divorced from the real-world situation of the context considered. By political ideal, I mean a sense of an overarching aim of politics—a sense of the nature of politics and what reflection on it ought to be about. Against this background, we can say that thinking about politics in light of ideals signals an engagement with the task of remaking our sense of the political, given the context-specific experiences of people. For the African context, the necessity to revise the sense of the political arises from experiences of normative instability, which are the consequence of the unsettling of the African conceptual world.

As such, deliberative agency is the imagination of the structure of the sphere of human action we regard as politics. It is an imagination that politics is a phenomenon whose nature entails the cocreation of meaning by individuals. Without the manifestation of the cocreation of meaning, this sphere of human action loses its intelligibility. It cannot be imagined as anything but that which necessarily presupposes the cocreation of meaning. The question is what this proposal concretely entails. What does it mean for a sphere of human action to be of this nature? How are we to understand this construction of the sense of the political? The answer I propose emerges from discussion of the basic human orientation to reality. To know what the construction of politics as deliberative agency implies, we ought to consider it as a construction of our basic orientation to a sphere of reality.

To know the world around us, we must be oriented toward it from a specific angle. For instance, we apprehend the world through the climatic seasons because we are oriented to the experience of the world through the feelings these seasons invoke in us. Winter, summer, autumn, and spring inspire specific imaginations about the world in people located in regions of the world where these divisions of climate obtain. The cold of the winter and heat of the summer lead people to orient themselves in specific ways to perceiving reality, and due to this perception, certain ways of dealing with reality follow suit. You do not just strive for ways to keep warm in the winter. You orient yourself to it in terms of an imagination that helps you to live through the feelings and twists and turns it invokes in you.

Although this is an imperfect analogy, the point I want to underscore is very simple. I want to emphasize through construal of the nature of the political sphere as deliberative agency that political life is of a definitive form due to our orientation to the world. But this orientation to the world is contingent on specific experiences that lead us to form certain imaginings regarding how to deal with reality. Having experienced political life as deliberation, both its manifestation as a given in traditional settings and its occlusion in the modern context, political life in the African context takes the form of a contestation in which the center is the exercise of agency in the form of the cocreation of meaning.

Normative instability premised on the experience of the destabilization of African conceptual resources recreates politics for this context to necessarily entail a form of dialectical cocreation of meaning. The understanding of political life as one in which the cocreation of meaning is central is, therefore, a perception of politics as inherently inflected by a specific form of contestation—namely, the struggle to create new meaning about a sphere of human life. From this emerges a proposal that the unity of all forms of action taken to constitute the core of political life consists in the cocreation of meaning. Where this collaboration manifests positively, the result is the entrenchment of conditions that enable people to thrive. Where the opposite outcome manifests, unsavory consequences follow in terms of conditions necessary for people to thrive.

DELIBERATIVE AGENCY AND POLITICAL FAILURE

Given this conception of deliberative agency, the question to ask is, what should we do about the phenomenon of political failure? Asking this question is an invitation to determine the nature of the relationship between deliberative agency and the experience of political failure. Can deliberative agency help us deal with the challenge of political failure? The answer to this question emerges if we consider what the quest for an adequate orientation to politics means for a broken self. To consider this question is to ask whether it is possible for a broken self to create meaning. I suggest that the possibility of creating meaning for such a person necessitates reflection on the nature of agency in times of political failure. What is the nature of the agency of one who experiences cognitive disorientation? What would it mean to talk about agency in relation to such a person?

There are at least two possibilities here. One is to postulate and make recommendations on the basis of a nostalgic form of agency. The other is to postulate a balancing agency that is capable of bridging different systems of reality. Nostalgic agency can be described as a never-ending mourning of lost concepts. It is a form of agency mirrored in efforts aiming to recreate the past in ways that can respond to the changed context of existence. Essentially, it is *mourning of the indigenous* because it holds up the ideal of the indigenous context as a pivotal lesson for all of the future. The injunction of nostalgic agency is this: do not look beyond your past for therein lies redemption and the authenticity of hope. Nostalgic hope is the goal of nostalgic agency.

Its appeal is that it offers the subject of cognitive disorientation a hope that is premised on the victories of a world that obtained prior to the experience of cognitive disorientation. Rather than say to the subject of cognitive disorientation, "You did it in the past, so you can do it again concerning creating a conceptual system of meaning," nostalgic agency insists, "Because you did it in the past, you must hold on to it forever." This is the shortcoming of this approach. Nostalgic agency recommends that subjects of cognitive disorientation must resist being torn between contradictions because there is a reality that is appropriate to subjects of cognitive disorientation. This approach is inadequate because it denies a fundamental aspect of the subject's experience. It denies the dimension of this experience that has to do with the exhaustion of the past as such because the conceptual resources of the past no longer suffice as guides to apprehending reality.

To sidestep nostalgic agency, balancing agency proposes marrying the two worlds that subjects of cognitive disorientation confront: a past not free from blemish and a present not respectful of ideals of the past. This proposal is often couched in the language of finding a proper formula to resolve the covariance of the relationship between individuals and the community—that is, finding a resolution to questions regarding who among the two should have primacy. Sometimes, the proposal manifests in skepticism about such a formula, leading to suggestions that the relevant question ought not to be balancing the contest about primacy between individuals and community but reinforcement of rights and duties.

Regardless of the form it takes, the balancing agency view assumes that the experience of cognitive disorientation allows a break for contemplation. The issue, alas, is that this is not the case. The reality is that subjects of cognitive disorientation must find a way to engage the task of meaning making while still living with the reality of cognitive disorientation. Subjects of this experience are confronted with a situation similar to the case of Otto Neurath's (1944) sailors on the high sea with a leaking boat. They are a people whose challenge is to repair the boat while on the high sea to avoid sinking. That is the task. In this light, the postulation of a balancing agency is inadequate because there is already the reality of a conceptual mismatch that makes talk about two worlds unintelligible. There is no such thing as a world properly belonging to subjects of cognitive disorientation and another that is alien to them.

Both worlds belong to subjects of this experience because they perceive reality as a totality. In such a situation, there is no reason to assume there can be clarity about the different traditions such that one can appropriate what is useful in both traditions to conceive ways of engaging the balancing act. Everything is in a flux, which is to say that the imperative is to think beyond distinctions in terms of the traditions that necessitate the postulation of a balancing agency. The aim should be to create a new horizon of meaning making for the subject of cognitive disorientation. Creating such a horizon is possible through creative agency, through engagement with the reality of living with contradictions.

The exercise of creative agency is like recycling, which is an imagination of sustainability through resilience. In recycling, discarded bottles can be used as materials for creating new bottles. However, this does not suppose that the new product is necessarily similar to the old one. In addition, the practice of recycling shows that it is not necessarily the case that only old bottles can be used as the core material for creating new bottles. It is perfectly possible to create bottles with anything that already exists. Most importantly, though, creative agency proposes to subjects of cognitive disorientation that the way forward is to adopt the attitude of orientation to reality as a contradiction. Orienting oneself to reality as a contradiction is neither an aberration nor cynicism. It is instead a resolute conviction that hope, in contexts such as the one the subject of cognitive disorientation must live through, inheres in having faith in the power of human imagination.

However way colonialization and the other factors responsible for entrenching cognitive disorientation operated, they did not succeed in killing imagination. On this basis, creative agency proposes to the subject of cognitive orientation that having faith in human imagination is the best way to approach reality while going through this experience. This amounts to an injunction that subjects of cognitive disorientation ought to accept as a necessary part of the human condition the reality of living in between nostalgias and with contradictions—where what was is no longer possible and what could become is not yet a reality, where what is in their best interest is not what they often choose to do but what they do is not always irrational. In this regard, the factors defining political failure are interpreted as more than mere deficiency of the subjects of those experiences. Instead, they are the outcomes of uncertainty bred by an absence of the security normally provided by an intact conceptual scheme.

The principle of orientation to reality as contradiction can be stated as follows: act in a way that is aligned with the true nature of your reality. Knowing that one's reality is shaped by contradictions, one ought to act in alignment with this understanding. The implication is to strive always to act in a way that truly recognizes the challenge posed by the situation. For someone whose reality is shaped by contradictions, acting in full cognizance of this reality means to rely on one's companions as equal partners in the struggle for the creation of meaning. It means to recognize that though no single individual subjected to the experience of cognitive disorientation has answers to the problem, having faith in the possibilities of collective effort could yield unexpected, fruitful results.

As cocreators of meaning, the subjects of cognitive disorientation rely on each other to transcend the debilitating normative instability they experience. They collaboratively overcome deficiencies of a destabilized conceptual scheme by asserting, first, that the potential of human imagination is at core indestructible and, second, that since imagination survives all attempts to obliterate its potential, there is always a possibility for the creative remaking of any given people's tools of cognition to respond to the challenge of normative instability. This is, in essence, to say that orienting oneself to reality as a contradiction is a learning process. It is a move away from the performance of collective oppression and sympathetic gaze on each other as adequate responses to the experience of cognitive disorientation. It is a move toward the embrace of adopting a way of being in the world fixated on reshaping reality to enable *becoming*, in the sense of bringing forth a new form of existence as a more viable response to the situation.

One might wonder whether this is enough—that is, whether, indeed, this orientation to reality is not another form of paralysis. The reason for this uncertainty is the absence of a positive command in deliberative agency regarding the concrete action to undertake to mitigate cognitive disorientation and restore symmetry to the political sphere. This is certainly justified. After all, the challenge of political failure is so paralyzing that any attempt to tackle it must point out how to redirect politics in the African context. Taking seriously the dire consequences of political failure presented at the outset of this book lends support to this view. Like we saw in chapter 1, the consequence of political failure is unsavory, implying in most cases a risk to life and limb. To this end, the argument that a concrete plan of action needs to emerge from consideration of this issue is understandable.

Although I grant all this, it is important to be circumspect about hurried attempts to make this kind of move. I already argued that the challenge of political failure should not be reduced to an issue to resolve through reliance on what I called in chapter 1 a problem-solution logic. The reason, I suggested, is the specific nature of the challenge of political failure. Understood properly, the experience of political failure demands a conception of an orientation to politics that responds adequately the challenge of cognitive disorientation, which breeds normative instability. It requires thinking holistically about the domain of politics as a sphere of human action. It means thinking about this issue without aiming to infer specific actions, such as a command to build institutions, infrastructure, or a vibrant economy. To be meaningful, these activities require a conception of the overarching vision of the nature of the political. Thus, articulating an overarching goal of politics is the adequate goal to pursue in attempting to respond, from a philosophical perspective, to the challenge posed by political failure.

Besides, recognizing the magnitude of the challenge posed by political failure implies that one ought to be humble about the potentials of a theory to magically change the situation. The argument that adopting an orientation to reality as a contradiction is meant to underscore this point because it is an invitation to be mindful of the value of relying on one's companions as cocreators of meaning and sense of purpose. It is just in the nature of human response to tragedies to turn to this approach to dealing with reality.

As we can imagine, in times of confrontation with a tragedy defying comprehension through the lenses of a community's mode of thinking, the natural response is to turn to each other as agents of meaning making. It is natural for people in situations of tragedy to band together to collectively share their stories, fears, and hopes to make sense of what they are experiencing. They do so not because any of them believes that a member of the community has all the answers sought to explain the tragedy confronted. They do so because of a firm conviction that the imaginative capacity of all the members of the community can contribute, however imperfectly, to the task of making sense of the situation.

We, of course, know that there are limitations to what each person can offer in terms of imagination. This is certainly true and decipherable if we consider instances when we were mistaken in our assumptions. As a result, the challenge is to consider what we can really hope to gain by relying on other subjects of cognitive disorientation to create meaning in politics. It is the realization that, individually, we are all limited in terms of the power of our imagination that makes it vital for us to rely on others as cocreators of meaning in dealing with political failure. The nature of political failure necessitates this orientation because it entails an absence of clarity about what should form the core of political life. This problem, surely, will persist if people do not talk to and listen to each other. This is the case because meaning emerges through engagement with others living through the experience of political failure.

By challenging each other and striving together to produce meaning in the sphere of politics, subjects of cognitive disorientation do not only transcend the normative instability driving political failure but also develop an attitude that is essential to the establishment of social solidarity. Rather than focus exclusively on imagining politics as something external to individuals, they, by this means, rededicate themselves to interpersonal interaction as a fertile ground of politics. Looked at this way, the failure of an action in the political sphere becomes not a matter occurring in a separate realm of reality but a failure of real human beings one is engaged with in a web of interaction. This is what will enable subjects of cognitive disorientation to transcend the despondency that results from the bifurcation of survival and the exercise of political agency. This is the means by which they can sharpen each other's political alertness as they create a form of moral sensibility necessary for developing the motivation to act appropriately. We can understand this issue better when we consider the justification of the proposal advanced.

The question to ask, therefore, is as follows: Why is deliberative agency, as an ideal of politics, justified? In other words, why is the nature of politics proposed by this view acceptable? The question of justification is necessary because it presents the ground for the acceptance of the proposition advanced under the umbrella of deliberative agency. At this juncture, we should recall the sense in which deliberative agency is a conception of the overarching goal of politics. This will enable us to have a sense of its plausibility. Deliberative agency is an ideal of politics because it is an articulation of the nature of politics in a context with specific experience.

By envisioning the nature of politics in the context of political failure, deliberative agency embodies a view of politics as a sphere where human beings can enact meaningful action or create meaning. When we recall that the core of political failure is a lack of meaning in politics, then it becomes clear the grounds on which deliberative agency is a plausible articulation of the nature of politics. To be meaningful, politics ought to be a sphere of human action where individuals are cocreators of meaning. This is the concrete proposal of deliberative agency. Given this, the question of justification relates to the reason we should accept that politics should be a sphere of action where individuals are cocreators of meaning. Why should we accept this view? That is the question of justification to address.

The proposition is justified because it captures the condition for the re-creation of meaning in a context challenged by meaninglessness in politics. It provides the foundation that allows for the generation of meaning and purpose. This foundation relates to the transcendence of agential paralysis through the recognition of each other as bearers of imagination that could be put to use in generating meaning. This means to propose that politics is a sphere of human action, not an alien behemoth far removed from individuals. Because individuals are cocreators of meaning, politics becomes a form of action that demands individual conviction. This implies that adopting an orientation to politics as contradiction is, first and foremost, a duty of the individual person.

Relating to the sphere of reality regarded as politics as a contradiction enables one to recreate the symmetry occluded by normative instability. Thus, a failure to act in accordance with the principle of action derived from deliberative agency, described as creative agency, is a personal dereliction of duty to be true to oneself by aligning one's action to the true nature of one's situation. Based on this explanation, deliberative agency is a justified conception of the ideal of politics in the context considered. The proposition is justified both necessarily and sufficiently. The necessary justification consists in the fact that deliberative agency provides a possibility of meaningful action in a situation where meaning is occluded. The idea is sufficiently justified because deliberative agency shows how we can overcome the agential paralysis that is the core of the experience of political failure.

Even with these clarifications, there remains confusion about whether the proposition of the idea of deliberative agency does not imply that there is only one way to conceive the nature of political life. In other words, does the suggestion of this view not imply an assumption that politics in the African continent is the same everywhere and, thus, that a unilateral solution applies to the political problems across the continent? This would be a mistaken understanding of the goal of this book. The reason is that arguing for a perspective on how to deal with political failure is not an attribution of uniformity to the entire spectrum of the political experience of disparate groups.

The point of deliberative agency is to underscore the unifying dimension of the different experiences of political failure. As I have argued, the unity of the different experiences of political failure in Africa inheres in the inertia it induces in individuals regarding the social and political conditions shaping their lives. As such, the solution I advocate addresses the crisis of meaning behind this inertia. Thus, my argument that deliberative agency is an appropriate response to the situation of political failure is therefore not an argument that there is only one way to understand the nature of political life in all of Africa. Deliberative agency is an attempt to make a case for a perspective that is viable given the circumstance of political failure.

DELIBERATIVE AGENCY: MATTERS ARISING

An objection against this explanation could be that deliberative agency is not the most viable option available to address the challenge of inertia. Activism, for instance, can be taken to constitute a better chance of overcoming the inertia. The claim would be that, instead of adopting the perspective of orienting oneself to reality as contradiction and acting in accordance with the principle of creative agency, what we need to do is to engage more in activism because it has greater potentials to lead to practical results. In fact, the argument could be stretched further to mean that such proposals as the one articulated through the idea of deliberative agency are perfect examples of how theory actively impedes practical action.

Responding to the objection requires us to do more than suggest that activism needs to first articulate a vision of the world it seeks to create. We cannot merely respond to this objection by suggesting that deliberative agency supplies the vision of a world and is, as such, the important first step for a viable engagement in activism. An appropriate response must explain the relationship assumed to exist between theory and praxis in deliberative agency. Does this theory also assume a bifurcation of theory and praxis?

The proposal of deliberative agency does not assume a bifurcation of theory and praxis. In fact, deliberative agency aims to show that the assumption of a bifurcation between theory and praxis becomes spurious once we delineate correctly the nature of political life in a situation of political failure. The reason is that political failure does not admit of dichotomies. Everyone in the context it manifests is affected. It should be clear from the explanation of deliberative agency above that the concept does not aim to address current African political experience in the fashion of previous attempts described in chapter 1 as beholden to the problem-solution logic. Deliberative agency begins with recognition of the fact that distinctions between an "us" and a "them" do not apply in the situation of political failure. This is to say that the political problem Africa confronts in the present century cannot be properly understood through the prism of dichotomies.

For instance, it is not a problem of the elites and masses; nor is it a divergence of interest between capitalists and proletariats. It is not an issue of differences between Christians and Muslims; nor is it a consequence of a mismatch of spiritual empires of world religions and local fiefdoms of the nonproselytizing indigenous African religions. In fact, it is not a problem arising from incongruousness of indigenous ways of knowing and imported ways of doing or, to put it differently, an incommensurability of African modes of being and foreign ways of life. As already indicated, however nice and psychologically soothing these dichotomies are, they do not get to the heart of the matter. And the reason is that human beings perceive reality as one single occurrence. The subject of cognitive disorientation, whose challenge of inertia is addressed by the postulation of deliberative agency, perceives reality as one single occurrence. The implication thus is that events occur in that subject's world as a continuum, the dichotomies included.

The proposal of deliberative agency avoids the allure of dichotomies, which is not the case for an exclusive focus on protest as a means of dealing with the current political reality in Africa. By suggesting cocreation of meaning as the core of political life, deliberative agency moves beyond thinking in the mode of dichotomies. This is because its construction of the nature of the sphere of reality called politics already involves the integration of an intersubjective aspect. I cannot validly accept the conception of politics implied by deliberative agency and at the same time fail to recognize the necessity of *an other*. Both the dimension of the self and that of others are intertwined. There is, however, another dimension of deliberative agency that demonstrates its immunity to the objection that it impedes practical action. This has to do with the fact that deliberative agency cuts in two directions—namely, the inward and outward directions.

By recommending that people experiencing cognitive disorientation should adopt an orientation to politics as contradiction, deliberative agency demands two-dimensional action. One aims at the individual and the other at external reality. It requires of the individual to see her or his experience as personal, not an occurrence that is wholly external. At the same time, it requires a collective pursuit of structural and nonstructural changes that will enable the creation of new meaning.

The individual must, therefore, simultaneously act in two ways—on oneself and with others. This is essential because it is only when we are able to act in this manner that we can develop the sort of attitude to reality that will guarantee success. Without making the changes required at the personal level, one will be ill prepared for the task of acting in concert with others. The opposite is also the case because focusing exclusively on outward-oriented action does not produce the disposition necessary to realize personal transformation. Both are required by the orientation to reality as contradiction.

Even if it is accepted that deliberative agency does not impede practical action, should this point be taken to mean it is better than activism in responding to the current political problem in Africa? After the experience of the Arab Spring in North Africa and similar social-media-driven protests in Africa, it has become pretty obvious that modern forms of activism in the continent are powerful. Not only are people able to organize collective action from the safe spaces of their homes both in Africa and overseas; there is also the sheer efficiency of reaching out to millions in real time.

Thus, why would it not suffice to argue that activism is the best way to tackle current political problems in Africa? Why should we seek another explanation, given especially that social media puts the youth whose future is at stake at the center? There are two reasons it will not suffice to say activism is a sufficient response to the experience of political failure. First, activism relies on an unsustainable dichotomy incapable of dealing with the magnitude of the challenge. Secondly, the response of activism is one-dimensional. It is a response focused on realizing desirable virtues without understanding the role of vices in the overall political experience in question.

In general, it is necessary to construct an us-versus-them dichotomy to ensure that activism leads to envisaged goals. One could argue that it is not always the case that activism has to rely on dichotomies demonizing others. The dichotomy could simply entail the separation of evil and good. It could, for instance, be a dichotomy between society and thieves or natural disasters and the entire community. The issue is that political activism does not thrive on this sort of dichotomy. Politically oriented activism aims to reform institutions and general political praxis in a given context.

This should at least constitute a desirable ideal for any political form of activism worth its salt. Thus, it relies on the construction of a dichotomy between an us and a them. In some instances, this might entail the separation of political institutions from the people in a given society so that the people can combat institutions to change them. The problem with this approach is that the dichotomy assumes too much about the separating lines between the people and their institutions. This is a false assumption that removes from the equation the necessity of action on oneself as the prerequisite for attaining real change. This is precisely why activism does not bring real and lasting changes but mostly admirable changes here and there. Real and lasting changes of the sort required to tackle the problem of political failure can only emerge when both the personal and outward dimensions of action form part of the equation defining political orientation.

The second issue is rather straightforward. Suggesting activism as an approach to deal with the challenge of political failure amounts to sidestepping the need to understand the role of vices in the experience of political failure. By vices here, I mean the cognitive habits bound up with cognitive disorientation. Without dealing with these vices, it is impossible to see the difference between what is merely rational and what is reasonable. As discussed earlier, it was rational for Africans to conceive survival as the very end of existence after the experience of the evils of wars and economic catastrophes induced by the imposition of structural adjustments by one of the world's unholy trinity, the IMF. Abandoning other concerns to focus on the pursuit of survival was rational because it was a logical step. This is just like someone responding to pain by running away from it.

But sometimes, such a logical step might not be the best decision. The reasonable thing might require us to face certain discomforts with equanimity and grace. If we respond to the challenge of political failure only through activism, it becomes impossible to understand the role of the vices that sustain the current status quo. This might mean that we will be back to where we started because, rather than change, these vices could just reconstitute themselves in different ways to give an inkling of change. These two reasons make imperative the need to adopt the proposal of deliberative agency instead of activism as the solution to the challenge of political failure. This is certainly not to say that activism is bad or useless. The point is that, as a political form of action, activism is an insufficient approach to tackling the problem of political failure. At least, this is the case compared to the proposal of deliberative agency, which in my view is the path to a better future in Africa.

EPILOGUE

MY MATERNAL GRANDMOTHER, EKAERU OMADA, was an accomplished woman bestowed with one of the highest titles in our part of the world. Ekaeru was also a poet and an admired singer. The refrain of one of the songs she cherished and sang goes: "A government that has hands but no legs is about to walk, to make progress. A people who have hands but no legs about to walk? This progress is a disease!" Whether this was her own song, in the sense that she authored it, I do not know. What I know, however, is that she responded with the song to the confusions and contradictions she would quite frequently observe about the modern governance she had to confront. She would often quip, "Uwa kporo isi na ana" ("The world is confused"), before she sang this song. As a child, I could not understand what she wanted to convey through this rather dramatic song. Somehow, though, I felt she felt seriously injured by all that the modern system of government represented. I imagine she was trying to deploy jest as a way to humanize her world, while dealing at the same time with the problem of not being able to understand. Of course, I say this with the hindsight of an adult who has taken a great deal of time to reflect on the goings-on in Africa.

Ekaeru knew intuitively that something did not add up in the space in which she lived. And she found new idioms to convey the paralysis resulting from this situation. Looking back, I now conceive her song, quoted above, as a reference to the fact that modern politics as she experienced it, although able to constrain individuals, lacks a normative foundation. With its metaphoric hands, the government controls the fate of individuals in this political space, although it lacks the metaphoric legs—foundations—upon which it can securely stand. This book is an attempt to address this problem—namely, how we should tackle the situation of political failure that emerges from the lack of normative roots of the modern forms of governance in Africa. The book is an attempt to find a way out of the quagmire created by the normative instability in modern African politics.

Menkiti was correct in his observation that normative instability breeds a serious problem of political disorder in Africa. If it is not clear why an action should be performed in the sense of the grounding of that particular way of doing things, the people compelled to perform that action for whatever reason cannot but feel disoriented. For a keen observer of politics in Africa, one thing that is clear is the need to understand why things are at a standstill—that is, why a debilitating sense of inertia characterizes everyday life in contemporary Africa. Certainly, people in the continent eat, drink, establish businesses and become rich, follow football games, plan for the immediate future, and so forth, just like people around the world do. However, there is a specific sense of emptiness, of lack of meaning, that is acutely felt in the continent.

In this book, I argued that the first challenge in conceiving a contemporary political theory that can respond to this situation in the continent is to find a way to name this experience of meaninglessness. As such, I argued that, in relation to political experience, we ought to understand the situation as a phenomenon of political failure. This refers to a situation in which individuals experience a peculiar form of powerlessness in relation to the social and political factors shaping their lives. I argued that this diagnosis is philosophical in the sense that it is a means through which we are put in a position to think of the whole, not just aspects of political experience in Africa. Given this way of naming the experience of meaninglessness confronting individuals in Africa, the question to ask is what it means and what ought to be done in terms of finding a solution.

Contextualization, I have shown, matters for any answer we proffer. Thus, the approach I suggested was to begin the search for an answer by analyzing the deficiencies that make positions advanced in extant literature on African social and political theory deficient. When we examine the different perspectives advanced in normative African political thought, a general deficiency we notice is the reliance on a specific form of logic in dealing with political challenges in Africa. Designating this logic as a problem-solution logic, I showed that the specific shortcoming of this approach is that its linearity and focus on linking causes to effects is incapable of helping us understand and resolve the problem posed by current political experience in Africa.

The attempt by sub-Saharan pan-Africanist thinkers and African political philosophers to respond to the challenge by retrieving and reconstructing concepts from the traditional African past is also insufficient. Although these thinkers approached this task in ways that were creative, the limitation of their answer inheres in the absence of clearly worked-out parameters regarding how to make African conceptual resources fit again for the task of theory formation. The reason it is important to ensure the reconfiguration of African conceptual resources is part of the answer we develop is because the long history of denigration and humiliation of the African person and most things African implies the delegitimization of African concepts as dependable tools to employ in knowing reality. Since concepts are the lenses through which we are able to experience, shape, and create reality, one whose conceptual resources are considered unreliable ways to know reality is indeed placed in a difficult situation.

The point of this argument, of course, is not to suggest that this situation obtains merely due to impositions by some sinister non-African groups. By coming into contact with other traditions of knowledge and seeing the clear limitations of African conceptual resources in terms of creating and interpreting this new reality, Africans have found themselves at a juncture where what they have in terms of conceptual resources is no longer sufficient. This is the reason people have resorted to either of two ways of dealing with reality— either wholesale return to original African ways as the answer or tenacious pursuit of full-scale Westernization. I showed why the two perspectives miss the point regarding the challenge posed by African political experience. They miss the point because people experience themselves as a continuum, and the challenge is to develop a new way of interpreting experience in a situation where concepts are in a flux.

Against this background, I argued that African conceptual resources, given the reality of life in contemporary Africa, have become destabilized. Thus, the most promising way to deal with the challenge of politics in this context is to work out the possible way to remake these conceptual resources in the interest of accomplishing what can be regarded as existential repair. To this end, I developed the idea of conceptual creativity as a method of political philosophy in a context where conceptual destabilization defines experience. Following the steps of conceptual creativity, I developed an account of contemporary African political philosophy that is capable of helping us overcome the challenge posed by political failure. The account is a theory of deliberative agency, which is a reimagination of African political culture in its manifestation as public deliberation.

In a nutshell, the above is a cursory outline of the book. Given the current political climate in the world, it seems that there are general lessons to learn from the exploration in this book. I highlight three such lessons and point out the implication of my argument in this book that a viable political philosophy requires of us to develop an orientation to politics as a contradiction. These three lessons relate to the following: (1) imagination and politics, (2) new forms of tribalism, and (3) collective responsibility vis-à-vis cognitive damage.

In explaining how the destabilization of African conceptual resources informs current political experience in Africa, I made the remark that regardless of the way colonization manifested, it did not destroy human imagination. As such, rather than talk about complete conceptual loss regarding Africans, the appropriate reference would be conceptual destabilization—that is, the weakening of faith or trust in African conceptual resources as reliable ways of knowing, shaping, and creating new reality. When we look beyond this specific context, we can see the myriad ways the weakening of trust in extant conceptual resources manifest. In fact, the current political climate seems to me to suggest that anxieties about democracy in so-called advanced countries is related to uncertainty about the conceptual resources of these societies.

Recent developments have made people unsure about how to make sense of reality through the concepts available to them. People are unable to name what they experience socially and politically precisely because the concepts of democracy, human rights, and so on available to them seem inadequate to capture the goings-on. To this end, their faith in the available conceptual resources seems to have weakened. Just like we find in the African case, some attempt to respond to this situation by fighting to return to old ways of knowing, manipulating, and dealing with reality.

This, alas, is doomed because it does not lead to anything that is useful in the situation. Returning to a pre-"woke" world, a pre-"cancel-culture" world, and so forth is not only impossible but an unviable way to tackle this reality. Nonetheless, adopting a new, anterior approach to conceiving reality is also unviable because it will lack normative grounding. Thus, it has become imperative to ask questions about the way forward. I think having faith in the power of human imagination is the only way forward. This is the only way to engage in the creative refashioning of the conceptual resources of so-called advanced societies to make them fit again for the task of theory formation.

The second point I would like to make is about the current form of tribalism. It is no longer a secret that political tribalism currently constitutes one of the major challenges of politics in many parts of the world. To tackle this challenge, however, it seems to me that it will be insufficient to treat it as the outcome of social media echo chambers. To see why this is the case, one must simply ask why in the first instance there developed echo chambers that are so far apart in their perception of reality such that they could result in vicious political tribalism. I think the most viable approach is to conceive of the situation as a manifestation of cognitive disorientation of the sort I noted that afflicts Africans today.

Due to the perplexing situation of finding that the conceptual resources available to them have become inadequate to understand the new forms of political experience they must deal with, people turn to explanations that purport to offer new alternatives to conventional views. This is the reason faith in conspiracy theories, alternative facts, and so on is hardly shaken in the light of evidence showing they are wrong. People refuse to give up on these explanations precisely because they promise and offer alternative ways to deal with reality in a situation where available concepts have become unsuitable.

They will not give up on these alternative ways simply because someone has provided evidence to show they are wrong. So long as the evidence is articulated in the conceptual idioms they already know, and now find inadequate, they will continue to hold on to the alternative views. Thus, the thing to do is to attempt to reimagine central conceptual categories in this context to find new, adequate meanings of the idioms of politics as a sphere of human action. In this regard, the insights offered in this book about the African example could be instructive.

Finally, we ought to learn the lesson of cognitive damage to see why it is our collective duty to ameliorate and transcend it. Alternative facts, conspiracy theories, and related factors are currently operating to cause an implosion of the political self-understanding of many advanced democracies. Why is this the case? Drawing from the explorations in this book, an explanation we ought to take seriously is that these ways of orienting oneself to reality entail a form of gaslighting. The main problem gaslighting creates is to weaken confidence in our taken-for-granted orientation to reality. Thus, as a result of gaslighting propelled by alternative facts, conspiracy theories, and related factors, the conceptual resources of different groups are suffering gradual but serious damage. This can lead to cognitive damage because consistent, long-term doubt about an established orientation to reality blunts the power of concepts. This is the case regardless of whether the doubt is substantiated or not. What matters is for the momentum to be sustained. Cognitive damage is a situation where unviable concepts become internalized as veritable ways of "fighting back" against the changing circumstances that define one's experience of reality. The situation can get to a point where dialogue with those holding contrary but true perspectives becomes impossible.

As I have argued elsewhere (Okeja 2019), this experience is neither new nor restricted to current political experience in the West. In fact, the situation does not arise because of one single factor, like the attempt to push back against one's changing circumstances. In the African context, for example, the main factor that is behind the experience of cognitive damage is the attribution of universality to Western ideas and concepts. Because universality is assumed to inhere in Western ideas and concepts, they are superimposed on African reality. In a sense, colonization can be seen as a *conceptual adjustment program*.

Africa and other colonized places encountered colonization basically as a form of conceptual adjustment program. For instance, in terms of the law, colonization sought to adjust Africans conceptually by replacing the rule by customs that existed prior to colonization with rule by written laws. Concerning social life as represented by marriage, the aim was to conceptually adjust Africans by moving them from conjugal relations defined by polygamy to one that is shaped by monogamy. So too we find with religion. Here, the aim was to move Africans from the conceptual organizing principle of polytheism to monotheism. This experience led to the destruction of the normative foundations of social, cultural, economic, and political life in this context.

This is part of the reason Africans find themselves in a situation of cognitive disorientation, which is complicating agency in politics and others spheres of life. Given that every society can be afflicted by this epistemic vice, there is a collective responsibility to ameliorate or resolve the problem. And philosophers are particularly implicated in this task because they raise and discuss some of the most fundamental questions about reality. We can tackle the challenge by engaging in conceptual repair where the problem already exists, like in postcolonial societies, or by attempting to forestall the uncritical universalization and superimposition of our own concepts on others. We ought to note the overall value of conceiving and orienting ourselves to politics as contradiction. It is simply unreasonable to think that our cherished concepts that define our orientation to reality apply to all similar contexts. The essential thing is to always be alert to the sense in which we are all potential contributors to giving meaning to experience. Regarding politics, the orientation to reality as contradiction is necessary because we are cocreators of meaning.

BIBLIOGRAPHY

Achebe, Chinua. *Arrow of God*. London: Heinemann, 1964.

———. *Hopes and Impediment*. London: Heinemann, 1988.

———. *Things Fall Apart*. Oxford: Heinemann Educational Publishers, 1996.

Adejunmobi, Moradewun. *Vernacular Palaver: Imaginations of the Local and Non-native Languages in West Africa*. Clevedon, UK: Multilingual Matters, 2004.

Ajei, Martin. "Kwasi Wiredu's Consensual Democracy: Prospects for Practice." *European Journal of Political Theory* 15, no. 4 (2016): 445–466.

Ake, Claude. *Building on the Indigenous*. Accessed July 10, 2018. http://repository .uneca.org/bitstream/handle/10855/13951/Bib-55375.pdf?sequence=3.

———. *Democracy and Development in Africa*. Washington, DC: The Brookings Institution, 1996.

Ani, Emmanuel. "On Traditional African Consensual Rationality." *Journal of Political Philosophy* 22, no. 3 (2014): 342–365.

Appiah, Kwame A. *In My Father's House: African in the Philosophy of Culture*. New York: Oxford University Press, 1992.

Armstrong, Robert. "The Public Meeting as a Means of Participation in Political and Social Activities in Africa." In *Socio-Political Aspects of the Palaver in Some African Countries*, edited by UNESCO, 11–26. Paris: UNESCO, 1979.

Asouzu, Innocent. *Ibuanyidanda: New Complementary Ontology; Beyond World-Immanentism, Ethnocentric Reduction and Impositions*. Münster, Germany: Lit Verlag, 2007.

Atanga, Benoît. "Actualité de la Palabre?" *Revue Études* 324 (1966): 460–466

Awolowo, Obafemi. *Awo: The Autobiography of Chief Obafemi Awolowo*. Cambridge: Cambridge University Press, 1960.

Ayandele, Emmanuel Ayankanmi. *The Educated Elite in the Nigerian Society*. Ibadan, Nigeria: Ibadan University Press, 1974.

Ayittey, George B. N. *Indigenous African Institutions*. New York: Transnational Publishers, 2006.

Azikiwe, Nnamdi. "From Tribe to Nation: The Case of Nigeria." In *Themes in African Social and Political Thought*, edited by Onigu Otite, 274–280. Enugu, Nigeria: Fourth Dimension, 1978.

———. *Ideology for Nigeria: Capitalism, Socialism or Welfarism?* Lagos: Macmillan Nigeria, 1979.

———. *My Odyssey: An Autobiography*. New York: Praeger, 1970.

———. *Renascent Africa*. London: Frank Cass, 1968. First published in 1937 (Lagos).

Bell, Richard. *Understanding African Philosophy: A Cross-Cultural Approach to Classical and Contemporary Issues*. New York: Routledge, 2002.

Bello, A. G. A. "Some Methodological Controversies in African Philosophy." In *A Companion to African Philosophy*, edited by Kwasi Wiredu, 263–273. Malden, MA: Blackwell, 2004.

Bidima, Jean-Godefroy. *Law and the Public Sphere in Africa: "La Palabre" and Other Writings*. Translated by Laura Hengehold. Bloomington: Indiana University Press, 2014.

Bodunrin, Peter. "Philosophy in Africa: The Challenge of Relevance and Commitment." In *Postkoloniales Philosophieren: Afrika*, edited by H. Nagl-Docekal and Franz M. Wimmer, 15–39. Vienna: Oldenburg Verlag, 1992.

———, ed. *Philosophy in Africa: Trends and Perspectives*. Ile Ife, Nigeria: University of Ife Press, 1985.

———. "The Question of African Philosophy." *Philosophy* 56, no. 216 (1981): 161–179.

Bujo, Benezet. Wider den Universalanspruch westlicher Moral: Grundlagen afrikanischer Ethik. Freiburg: Herder, 2000.

Busia, Kofi A. *The Challenge of Africa*. London: Praeger, 1962.

Cabral, Amilcar. "National Liberation and Culture." *Transition* 45 (1974): 12–17.

———. *Return to the Source: Selected Speeches by Amilcar Cabral*. New York: Monthly Review, 1973.

———. *Revolution in Guinea: Selected Texts by Amilcar Cabral*. New York: Monthly Review, 1969.

Chabal, Patrick. *Africa: The Politics of Suffering and Smiling*. London: Zed Books, 2009.

Chabal, Patrick, and Jean-Pascal Daloz. *Africa Works: Disorder as Political Instrument*. Oxford: James Currey, 1999.

Chinweizu, Onwuchekwa Jemie, and Ihechukwu Madubuike. *Towards the Decolonization of African Literature: African Fiction and Poverty and Their Critics*. Washington, DC: Howard University Press, 1983.

Clark, Phil. *The Gacaca Courts, Post-Genocide Justice and Reconciliation in Rwanda: Justice without Lawyers*. Cambridge: Cambridge University Press, 2010.

Eboh, Marie P. "Democracy with an African Flair." *Quest: An International African Journal of Philosophy* 7, no. 1 (1993): 92–99.

Echeruo, Michael. "Nnamdi Azikiwe and Nineteenth-Century Nigerian Thought." *Journal of Modern African Studies* 12, no. 2 (1974): 245–263.

Ekeh, Peter. "Colonialism and the Two Publics in Africa: A Theoretical Statement." *Comparative Studies in Society and History* 17, no. 1 (1975): 91–112.

Erdmann, Gero, and Ulf Engel. "Neopatrimonialism Reconsidered: Critical Review and Elaboration of an Elusive Concept." *Commonwealth and Comparative Politics* 45, no. 1 (2007): 95–119.

Erumevba, J. T. "The Concept of African Brotherhood and Praxis of Unity: Nyerere Revisited." In *Philosophy in Africa: Trends and Perspectives*, edited by Peter Bodurin, 190–199. Ile-Ife, Nigeria: University of Ile-Ife Press, 1985.

Etounga-Manguelle, Daniel. "Does Africa Need a Cultural Adjustment Program?" In *Culture Matters: How Values Shape Human Progress*, edited by Lawrence E. Harrison and Samuel P. Huntington, 65–77. New York: Basic Books, 2000.

Eze, Emmanuel Chukwudi. "Democracy or Consensus? A Response to Wiredu." In *Postcolonial African Philosophy: A Critical Reader*, edited by Emmanuel Chukwudi Eze, 313–323. Cambridge: Blackwell, 1997.

Eze, Michael Onyebuchi. "What Is African Communitarianism? Against Consensus as a Regulative Ideal." *South African Journal of Philosophy* 27, no. 4 (2008): 386–399.

Flikschuh, Katrin. "The Arc of Personhood: Menkiti and Kant on Becoming and Being a Person." *Journal of American Philosophical Association* 2 no. 3 (2016): 437–455.

———. "The Idea of Philosophical Fieldwork: Global Justice, Moral Ignorance, and Intellectual Attitudes." *Journal of Political Philosophy* 22, no. 1 (2014): 1–26.

———. "Nkrumah's Philosophy in Action: Between Ideology and Ethnophilosophy." In *Disentangling Consciencism: Essays on Kwame Nkrumah's Philosophy*, edited by Martin Ajei, 93–112. Lanham, MD: Lexington Books, 2017.

———. *What Is Orientation in Global Thinking? A Kantian Inquiry*. Cambridge: Cambridge University Press, 2017.

Fortes, M., and E. E. Evans-Pritchard, eds. *African Political Systems*. New York: Paul Keagan, 1987.

Fourie, Pieter. "Ubuntuism as a Framework for South African Media Practice and Performance: Can It Work?" *South African Journal for Communication Theory and Research* 34, no. 1 (2008): 53–79.

Gyekye, Kwame. *An Essay on African Philosophical Thought: The Akan Conceptual Scheme*. Cambridge: Cambridge University Press, 1987.

———. "Person and Community in African Thought." In *Person and Community: Ghanaian Philosophical Studies I*, edited by Kwasi Wiredu and Kwame Gyekye, 101–122. Washington, DC: Council for Research in Values and Philosophy, 2004.

————. *Tradition and Modernity: Philosophical Reflection on the African Experience.*
   Oxford: Oxford University Press, 1997.

Hallen, Barry. *The Good, The Bad and The Beautiful: Discourse about Values in
   Yoruba Culture.* Bloomington: Indiana University Press, 2000.

Hallen, Barry, and J. Olubi Sodipo. *Knowledge, Belief, and Withcraft: Analytic
   Experiment in African Philosophy.* Stanford, CA: Stanford University Press, 1997.

Harrison, Lawrence E., and Peter Berger. *Developing Cultures: Case Studies.* New
   York: Routledge, 2006.

Harrison, Lawrence E., and Samuel P. Huntington, eds. *Culture Matters: How
   Values Shape Human Progress.* New York: Basic Books, 2000.

Helfrich, Ann. *Afrikanische Renaissance und Traditionelle Konfliktlösung: Das
   Beispiel der Duala in Kamerun.* Münster: Lit Verlag.

Helle-Valle, Jo. "Seen from Below: Conceptions of Politics and the State in a
   Botswana Village." *Africa* 72, no. 2 (2002): 179–202.

Helman, Gerald B., and Steven R. Ratner. "Saving Failed States." *Foreign Policy* 89
   (1992–1993): 3–20.

Herbst, Jeffrey. "Responding to State Failure in Africa." *International Security* 21,
   no. 3 (1996–1997): 120–144.

Hernaes, Per O. *Palaver: Peace or "Problem"? A Note on the "Palaver-System" on the
   Gold Coast in the 18th Century Based on Examples Drawn from Danish Sources.*
   Copenhagen: Center for African Studies Working Papers 1, 1988.

Hountondji, Paulin. *African Philosophy: Myth and Reality.* Translated by Henri
   Evans with Jonathan Ree. Bloomington: Indiana University Press, 1983.

Ibhawoh, Bonny, and J. I. Dibua. "Deconstructing Ujamaa: The Legacy of Julius
   Nyerere in the Quest for Social and Economic Development in Africa." *African
   Journal of Political Science* 8, no. 1 (2003): 59–83.

Idahosa, Pablo Luke Ehioze. "Going to the People: Amilcar Cabral's Materialist
   Theory and Practice of Culture and Ethnicity." *Lustopie* 9, no. 2 (2002): 29–58.

Irele, Abiola. "A Defence of Negritude." *Transition* 13 (1964): 9–11.

Iroegbu, Pantaleon. *Metaphysics: The Kpim of Philosophy.* Owerri, Nigeria:
   International Universities Press, 1995.

Janz, Bruce. *Philosophy in an African Place.* Lanham, MD: Lexington Books, 2009.

Jones, Ward. "Philosophers, Their Context, and Their Responsibilities."
   Metaphilosophy 37, no. 5 (2006): 623–645.

Jones, Ward, and Thaddeus Metz. "The Politics of Philosophy in Africa: A
   Conversation." *South African Journal of Philosophy* 34, no. 4 (2015): 538–550.

Kiros, Teodros, ed. *Explorations in African Political Thought: Identity, Community,
   Ethics.* New York: Routledge, 2001.

Lewis, Stephen R. "Explaining Botswana's Success." In *Developing Cultures: Case
   Studies,* edited by Lawrence E. Harrison and Peter Berger, 3–22. New York:
   Routledge, 2006.

Mair, Lucy. "Tradition and Modernity in the New Africa." *Transactions of the New York Academy of Sciences* 27, no. 4 (1962): 439–444.

Makinde, Akin M. "Teaching Philosophy in Africa." *Teaching Philosophy* 10, no. 3 (1987): 227–238.

Mamdani, Mahmood. *Citizen and Subjects: Contemporary Africa and the Legacy of Late Colonialism*. Princeton, NJ: Princeton University Press, 1996.

Masolo, Diamas. *Self and Community in a Changing World*. Bloomington: Indiana University Press, 2010.

Matolino, Bernard. *Afro-Communitarian Democracy*. Lanham, MD: Lexington Book, 2019.

———. "A Response to Eze's Critique of Wiredu's Consensual Democracy." *South African Journal of Philosophy* 28, no. 1 (2009): 34–42.

Maurier, Henri. "Do We Have an African Philosophy?" In *African Philosophy: An Introduction*, edited by Richard Wright, 25–40. Lanham, MD: University Press of America, 1984.

Mazrui, Ali. "The Blood of Experience: The Failed State and Political Collapse in Africa." *World Policy Journal* 12, no. 1 (1995): 28–34.

———. "Edmund Burke and Reflections on the Revolution in the Congo." *Comparative Studies in Society and History* 50, no. 2 (1963): 121–133.

———. "Ideology and African Political Culture." In *Explorations in African Political Thought: Identity, Community, Ethics*, edited by Teodros Kiros, 97–132. New York: Routledge, 2001.

———. "The World Bank, the Language Question and the Future of African Education" *Race and Class* 38, no. 3 (1997): 35–48.

Mbonu, Ojike. *My Africa*. New York: John Day, 1946.

Menkiti, Ifeanyi. "The Concept of a Person and Citizen, Lecture Delivered at the University of Chicago." Unpublished manuscript shared with the author, October 2017.

———. *Of Altair, the Bright Light*. Chelsea, MA: Earthwinds Editions, 2005.

———. "Person and Community in African Traditional Thought." *African Philosophy: An Introduction*, edited by Richard Wright, 171–182. Lanham, MD: University Press of America, 1984.

———. "Philosophy and the State in Africa: Some Rawlsian Considerations." *Philosophia Africana* 5, no. 2 (2002): 35–52.

Mkandawire, Thandika, and Charles Soludo. *Our Continent, Our Future: African Perspective on Structural Adjustment*. Dakar, Senegal: Council for the Development of Social Science Research in Africa, 1998.

Mouser, Bruce L. "The 1805 Forekariah Conference: A Case of Political Intrigue, Economic Advantage, Network Building." *History in Africa* 25 (1998): 219–262.

Neurath, Otto. *Foundations of the Social Sciences*. Chicago: University of Chicago Press, 1944.

Nkrumah, Kwame. *Consciencism: Philosophy and Ideology for Decolonization and Development with Particular Reference to the African Revolution*. New York: Monthly Review, 1965.

Nwala, Uzodinma. *Igbo Philosophy*. Lagos: Lantern Books, 1985.

Nyerere, Julius. *Ujamaa: Essays on Socialism*. Dar es Salaam, Tanzania: Oxford University Press, 1962.

Nzimiro, Ikenna. "Zikism and Social Thought in the Nigerian Pre-independence Period: 1944–1950." In *Themes in African Social and Political Thought*, edited by Onigu Otite, 281–301. Enugu, Nigeria: Fourth Dimension, 1978.

Odhiambo, Atieno E. S. "The Cultural Dimension of Development in Africa." *African Studies Review* 45, no. 3 (2002): 1–16.

Ojukwi, Odumegwu C. *Random Thoughts of C. Odumegwu Ojukwu General of the People's Army: Biafra*. New York: Harper and Row, 1969.

Okafor, Fidelis U. *Igbo Philosophy of Law*. Enugu, Nigeria: Fourth Dimension, 1992.

Okeh, Moses. "Modeling the Contemporary African Philosopher: Kwasi Wiredu in Focus." In *The Third Way in African Philosophy: Essays in Honour of Kwasi Wiredu*, edited by Olusegun Oladipo, 19–35. Ibadan, Nigeria: Hope Publications, 2002.

Okeja, Uchenna. "Justice through Deliberation and the Problem of Otherness." *Angelaki: Journal of the Theoretical Humanities* 24, no. 2 (2019): 10–21.

———. *Normative Justification of a Global Ethic: A Perspective from African Philosophy*. Lanham, MD: Lexington Books, 2013.

———. "On Kant's Duty of State Entrance." *Philosophy and Public Issues* 9, no. 3 (2019): 83–108.

———. "Palaver and Consensus as Metaphors for the Public Sphere." In *Oxford Handbook of Comparative Political Theory*, edited by Leigh K. Jenco, Murad Idris, and Megan Thomas, 565–579. Oxford: Oxford University Press, 2020.

———. "Space Contestation and the Teaching of African Philosophy in African Universities." *South African Journal of Philosophy* 31, no. 4 (2012): 664–675.

Okere, Theophilus. *African Philosophy: A Historico-Hermeneutical Investigation of the Conditions of Its Possibility*. Lanham, MD: University Press of America, 1983.

Oladipo, Olusegun. *The Idea of African Philosophy: A Critical Study of the Major Orientations in Contemporary African Philosophy*. Ibadan, Nigeria: Hope Publications, 2000.

Omotoso, Kola. "Expressing One Culture in the Language of Another." *Quest: An African Journal of Philosophy* 12, no. 1 (1998): 77.

Orizu, A. A. Nwafor. *Without Bitterness: Western Nations in Post-War Africa*. New York: Creative Age, 1944.

Orobator, S. E. "Tradition and Modernity in African Polity: Conflict or Co-existence?" *Africa: Rivista trimestrale di studi e documentazione dell'Istituto italiano per l'Africa e l'Oriente* 46, no. 2 (1991): 273–281.

Oruka, Odera. "Four Trends in African Philosophy." In *Philosophy in the Present Situation of Africa*, edited by Diemer Alwin. Wiesbaden, Germany: Franz Steiner Verlag, 1981.

———. *Sage Philosophy: Indigenous Thinkers and Modern Debate on African Philosophy*. Leiden, Netherlands: Brill, 1990.

Parson, Jack, ed. *Succession to High Office in Botswana: Three Cases*. Athens: Ohio University Center for International Studies Monograph Series, 1990.

p'Bitek, Okot. *African Religions in Western Scholarship*. Nairobi, Kenya: East African Literature Bureau, 1970.

Rawls, John. *A Theory of Justice*. Cambridge, MA: Harvard University Press, 1971.

Senghor, Leopold. "Negritude and African Socialism." In *The African Philosophy Reader*, edited by P. H. Coetzee and A. P. J. Roux, 438–448. London: Routledge, 1998.

Serequeberhan, Tsney. *The Hermeneutics of African Philosophy: Horizon and Discourse*. New York: Routledge, 1994.

Smet, A. J. "The Teaching of Philosophy in Africa: The Colonial Heritage." In *Teaching and Research in Philosophy: Africa*, edited by UNESCO, 81–88. Paris: UNESCO, 1984.

Sogolo, Godwin. "Options in African Philosophy." *Philosophy* 65, no. 251 (1990): 39–52.

———. "Philosophy and Relevance within the African Context." *Journal of Humanities* 2 (1988): 97–114.

Soyinka, Wole. *Myth, Literature and the African World*. Cambridge: Cambridge University Press, 1976.

Taiwo, Olufemi. "Post-Independence African Political Philosophy." In *A Companion to African Philosophy*, edited by Kwasi Wiredu, 243–259. Malden, MA: Blackwell, 2004.

Udo, Etuk. "Philosophy in a Developing Country." *Philosophy* 62, no. 239 (1987): 59–66.

Wamala, Edward. "Government by Consensus: An Analysis of a Traditional Form of Democracy." In *A Companion to African Philosophy*, edited by Kwai Wiredu, 435–442. Malden, MA: Blackwell, 2004.

Wamba dia Wamba, Ernest. "Experiences of Democracy in Africa: Reflections on Practices of Communalist Palaver as a Method of Resolving Contradictions among the People." *Philosophy and Social Action* 11, no. 3 (1985): 5–23.

———. "Pan-Africanism, Democracy, Social Movements and Mass Struggles." *African Journal of Political Science* 1, no. 1 (1996): 9–20.

wa Thiong'o, Ngugi. *Decolonizing the Mind: The Politics of Language in African Literature*. Nairobi, Kenya: East African Educational Publishers, 1986.

Wiredu, Kwasi. "Brief Remarks on Logical Positivism." In *The Way in African Philosophy: Essays in Honour of Kwasi Wiredu*, edited by Olusegun Oladipo, 315–340. Ibadan, Nigeria: Hope Publications, 2002.

———, ed. *A Companion to African Philosophy*. Malden, MA: Blackwell, 2004.

———. *Cultural Universals and Particulars: An African Perspective*. Bloomington: Indiana University Press, 1996.

———. "An Oral Philosophy of Personhood: Comments on Philosophy and Orality." *Research in African Literatures* 40, no. 1 (2009): 8–18.

———. "Philosophical Research and Teaching in Africa: Some Suggestions." In *Teaching and Research in Philosophy: Africa*, edited by UNESCO. Paris: UNESCO, 1984.

———. *Philosophy and an African Culture*. Cambridge: Cambridge University Press, 1980.

———. "Some Comments on Contemporary African Philosophy." *Florida Philosophical Review* 3, no. 1 (2003): 91–96.

———. "Toward Decolonizing African Philosophy and Religion." *African Studies Quarterly* 1, no. 4 (1998): 17–46.

Wright, Richard, ed. *African Philosophy: An Introduction*. Lanham, MD: University Press of America, 1984.

Young, Crawford. *The African State in Comparative Perspective*. New Haven, CT: Yale University Press, 1994.

INDEX

UCHENNA OKEJA is Professor of Philosophy at Rhodes University. He is affiliated with Nelson Mandela University as a research associate.